SHELL GAME

to Bud,

Words from the heart,

Jerry Martien

SHELL GAME

A TRUE ACCOUNT
OF BEADS AND MONEY
IN NORTH AMERICA

by Jerry Martien

*with a foreword
by Gary Snyder*

MERCURY HOUSE
SAN FRANCISCO

Grateful acknowledgment for the use of selections from the following:
The chapter "In the Land of Loose Money" first appeared in slightly dif-
ferent form in *Raritan;* reprinted by permission. Selection from *The
Great Dimestore Centennial,* published by Station Hill Press, © 1986 by
Don Byrd. Reprinted by permission of the author. From *The Cantos of
Ezra Pound,* published by New Directions Publishing Corp. Copyright ©
1934, 1937, 1940, 1948, 1950, 1956, 1959, 1962, 1963, 1965, 1966, 1968,
1970 by Ezra Pound. Copyright © 1969, 1971 by the Estate of Ezra Pound.
Reprinted by permission of the publisher. From *The Good
Message of Handsome Lake,* published by Unicorn
Press. Copyright © 1979 by Joseph Bruchac.
Reprinted by permission
of the author.

United States Constitution, First Amendment: Congress shall make no
law respecting an establishment of religion, or prohibiting the free exer-
cise thereof; or abridging the freedom of speech, or of the press; or
the right of the people peaceably to assemble, and to petition the
Government for a redress of grievances.

Library of Congress Cataloging-in-Publication Data:
Martien, Jerry
Shell Game : a true account of beads and money in North America / by
Jerry Martien ; with a foreword by Gary Snyder. — 1st ed.
p.   cm.
Includes bibliographical references.
ISBN 1-56279-080-3 (pbk. : alk. paper) : $14.95
1. Indians of North America—money. 2. Wampum—History. 3.
Indians of North America—Commerce. 4. Indians of North America—
Finance. 5. Exchange—United States—History. 6. Money—United
States—Philosophy. I. Title.
E98.M7M37 1995   95-16875
306.3'4—dc20   CIP

FIRST EDITION
5 4 3 2 1

CONTENTS

FOREWORD BY
GARY SNYDER

Jerry Martien tells a rich story. He went back east, three thousand miles overland, from his home at the western edge of north America, without much money. He went to revisit his past and pursue an obsession. The wry tale of his own loves and losses, and the backpack of scholarly books that walks the night streets with him, is stitched into this study of misunderstanding, loss, and also persistence of a way of life based on reciprocity. His tale starts with beads.

Seashells. Clams and conches, bivalves and univalves. A hard white surface secreted line by line from an edge of the soft mantle, using precious molecules of calcium sucked in from the sea. Protects soft flesh, and then, the shell, lives on for years. Durable, smooth, hard, pale or purple or pink, ground and polished, drilled for beads. Beads in strings or belts or necklaces make us look and feel special, and became bonds and tokens, even (Martien suggests) "messages" in a virtual language of gift and agreement. They were a key item in the ancient gift economy and its exchanges of love, land, condolences, spirit, art, resistance. We learn that the earliest coins, from Tyre, had a seashell on one side and a dolphin on the other.

Folded into Martien's account is his research on the history and complex logic of wampum (shell bead strings or belts) as used by the highly organized native nations of what's now New York and New England, the peoples of the Longhouse. The Dutch, English, and French traders and settlers apparently failed to grasp that wampum, with its many ceremonial and political uses, was not just an Indian equivalent of money. This added a peculiar semantic confusion to the already perplexing and depressing story of the slow and steady expropriation of native lands even prior to the existence of the United States. American History has been "centuries of denial" of deliberate lying, cheating, and massacres. "This is how the New World was 'conquered,'" Martien says, "not with a bang, but one crooked deal at a time."

The Iroquois and their neighbors were a remarkably productive, gifted, socially sophisticated and sizable population that played a significant role in the early Euro-American economy. In the end what they got was scorn and pain. And Martien suggests that the economic rationale of the early Atlantic traders (many of whom believed that it was not merely profitable but *virtuous* to commodify the world) has finally tricked and cheated us all. We live in a blighted social and ecological landscape, with most people increasingly confined to the poverty of the "National Rez" (Leslie Silko).

Shell Game's special contribution is as a meditation on history, economy, and the human heart. Martien draws on the seminal work by the anthropological economist Marcel Mauss, *Essai sur le Don* ("Essay on the Gift"), and Lewis Hyde's useful extension of that called *The Gift*. He reminds us that although the old gift exchange modes have expired, they still offer insights for social, spiritual, and moral life.

Jerry Martien's narrative brings him back to the northern California Pacific Coast to note there too the power of dentalia-shell and abalone beads among the Native Californians, and sums up his lessons. Stewardship, restoration, generosity, and "investment in the longer-term bonds" in "communities where kinship means both family and place, in watersheds where salmon [or forests, or grasslands, or well-tended orchards] are the primary indicator of riches" are all part of the "re-opening of the gift relationship." In our families and communities, friendships and crafts, at least, we can do this. *Shell Game* itself is a gift. And this foreword is a small return for poems of Jerry's that touched me long ago, as well as an appreciation for the present text. We can hold some space open for a path with heart.

—G.S.

ACKNOWLEDGMENTS

This is a book of acknowledgment, and a pilgrimage to the re-payment of unsettled accounts. As with our general indebted-ness, however, the personal debts are almost beyond reckoning. To acknowledge them all here would be another kind of bookkeeping;

    ☙ but to the generous guides and providers, who made the journey possible: John Taylor, Paul Ryan, Lori Longbotham, Rosey Rounds, Paul Morgan, Don and Marge Byrd, the Varsity Cafe, David Yarrow, Doug and Amy Unger, Ted and Virginia Solotaroff, Mike Raab and Michi Blixt, Jane Raab, Felicia Oldfather, Jenna Magnuson,

    ☙ to the State Museum of New York at Albany, their help-ful staff, particularly Raymond Gonyea, then of the Depart-ment of Historical Services,

    ☙ to the keepers of the door and the texts at the Heye Museum of the American Indian Library, the Bronx,

    ☙ to Planet Drum Foundation and *Raritan* for publish-ing earlier installments of this investigation into the causes of our poverty,

    ☙ to the readers and advisers who provided both insight and a place to first exchange this gift, particularly Richard Cortez Day, Ellen Givins, and Matina Kilkenny for editorial guidance,

❦ to Tom Christensen and the people at Mercury House, and to Joan Martien and Jenny Finch, who have generously polished and made of it this present,

❦ to the makers and keepers of the names, my teachers and accomplices, and to friends and family who have accepted and supported these years of absentminded obsession,

❦ to the scholars of money and beads and the history of North America, who have opened the paths I have followed and occasionally wandered from,

❦ and to the Longhouse People and the adherents of the Great Law of Peace, for their bright fire and enduring example, with condolence and apology,

❦ my deepest gratitude, and this down payment on what is due.

SHELL GAME

*Here are the pieces. Text and dream, beginning here. Pieces,
strung out across the continent. This is how it begins.*

*Our history is a beaded string of transactions, leading back
from today to the first exchanges of the social contract. And
just as in our personal lives we see how a long-ago loss adds
up to a present impoverishment, and the only remedy to recount the loss—so we require an audit of the collective
soul, to weave again the picture
of its true history.*

*To see and acknowledge,
to begin to redeem our hearts.*

IN THE LAND OF LOOSE MONEY

In the small dark hours of a late twentieth-century April night I am crossing North America. Down there in the heart of the continent they are sleeping with the lights on—lost and dreaming souls hovering in the darkness over corner and backyard lights, in the vaporous illumination of empty shopping centers and crowded graveyard parking lots. Souls afraid of what comes in the dark to collect.

I am on an errand. In common with the people on the plane around me, my errand has to do with money. It is a summons, calling me back east into another life and time. I am carrying history. History is waiting to be repeated.

The lights are dim inside the plane. Only three or four other passengers have their reading lights on, briefcases open to calculators and printouts and data spreads, accountant-messengers driven not here not there, between the stars and the Ohio valley, crossing toward tomorrow's untransacted business. Below us the troubled short-sold spirits mingle with the ancient ghosts of the Great Forest. So much missing, so many lost.

Before turning out the light I study again the dog-eared footnote to Mauss's *Essay on the Gift*. My place in the text still marked by an old ticket on the Kerrville Texas Bus Line. I have been on this errand a long time. History repeating and repeating. I read, then read again.

We hold that mankind made a number of tentative steps. At first it was found that certain things, most of them magical and precious, were by custom not destroyed, and these were endowed with the power to exchange. . . . In the second stage, mankind having succeeded in making things circulate within the tribe and far outside it, found that these purchasing instruments could serve as a means to count wealth and make it circulate.[1]

1. MARCEL MAUSS'S ESSAI comes to us like an old coin, a token of great value lost and found again. Trained as a Sanskrit scholar and religious historian, Mauss took up the new "science" of sociology and the history of human exchange in response to the horrible losses he observed in postwar 1920s Europe. The beginning of Mauss's note—it runs more than two pages—is also marked in my copy by a ballot stub from the national elections of 1988:

These precious objects differ, it is true, from what we are accustomed to consider as purchasing instruments. Beyond their economic nature they have a mystical nature. . . . Moreover, they have a very general circulation within a society and between societies, but they are still attached to persons or clans (the first Roman coins were struck by gentes), and to the individuality of their former possessors and to contracts made between moral beings. (Essay on the Gift: Forms and Functions of Exchange in Archaic Societies, *trans. Ian Cunnison [New York, 1967], 93–94 n.25)

For that sense of connection we return to Mauss's book—and to our own back pages.

It had always been a question of value. What was the value of a life, what made it worth living? The books and papers in my knapsack, the pictures in my mind, the little money in my pocket—all taking me on an errand of ancient commerce. I had slowly come to understand that all wealth has its origin in a gift relationship, beginning with the gift of life itself. That through the ages of human community on this planet, through its oldest and deepest wisdom, ways had been found to acknowledge that gift and so keep it and ourselves alive. Receipt was acknowledged by what came to be our words of prayer and thanksgiving. The words were marked by precious and magical objects. The objects were valued and exchanged because they bespoke the gift and reenacted the giving.

Bead. Of ancient origin, related to Sanskrit *bhed*, meaning to bend, as when we bow or kneel. Coming out as Old English *biddan*, to pray, as in I bid thee, hear what I ask. In the name for *please*, as German *bitte*. And in the name of prayer itself, *gebed. Bede*, the mnemonic and numinous objects by which prayers are told. Among our oldest human artifacts. Pieces of shell or bone or stone, porcelain or glass, rose seeds of the rosary, pierced and strung together, each one a prayer and an offering.[2]

But it came to this: the spirit-thing became money—a marker that could transfer the gift of one place to the gift of another, without the actual object. Stand for—change, as it always had. One thing to another. But now abstracted from the thing itself, a word of ambiguous reference. It was a powerful convenience. Sublimated from the names of things into number, it became more than a person could count. It could buy and sell the souls of men, dress them in suits and ties and send them on errands of self-destruction. And the life and spirit, the gift of an entire continent—taken and spent.

I had come to see the pieces. To look at the beads and study the accounts. How it had come to this. I had read and reread the books. Strung the pieces in my mind over and over. Lived as close to the gift as possible, saved up $324 for the plane ticket, and what I hoped would cover expenses. And I was bringing something to sell.

I had to know I was looking for things lost beyond recovery. Things I hadn't been able to get away from. Money, I thought. Promises, agreements. The wealth of North America. Even from the beginning, it was too late.

From the first encounter then. Go back and repeat:

*Here arrived yesterday the ship the Arms of Amsterdam.
. . . They report that our people there are of good courage and live peaceably. Their women also have borne Children there, they have bought the island Manhatas from the wild men for the value of 60 guilders.*[3]

As the shuttle approaches the island now, the World Trade Center rises beyond the marshes of Bayonne, the little Dutch outpost having outlived both courage and peace, still buying and selling the pieces nonetheless. It's been twenty years. The underground walk from Port Authority to subway only confirms the colony's brash new announcement—it's all still for sale, only this much bigger and faster and more expensive. As to quality, the streets above are eloquent. If you're not buying or selling, don't even ask. How appropriate that this first letter from Manhattan is a bill of goods.

The cargo of the aforesaid ship is:

2. THE RECONSTRUCTED Indo-European base word is *bhidh,* related to our bide, abide, and to Latin *fidus* (confide, fidelity), connoting an object of faith. Possibly related also to I-E *bheudh,* to make an offering, and thus by association to *buddha,* one whose prayer is answered. See Julius Pokorny, *Indogermanisches Etymologisches Wortebuch* (Bern, 1959), 117, 150. I thank Richard Arthur for correcting my initial derivations.

3. LETTER DATED 5 November 1626 from Mr. P. Schagen, Deputy of the States-General at the meeting of the West India Company, to The Hague. Transcribed from the document on display at the Museum of the City of New York. Also in E. B. O'Callaghan, ed., *Documents Relative to the Colonial History of the State of New York* (Albany, 1853–87), 1:37–38.

7,246 beaver skins
178 ½ otter skins
675 otter skins
48 mink skins
36 wild cat skins
33 mink
34 rat skins
Many logs of oak and nut-wood.

4. While the English and Dutch national interests were in fierce and ultimately violent competition, the colonists had to depend on each other and the inhabitants for their survival. Neither colony had a valid claim to the land they had settled nor a sustainable means by which to live there. For the role of beads in resolving these awkward circumstances, see William Beauchamp, *Wampum and Shell Articles Used by the New York Indians*, Bulletin 41 of the State Museum of New York (Albany, 1901).

My flea-market suitcase is heavy with the customary burden of those driven from their libraries by obsession. Raincoat and hat, knapsack and bedroll, like a pilgrim from another planet I get on the wrong subway and have to walk west out of Harlem plain, drag all that history up the rocky paths of Morningside Park. Remembering not to let eyes meet. Try not to look like an easy mark. Don't think about money. It's the only thing on these streets that's talking. Imagine landing here without it.

> *To the Governor & Council of New Plymouth from the Manhatas in the Fort Amsterdam March 9, Anno 1627....*
>
> *And if it so fall out that any good that come to our hands from our native country may be serviceable unto you, we shall take ourselves bound to help and accommodate you therewith, either for beaver or any other wares or merchandise that you should be pleased to deal for.*
>
> *And if in case we have no commodity at present that may give you content, if you please to sell us any beaver or otter or such like commodities as may be useful for us for ready money, . . . we shall appoint one to deal with you at such place as you shall appoint.*
>
> *—Isaak de Rasieres, Secretaris*[4]

"As may be useful for us for ready money"—stranded in a tight-ass Dutch town on a very hard rock at the edge of an unimaginably wild continent, and they were broke. They had

nothing for ready cash. In what they thought was a land purchase from the Manhata, "the value of 60 guilders" had been
in merchandise—implements of iron, woolen stockings that
were thought to be useful tobacco pouches, probably some of
the beads that were already working the trade in Africa. Not
what their letter had in mind—not "ready money." And they
were not disappointed in supposing their English cousins
might be thinking along the same lines. They had answer in
ten business days.

5. THE DATE OF THE
English letter in reply
is 19 March, 1626,
the two nations being
on different calendars.

> Likewise for your friendly tender and offer to accommo-
> date and help us with any commodities or merchandise
> you have or shall come to you, either for beaver, otters or
> other wares, it is to us very acceptable, and we doubt not
> but in short time we may have profitable commerce and
> trade together.
>
> For this year we are fully supplied with all neces-
> saries, both for clothing and other things. But hereafter
> it is like we shall deal with you if your rates be reason-
> able.
>
> And therefore when you please to send to us again by
> way of any of yours, we desire to know how you will take
> beaver by the pound and otters by the skin.
>
> And how you will deal per cent for other commodi-
> ties, and what you can furnish us with. As likewise what
> other commodities from us may be acceptable to you, as
> tobacco, fish, corn or other things, and what prices you
> will give, etc.
>
>   —By the Governor & Council of New Plymouth,
>   Your Worships' very good friends & neighbors, etc.[5]

Beaver—or otter? inquireth the New Netherlander. Tobacco, fish—corn if you will, respondeth the New Englander.
Without a penny in pocket, they are issuing the coinage of
the New World. We don't need anything just now, but would
love to make some money in the Old World way. And so they
miss the wealth that is open before them, fail to understand

their own ancestral ways of reckoning. Of every new thing revealed to their unastonished eyes, they could only ask is this money,

6. THESE ARE THE WORDS
*Of Plymouth Plantation,
1620–1647, by William
Bradford, Sometime
Governor Thereof,* ed.
Samuel Eliot Morison
(New York, 1952),
144–45, Anno 1624.

*they having found the benefit of their last year's harvest,
& setting Corn for their Particular end in this year's
planting—6*

The *benefit*—meaning *profit*. Even their own word for gift, like their word for *good*, now means a monetary relation. Remember the story? The corn that was a present? The Pilgrims in the grade-school pictures, how hungry and thankful they were? Did it ever happen? The picture of Massasoit and his people bringing the corn and the knowledge to cultivate it—is there memory of this? Say it again:

& they having found the benefit of their last year's harvest, & setting Corn for their Particular end in this year's planting, began now highly to prize corn as more precious than silver, & those that had some to spare began to trade one with another for small things, for money they had none, & if any had, corn was preferred by the quart, pottle & peck.

And so turn the gift into money. Use surplus fish to feed the growing corn, use the corn to buy from your Brethren in Christ; grow tobacco for the Indian and the Dutchman, the profit returning as beaver for export. Corn by the quart, pottle, and peck. Beaver by the pound. Transmutable into credit in dollars—the silver Leewan-Dahlers minted of the plunder the Spanish had brought from their own colonial endeavors, which the Dutch in turn nickel and dimed from an improvident Spain. Now we're talking money.

The desired commerce between these New World friends and neighbors was not long in coming. It is with an accountant's pleasure that the good Bradford records the first visit of the New Netherlanders,

who sent again unto them from their Plantation both

*kind letters, also diverse commodities, as sugar, linen,
cloth, holland, finer and coarser stuffs, etc. . . . And
amongst other commodities they vended much tobacco
for linen cloth, stuffs, etc., which was a good benefit to
the people, till the Virginians found out their Plantation.*

> *But that which turned most to their profit in time
was entrance into the trade of wampumpeag, for they
now bought about £50 worth of it of them, in corn, &
they told them how vendible it was at their fort Orenia,
and did persuade them they would find it so at
Kennebec.[7]*

7. *OF PLYMOUTH
Plantation,* 202–3,
Anno 1628 of
Bradford's journal.

"Wampum?" says my host, politely.

"Only it wasn't money," I always had to add. "The little
beads made of shell. It was like money—only it wasn't." I had
to repeat it. "Your ancestors—they were broke and they
thought it was money. It turned out to be their ticket to the
New World."

I'm on the couch in the living room of his upper West-
Side apartment. My baggage and papers are spread around
the room. He has already been more than gracious. While I
wait for my soul to catch up with my too-suddenly trans-
ported body, I watch a video featuring the northwoods poet
Tom McGrath on the VCR's big-screen projector. You have to
know some place, the poet kept saying in sly, rough homilies.
Live there and get to know it. Ah yes—what I thought I'd
been trying to prove these past twenty years. Otherwise, I
keep saying, you don't know what things are really worth—
or where worth itself comes from. That must explain what
I'm doing here so far from home. How all this got started. I
have another of the potent screwdrivers he's serving up.

"It's like this," I say, waving my glass in the general direction of Long Island. The English had been building a boat at
Buzzards Bay. De Rasieres suspected they already had some
notion of how "vendible" the seashell currency might be.

They were building the boat, he explained to his superiors at The Hague,

in order to go & look after the trade in Sewan in Sloup's Bay, . . . which I have prevented for this year by selling them 50 fathoms of Sewan, because the seeking after sewan by them is prejudicial to us, inasmuch as they would, by so doing, discover the trade in furs, which if they were to find out, it would be a great trouble to us to maintain.[8]

"*Sewhounhocky,*" I said. "The place the shells came from. Long Island." My host, I had slowly come to realize, was near the end of a prolonged bout with his demon. The vodka was gone. He was in the kitchen, unwrapping the gift of smoked salmon I had brought from his sister. Too much money at too young an age, she had said. A small fortune from a sixties rock & roll band, squandered in the seventies. An inheritance controlled by his father. All this East Coast history and wealth, its causes and effects and the need it engendered—it was obviously beyond me, part of what I was here to sort out. The sister and I, after two or three years, seemed to be losing whatever agreement we had shared, and ideas about money seemed to be at the heart of the problem. So now, figuring in love, I knew less than nothing.

"It was a misunderstanding," I said, speaking again mostly to myself. A distinction was lost. The Dutch used the local word for beads made from the purple edge of the great clam, *Venus mercenaria*.[9] Sewan hacky they said—sewan for short. The English used the name for the strung white beads, *wanpun apiag,* which they pronounced *wampum peake* and shortened to *wampum* or *peage* or *peake*.[10] But if neither could hear the names or grasp their reference, how much less could they know that in the Algonquin language it was an animate noun. The significance of dark beads or light, the difference between the woven and strung and the handful, between adornment and ceremony and trade, between gift and obliga-

8. This Letter of New Netherland's Secretary de Rasieres is noted by William B. Weeden, "Indian Money as a Factor in New England Civilization," Johns Hopkins University Studies in Historical and Political Science (Baltimore, 1884), 20 n.3. His source for it is John G. Palfrey, *A Compendious History of New England from the Discovery by Europeans* (Boston, 1872), 1:283.

9. Also *Mercenaria Mercenaria*—the paquahog or quahog clam, still found in much diminished size and quantity. See cover photo and Percy A. Morris, *A Field Guide to Shells of the Atlantic and Gulf Coasts and West Indies* (New York, 1973).

10. See Frank G. Speck, "The Functions of Wampum among the Eastern Igonquin," Memoirs of the American Anthropological Association 6 (1919): 3–71. The significances of the name are summarized in Ruth Underhill's *The Red Man In America* (Chicago, 1953), 67.

tion—missing these, getting a few names wrong, thinking it was money, they lost the New World before they discovered it.

tion—missing these, getting a few names wrong, thinking it was money, they lost the New World before they discovered it.

"That's really very interesting," said my host. He offered me the last of the salmon. My stomach had not yet settled from the plane ride. "Too rich," I said. He asked if he could borrow twenty dollars. No problem. I dug out a bill and he went back to his room, leaving me to collect my thoughts and belongings and browse a while in his library. He was a formidable student of music, poetry, Tibetan Buddhism, and addiction.

I emptied my stash and counted it out after showering. It was already evident that my movie-detective budget (I get twenty-five a day—plus expenses) was as ridiculous here as the rest of my act. I would be wholly dependent on the couches and hospitality of people who knew little about me, aside from a few poems and a preoccupation with language and old beads. If I learned nothing else, I would know by the end of this journey whether the life of the scholar-gypsy was still marginally possible. Despite much evidence to the contrary, I had to believe that the laws of gift exchange and hospitality still sometimes prevailed.

He was sleeping peacefully when I left. I'd hoped the food and the little weed we shared would mellow him and not send him farther over the edge. I held some similar hope for myself and could imagine that I negotiated the elevator and found the street almost as if I lived here. I practiced the prevailing mode of walking, as if I were going to meet my broker or connection. Running over figures and dates, old texts like beads in my mind:

> . . . it was two years before they could put off this small quantity till the inland people knew of it & afterwards they could scarce ever get enough for them, for many years together. . . . And strange it was to see the great alteration it made in a few years among the Indians.[11]

It would be half a century before they had any idea who these "inland people" were, or that they were on the eastern

11. IN HIS TRANSCRIPTION of Bradford (*Of Plymouth Plantation,* 203), Beauchamp's version adds *and thus did our brethren so fall into this commodity that it became as ready money unto them.* This phrase clarifies the "great alteration" of the New England coastal people, who found the beads highly desired by the Mohawk and more eastern Iroquois nations, thus putting them in the lucrative position of middlemen between Europe and the interior of the New World. This new wealth would of course prove to be their ruin.

doorstep of a great confederate nation for whom these beads were a living symbol, a woven language in which their own recent arrival was already documented. To the eyes and hands of these desperate immigrants, the things of the fallen material world were soulless commodity. And every commodity must have its price, and another commodity in which to pay it —something portable and measurable by volume, weight, and number. So they turned the New World into a counting house.

> *. . . the Massachusetts had none or very little of it. . . .*
> *Only it was made and kept among the Narragansett and*
> *Pequots which grew rich and potent by it & these Mass-*
> *achusetts were poor & beggarly & had no use of it.*
> *Neither did the English of this Plantation or any other in*
> *the land, till now that they had knowledge of it from the*
> *Dutch, so much as know what it was, much less that it*
> *was a commodity of that worth & value.*

"That worth & value"—heading down Amsterdam Ave, I imagined everyone on the street understood what I was saying, as if the deal had just gone down this morning.

"It's too late—it was probably too late from the beginning. Nobody wants to hear it—not here. *Here* is the heart of the problem."

We were sharing a smallish Greek salad on 93rd Street. The time and money of my dinner partner were apparently as tightly budgeted as mine. It was difficult for me to imagine how much money people made here, or how they could be spending it all. He was at the end of his three days of teaching in town, had to get back to his office and finish the week's work before returning to home and family in the Berkshires. It turned out his apartment wouldn't be vacant, though— someone else was using it. We'd had an old friend of his in common, whose name I was told not to mention if I called him at home. And we shared some of that writer's gloom over a piece of work gone too many years unfinished. We talked language and money, history, and geography.

"I have a deadline on," he said. "For a 2,500-word history of the Berkshires."

"Good," I agreed. He politely let me eat the last olive. "People need to know where they are."

I admired with some envy his ability to turn money in a literary way. Editing a prestigious journalism review, teaching, freelancing—yet he seemed to have no more change or time to spare than I did. He found it amusing that I was trying to get an advance to write a book to make enough money to buy the time to write a book about money.

"Otherwise people think water comes from faucets—or food from microwaves." It clearly wasn't coming from the waiter—I was trying without success to get the attention of one of the four guys at a table near the kitchen, all of them apparently bosses. Three and a half centuries late, but they know the importance of a good location.

It had not been this rock but the long island to the north that was the source of wealth. *Sewhounhocky*,[12] meaning the place of unstrung shells—or as it would translate today, the land of loose money:

> *This point [on Gardiners Bay] is also well adapted to se-*
> *cure the trade of the Indians in Wampum (the mine of*
> *New Netherland), therein situate lie the cockles whereof*
> *Wampum is made, from which great profit could be re-*
> *alized by those who would plant a colonie or hamlet at*
> *the aforesaid Point.*[13]

But if the New World prospector did not care to move to the diggings on Long Island, he had only, as New York's first promotional book advertised, to wait and it would come to him:

> *the Indians, without our labor or trouble, bring to us*
> *their fur trade, worth tons of gold, which may be in-*
> *creased, and is like goods found.*[14]

12. SEE SPECK ("THE Functions of Wampum") and William W. Tooker, *Indian Place Names on Long Island* (New York, n.d.).

13. CORNELIUS VAN Tienhoven, secretary of New Netherland, Information Relative to taking up land in New Netherland, in the form of Colonies or private bouweries," delivered to the States-General 4 March 1650 (O'Callaghan, ed., *Doc Rel Col Hist NY*, 1:365–66).

14. ADRIAEN VAN DER Donck, *A Description of New Netherland* (1653), cited in *Doc Rel Col Hist NY*, 1:356. In what may be New York's first literary contract, van der Donck was granted fifteen-year exclusive rights to publish his advertisement. Unfortunately, he was detained in Holland by merchants who considered colonists an obstacle to business, and though he finally returned to his plantation (what is now Yonkers), he died before a new edition could be printed.

"People in this town don't see it," he said. I could feel in his voice some of the stress of living one place and doing business another. And maybe some comfort in talking to someone who had made other choices and come up against the same rock.

15. FROM THE RELATION OF 1642, Reuben G. Thwaites, ed., *The Jesuit Relations and Allied Documents; Travels and Explorations of the Jesuit Missionaries in North America 1610–1791* (Cleveland, 1896–1901), 22:290–91. The word "presents" translates *presens,* not Mauss's more generalized *don.*

"People in civilization don't see it," I had to add. "They think value comes from money, and money from banks. Or from other money—or from labor, for christ sake." I was warming to my ethno-numismatic rant.

"People don't see it's a gift. They think they can't afford to see it—they treat the world like money, get greedy, and lose it. Over and over, till it's gone—till it's too late."

He poured water from the pitcher he'd brought from a couple of tables away. The Socratic dialogue in the corner continued. We drank water and talked books. How Nancy was doing. He looked at his watch. We split the price of the dinner and tip. We walked a short way together and he gave me directions to my next destination. Both knowing we probably wouldn't meet again.

The presents among the peoples are all the affairs of the country: they dry the tears, they appease anger, they open the gate of the country to strangers, they deliver prisoners, they revive the dead.

Nothing is said, as it were, and nothing answered but by presents; it is on this account that in harangues the present passes for a word.

They make presents to animate men to war, to invite peace, to induce a family or nation to come and take a place and dwell near you, to satisfy or pay those who have received any harm or any wound, specially if blood has been shed.[15]

It was the Jesuits, primitive anthropologists already steeped in symbols of atonement and prayer, who first seemed to grasp the workings of this new land's economy. But they

brought beads of glass and shell from Europe, hoping to purchase souls, as if with money.

Not money—the present passing for a word. Here is my word—here, the palpable promise, something of value to mark my word. Beads on a string. The strings then woven, side by side, figures emerging. Pictures in darkness and light, signs to be held and spoken aloud. Voices woven out of the past.

Then new figures, new voices in the landscape of North America, refugees from the bankruptcies of Europe. You can still see them.

—Here, on the St. Lawrence, the Jesuit from France.

—Here, at the mouth of the Hudson and on Long Island, the Dutch trader.

—And here, from the Kennebec to Narragansett Bay, between piety and profit, the English dissenters.

Each of them holds a present in his outstretched hand. They know these strings of beads are highly valued. They have no idea why this is so. They think it must be money, and they are buying their way into North America. If you want a piece of it, talk to the man with the outstretched hand.

🝆 🝆 🝆

"It got to be too expensive," I said. "All around." I passed the number across the table. My editor poured us both another shot of whiskey and set the bottle down. The envelope with my manuscript lay on the table beside it. I had walked the few blocks to his apartment, found myself early, surprised how near it was. It was beginning to feel like a very small town. His wife and I were introduced, she cleared the leftovers of chicken dinner and excused herself.

He had wanted to know if I'd brought any to sell. He'd lost touch with his only other literary connection in northern California.

"Too many people got to know about it. It attracted cops and robbers and dealers in expensive habits. The feds saw another excuse to get the eco-freaks and political types out of the hills—Nancy Reagan's little war."

It remained to be seen whether he was actually going to be my editor. It had been twenty years since we'd seen each other—the connection had been lost and then made again, and then again more recently. I wasn't sure we had anything to talk about, but he had made the gesture and I was grateful. The losses of those years were getting painful to count. And though I hadn't brought the commodity in question, I'd brought some writing. He'd talked about an advance and had mentioned an amount of money.

To my ear, we had each become a voice of the place we lived, addressed to the kind of people we talked to. He had his name on credible stationery and was well employed at a mid-town address, but I could hear the same small circle of discourse. He talked about how times had changed.

"It's the end of the big-gun style of literary discourse. I told Poirier that—that those days are over."

To an outsider, like the proverbial easterner in the western saloon, the size of the guns is not the first thing you notice. Like the city itself, its writers seem to be one big well-armed subway car. If there is a noticeable decentralization of voice, it is overwhelmed by the way big money has tightened and centralized the market for language. Bigger sales, smaller talk. More insider trading. I wondered if the voice in the envelope would sound as provincial in their ears. Whether, in any sense of the word, it would find currency here.

Ten years after its "discovery" by the colonists, wampum was declared official exchange of the Massachusetts Bay Colony, at six white beads to the penny. Of course no one had a penny. So instead, now beads are money. And now a life is one of the commodities it buys.

> At length there came a Narragansett Indian boy, who
> had been in the Bay a-trading, and had both cloth and

beads about him—they had met him the day before, and
he was now returning. Peach called him to drink tobacco
with them, and he came and sat down with them.

> *Peach told the others he would kill him and take what*
> *he had from him, but they were something afraid. But he*
> *said, "Hang him, rogue, he had killed many of them." So*
> *they let him alone to do as he would.*

> *And when he saw his time, he took a rapier and ran*
> *him through the body once or twice and took from him*
> *five fathom of wampum and three coats of cloth and*
> *went their way, leaving him for dead.*[16]

The colonial authorities saw to it that the offense was paid
for. Plymouth could not afford bad relations with the Narraganset, nor could its council. Like the traffic in corn and
beaver, the trade in wampum was to be undertaken only by
license, which only that body had power to grant. Fines levied
by its court were payable in beads.

16. BRADFORD AGAIN
(*Of Plymouth Plantation,*
299–300, Anno 1638).
To this first New England
murder trial, he adds in
the defendant's behalf that
Arthur Peach was a veteran
of the massacre known
as the "Pequot War," thus
clarifying "he had killed
many of them." No doubt
then as now, the distinction
between peace and war
was less than clear.

🏵 🏵 🏵

It was late. My host was emptying the ashtray. We had been
smoking tobacco, which I was trying not to do in people's
houses. He was supposed to be quitting. He offered me back
the roach. Half of it had already been too much.

"Keep it," I said. "It makes me forget things. They should
have a law against it." He thanked me. Strange that such a
small commodity should be a big deal here. I got up to go.
Museums and libraries, people to see. I'd call when I got back
from Albany and Onondaga. We'd have dinner.

I walked over and up Broadway, drunk and paranoid. It
began to seem too late again. I didn't know where I was, or
what I was doing here. What did it matter how it all got
started. Or what had happened to the sixties, or where the
wealth of North America had gone. Bright busy people came
and went between cabs and restaurants and theaters. They
live in such forgetfulness.

A friend of John's was at the apartment, helping him get

to the hospital for detox. He had invested some of the twenty in more food, but it hadn't really helped much. He looked in pretty bad shape. He generously gave me a key and encouraged me to stay on. We would see each other in ten days, when both of us were back from where we were going.

It is unimaginable, too far gone, too close to see—the sheer isolate need of those first migrant souls. That anything would ever feed a hunger born of such dispossession—anything but money. The words of the good pastor Bradford mingle with the street sounds from below as I finally nod off on the couch.

> *. . . And it hath now continued a current commodity*
> *about this twenty years, & it may prove a drug in time.*

Here are the pieces. Text and dream, beginning here. Pieces strung out across North America. This is how it began.

AT THE MARGIN OF PROFIT

The hustle is on. Late April, afternoon, 155th and Broadway—everybody who is making the daylight move, they are *on* the move. Central Americans engage West Africans in deep uptown deals. Who in turn do trade with the local cousin, the long-term resident of this undeclared port of entry into the underclass. Who remain, as if to say, *the margin begins here.* I'm also in the neighborhood on business. It's where the old accounts are kept. Ten thousand years of human business, hanging out around the corner.

The Museum of the American Indian appears to have been in steady decline since its founding by George Gustav Heye, inheritor of a nineteenth-century oil fortune and a zealous collector of Indian artifacts, who endowed—but not abundantly, it appears—a foundation to hold on to them. Now it's the late '80s, and deregulated finance is again pumping out billions, but the downtown centers of power have not found it convenient to maintain the museum any better than the neighborhood. They would like to move it to a safer location, but there are so many artifact- and power-seeking forces at work that nothing happens. Recently the *Times* reported that it may all be carted off to D.C., where they have a wider tax base and a stronger Indian lobby. "New Yorkers Denounce Smithsonian Takeover,"[1] the aggrieved headlines read. I can't help but notice before entering that the museum

1. *NEW YORK TIMES*, 13 MAY 1987. The argument would continue for another seven years, while the traditional rival cities quarreled over the bones they would otherwise be built on. After Mayor Koch of New York suffered a mild stroke the next fall, he broke off negotiations to move the Heye collection (the city bearing a quarter of the expense) into its Museum of Natural History. It would appear that the continued possession of these artifacts justified the cultural occupation of Manhattan Island, explaining why the show of curatorship was more important than its substance; the director of the Heye Foundation denied reports that many of the million artifacts in storage had been lost. The original seal of New Amsterdam—a beaver inside a circle of wampum —is indicative of the city's priorities in this matter.

shares its gated courtyard and fountain with a remarkably well-kept and imposing edifice: the American Numismatic Society. A latter-day temple of Mammon, where the official account is kept, and certain valuations are maintained. People don't commonly realize how much it costs to keep our money believable.

I pay my two dollars to the well-groomed blonde behind the reception desk. *Which way to the wampum?* She stares, then points me straight ahead. A few steps into the yellowed marble hall, in half a dozen glass cases, the objects I've come all this way to see. Relics of the wealth of North America.

But not money. For most of human history, we have lived without this device that is supposed to denote wealth. Accustomed to the highly abstract notion of coin, we can't imagine life without it. Civilization would be impossible. Historians may object that the ancient moneyless empires of China, Egypt, and Peru contradict this, but we can confidently reply that coinage frees us from pharaohs and sun kings, allows us to escape the anthill bondage to economic function. Money frees each of us to be our own personal financial wizard. Except that this is unfortunately not true—the bond we carry in our pocket requires a third party. Its heads and tails represent the faceless guarantor of its currency, of its being a measure, a standard, and a repository of value. Whether we're talking krugerands or plastic, that third party is always there. The Crown. The Fed. The Market. Leviathan.

The beads are cylindrical and surprisingly small—less than half an inch long and no more than a quarter-inch in diameter. There is argument that before the Europeans—and the bow drill, the iron awl, and the notion of money—the beads were discoidal, like thick subway tokens. But these in the glass cases are the objects that are traditionally meant by "wampum," and they are clearly difficult of manufacture. A friend once brought me a sack of the shells from Fire Island, and I failed impressively in my attempts to work in this medium. Laboriously chipped from periwinkle or clam, drilled and rounded by bone and stone implement, they were

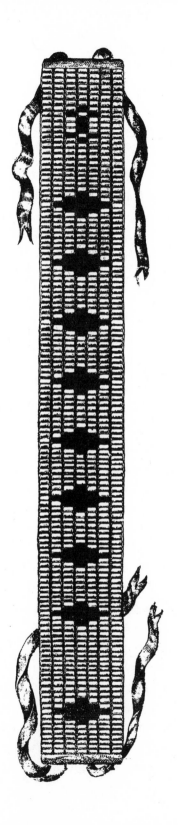

Wampum belt of seven rows (about 2 inches wide, 27 inches in length) woven from beads purchased by Lewis H. Morgan at Grand River, Ontario, in 1850. An "ethnographic" belt—woven from purchased beads, described, sketched, and then donated to the New York State Museum. The original drawing was colored to indicate that all but the white outlined diamonds are of purple beads, the pattern said to symbolize the peace between clans and villages. The bunch of eight purple shell strings was obtained by Morgan from a Grand River Onondaga. Its meaning is not known.

then strung by the hundreds, up to a fathom in length. Laid side by side, the strings wefted into wide belts. The belts would display, much like our dot matrix images, a woven pattern of white beads or of beads made from the dark purple-black edge of the clam's shell.

> *The Indians broke off about half an inch of the purple color of the inside, and converted it into beads. These, before the introduction of awls and threads, were bored with sharp stones, and strung upon sinews of animals, and when interwoven to the breadth of the hand, more or less, were called a belt of sewant or wampum. A black bead, of the size of a large straw, about half an inch long, bored lengthwise and well polished, was the gold of the Indians and always esteemed of twice the value of the white.*[2]

But if not money? Like a written agreement—a promise, and a promise to keep it. Like a gift—an object of beauty, which might be worn as adornment. I'm not sure that we who keep our arts and letters and money in different banks can fully comprehend this ancient way of accounting. In spite of our libraries and museums—and partly because of our dependence on them—we have lost nearly all memory of the most profound invention of our species—the forms and objects of exchange which marked the gift relation within the human community, and between it and the earth. I am here to see the pieces that are left, mark the transactions still within remembrance.

The earliest reference I find to Euro-American bead exchange mentions a 1613 agreement between two Dutch traders and certain chiefs of the Iroquois Longhouse.[3] The Dutch gave a silver chain. They received "a fathom of beadwork"—probably a woven belt of a thousand or more beads, its patterns a mnemonic key to the terms of the agreement. The seventeenth-century European was still accustomed to thinking emblematically, and so both parties probably understood this highly metaphorical exchange—including what

2. DANIEL DENTON, *A BRIEF Description of New York* (1670), quoted in Beauchamp's *Wampum and Shell Articles*. Vincent Wilcox's unpublished paper in the Heye library, "The manufacture and Use of Wampum in the Northeast" (1972), notes that the warp thread was sometimes of fiber, and that the single or double weft thread might come from any of a number of plants: black Indian hemp (dogbane, army root), *apocynum cannabinum;* swamp milkweed, *aspedias incarnata;* white Indian hemp (hairy milkweed), *aspedias pulchra;* toad flax, *linaria linaria;* and Indian mallow (velvet leaf), *abutilon butilon.* In his botanical research, Wilcox still sees the beads' symbolic intent: in use "wampum became the symbol of the power of the word." While Europeans quickly adopted the medium, the message was for the most part lost on them.

3. JEANNETTE HENRY, ED., *The American Indian Reader: Education* (Indian Historian Press, San Francisco, 1972), 204, cites L. G. Van Loon, *Tawagonshi* (*The Indian Historian* I, no. 3) as the authority for this exchange. These first Euro-American transactions are documented by oral tradition, keyed to the wampum that was given. As with the question of wampum's origins, these traditional stories ought to be considered primary authorities.

was signified by the silver, the links of the chain, and so on. And both parties no doubt appreciated the beauty of finely wrought objects, were surely curious and admiring, and saw benefit in further exchange. What is remarkable—and what opened the door of the New World—is how well they seemed to understand each other. They were rehearsing ancient gestures, by which our species has moved itself and its desired objects all over the planet. It was not an exceptional event, even for that time and place. The Atlantic dry cod fishery and the ensuing fur trade had been exchanging with the northern coastal people for over a century. In habitations along the St. Lawrence it was already possible to see metal pots, rats, and *porcelaine*,[4] the shell that had anciently been an article of commerce throughout the Mediterranean. By the early 1600s the Huron were so dependent on it that they had ceased to manufacture their own shells for exchange. Unlike the military assaults that characterized many colonial ventures, this "invasion" appears more like continuity than conflict.

But the Dutch exchange is of more than parochial interest, because there also occurred only a few years later another tragic bit of good fortune—the Dutch observed that these beads behaved very much like their money. Preceding the English colonists by a decade, they adopted the beads as the official currency of Manhattan. And so began to buy North America, with the money that lay waiting on its beaches. They were also, among themselves, extremely cash poor. It was a godsend.

4. THROUGHOUT THE *JESUIT Relations* and in other texts, the word *porcelaine* is translated "porcelain," erroneously suggesting a ceramic article of trade. It may denote a glass bead of European manufacture, but the general reference is to the Mediterranean cowrie shell, Europe's oldest medium of exchange, and by extension any such shell used in trade, or any beads made of shell—as the English used the word "wampum."

On the degree to which Europe had already affected the ecology and economy of the New World see Carl Sauer, *Seventeenth-Century North America* (Berkeley, 1980).

🦪 🦪 🦪

A soft late afternoon light comes in through high windows. The room is peaceful, quiet. I'm the only person in here. The varnished oak cases hold a remarkable hodgepodge of wampum articles, selected apparently at random from the Northeast Coastal and Woodlands cultures. In some way that we only dimly comprehend, these articles of shell had a kind of currency over a vast region, threaded by a common nomenclature, agreements about value, and a network of trails by which the beads moved through the Great Forest, inland and westward beyond the valley of the Ohio. A message system, and these its medium.

There are two Seneca message sticks in the case, which unless purchased or stolen would have been brought here by runner from western New York State. One string attaches thirteen black beads to the stick, marking the death notice of one of the chiefs of the Iroquois Confederacy. It invites the hearers to attend the Ritual of Condolence, the ceremony of loss and restoration that is the heart of the Longhouse culture. It carried the solemn news through the forest and then brought the healing reply, and the naming of another to fill the empty place in the Council of Chiefs.

The other message stick is an invitation to the Green Corn Dance. It has two long strings of white beads, and notches on it tell the day. There is a necklace all the way from the Winnebago—three feet of white beads with scattered black, attached to a pendant of German silver. From the Mohawk a woman's hair ornament, a diagonal pattern of black beads on white. A Penobscot collar, several rows wide, stripes of white across black beads. An Onondaga gathering of five white strings, one for each member nation of the Iroquois league; one string with four black beads, representative of their authority to open the councils of the Longhouse.

Message and ornament, record and symbol, article of exchange—in all these forms the beads moved through the forest. Strung as if on telegraph lines of hands, they not only represented but were the path between people and nations, the clear path from heart to heart, the agreement to agree. A string of three strands alternately black and white: the clan mothers urging a couple to live together.

It was only to be expected that the Dutch should perceive the beads with their own sense of what constituted wealth— valuations they were willing to enforce, the only description in town. The museum notes claim, with your usual Manna-

hatta insolence, that while in New England only the chiefs
wore wampum,

> *in New York, where shells were more plentiful, women*
> *wore necklaces, collars or bracelets of wampum, tied*
> *their hair and decorated their costumes lavishly with it.*

The tendency toward use-value and ornament, with less emphasis on exchange, is common enough where the supply of "mint" material is abundant. It didn't at all mean they were richer. Yet it must have seemed to the Dutch, founding their colony on the doorstep of the original clam,[5] that they had been handed the Bank of North America. The official rate of exchange was set at six white beads, or three of the purple, to a stiver (a unit approximate to the English penny). And with that they were open for business.

And are to this day.

The custodians of museums in New York State are keenly aware of the value of their holdings in beads. This one in particular has been informed, for example, that some of its wampum had come by way of a Chicago dealer in artifacts, a T. R. Roddy, who in 1899 had illegally purchased eleven belts that ended up in Gustav Heye's collection.[6] The Council Chiefs at Grand River have been requesting their return since the year before the museum opened, and the belts do not appear to be part of the present display. When I ask the woman at the desk where the rest of the wampum belts are, she studies me like a bank teller wondering if she can make it to the alarm button. Instead she says nothing. Stares at the phone till it rings. Answers that instead. No matter. They must be stashed with the million or so other artifacts the museum is unable to display, perhaps in their "research branch" out in the Bronx. Not available to undocumented alien scholars. I wander back to the wampum.

Of the four belts on display, two are beaded documents to mark the massive land transactions of William Penn. One is said to define the boundaries of his purchase, the other outlining additional territories ceded him by the Lenni Lenape.

5. *CLAM.* A DOLLAR. 1939: "I hit a crap game for about 80 clams" (J. O'Hara, *Pal Joey*), Harold Wentworth and Stuart Berg Flexner, *Dictionary of American Slang* (New York, 1967).

6. A CHRONOLOGY OF THE acquisition of the Heye foundation's wampum, and efforts for repatriation, is in *Akwesasne Notes* (Early Summer 1988): 9, along with the account of their eventual return to the wampum keepers at Grand River, Ontario.

The belts are about two feet long and are eighteen rows wide, the white shell and dark in patterns that bear little resemblance to our maps of Pennsylvania.

Two hundred years have left a fine patina, the purplish black and yellowed white far deeper and in every way richer than I had expected. Photos and description give little idea of their presence, their luminous beauty as objects. The patterns are clearly mnemonic, and would have been a very explicit memorandum of the agreement, recitable verbatim by those who directed the weaving and those trained to read them. But their *object*-ness was not lost in the transaction. They were also *a thing presented*, a gift from the inhabitants to Penn—not just a contract, and not that pseudo-contract, money (the "seller" here gave the beads to the "buyer"). Presented as a gift *and* a marker of the gift, the belts represented the formal opening of an ancient relationship.

But in another place, we know from our history books, is a piece of paper, and on it we see another version of this contract. We picture the great Penn, one hand on the wampum belt, the other holding a piece of paper across the Atlantic:

> *To have and to holde to the only behoof of the said William Penn his Heirs and Assigns forever To be holden of us as of our Castle of Windsor in free and common soccage paying only two Beaver Skins yearly.*[7]

A very different transaction appears to be marked here. Two beaver—only two beaver, a "token" amount—in soccage, signifying a feudal land tenureship in which the vassal owes a fee, but not actual service, to his lord. How strange, though, that this transaction should be directed not to the Lenni Lenape, but to the king of England. Both parties are paying their respects to their idea of the land's ultimate custodian—their gods, their God, or Charles II on God's behalf. But where one party extended a gift of use-relation, the other party thought he had come into possession, into an ownership-relation, "to have and to holde." The gift was of course not reciprocal: the land was surveyed and divided as if it were

7. THE ROYAL PATENT granting Penn his great tract is abundantly quoted in histories of Pennsylvania, but whether this grant's boundaries actually resemble the quadruple boundaries and territories indicated on the belts is not documented. In the 1890s Harriet Converse (*Myths and Legends of the New York Iroquois* [Albany, 1908], 143) noted that Penn's grandson gave the Pennsylvania Historical Society a belt delineating the figures of a white man and Indian shaking hands; five diagonal "props," perhaps delineating the five Iroquois nations, support these two figures. Such agreements commonly marked cessions of hunting territory or adoption of tribes/nations into a preexisting union.

just another parcel of English commons to be enclosed and leased and farmed for money. The Lenni Lenape were later known as the Delaware, for the river valley they no longer inhabited. We begin to see the breadth and depth of a tragic misunderstanding.

The third belt is probably a decade or so older than the others, dating from the last years in which the inhabitants were acknowledged proprietors of the eastern shore. It is longer, more elaborately designed, and apparently marked for some personal use. It bears the inscription *TYZACKE. 1609.*[8] There is no way of knowing what agreement or occasion it memorialized, in accord with the usual function of wampum. It may have been worn or displayed as a personal treasure, a use reflecting both the wearer's proximity to the coastal "mint" and the inflationary effects of the colonial adoption of wampum as a currency. The name in square Roman letters is that of Tyasks—John Tyasks, after the European nomenclature—a chieftain of the Wampanoag, southeastern Massachusetts people whose power and influence were greatly extended in the mid-1600s, due in part to their strategic location. Between the Narraganset—who soon followed the example of the Long Island manufacturers and used their own clam beds to supply the colonial bead connection—and the Massachusetts Bay Colony, which had followed the Dutch in adopting wampum as a currency, they were in the classic position of middlemen, an advantage that would prove their downfall.

Tyasks was an associate of Metacom, son of Massasoit, the Wampanoag chief famed for welcoming and provisioning the Plymouth colonists, a decision he lived to deeply regret. Metacom was known to the New Englanders as Prince (later King) Philip, and in both wealth and stature he was probably as royal a personage as the colonists would encounter, on this continent or the one they so recently had left.

Prince Philip a little before I came for New England coming to Boston had a coat and buskins on set thick with

8. THE BELT, ABOUT A hand's breadth by three feet long, also contains several geometrical figures; the date coincides with the first arrival of Dutch traders and may commemorate an agreement then made. As the only belt I've found that displays a personal name or European letters, it signifies the beginning of the end for the Wampanoag.

these beads in pleasant wild works and a broad belt of the same, his accoutrements we valued at twenty pounds.[9]

9. JOHN JOSSELYN,
An Account of Two Voyages to New England
(London, 1674).

10. SAMUEL G. DRAKE,
Biography and History of the Indians of North America
(Boston, 1837), cited by Converse (*Myths and Legends,* 144).

11. (LONDON, 1643).
Williams's small, invaluable treatise is variously reprinted, usually for its account of the first American money.

Another account a few years later records the same fascination, and the same wonder at the mingling of ornament and wealth:

King Philip had a coat all made of wampumpeage which, when in need of money, he cut in pieces and distributed plentifully among the Nipmoog sachems and others.[10]

This puts the Manhattan claim to wealth in another light. Having a lot of beads is one thing—having sufficient class and cultural force to wear them as tokens of power, a power that is enhanced by giving them away—this is value in another sense.

So what we see in these first encounters, inevitably fatal in the long run, is the failure of the colonist to see the beads as something distinct from money. Even that independently pious liberal Roger Williams, in his *Key into the Language of America,*[11] could not comprehend the shell adornment except as an ostentatious use of coin:

Machequoce—A Girdle: Which they make curiously one, two, three, four, and five inches thicknesse and more of this money which (sometimes to the value of ten pounds and more) they weare about their middle and as a scarfe about their shoulders and breasts. Yea the Princes make rich Caps and Aprons (or small breeches) of these Beads thus curiously strung into many formes and figures: their black and white finely mixed together.

The dissenting Dr. Williams was no doubt understanding of spiritual value and was able to appreciate fine objects, but it is likely that "rich," as used here, is more a term of monetary than aesthetic valuation. The distinction between wealth and money was further obscured by the inhabitants' willingness to cooperate in this misunderstanding:

The Indians are ignorant of Europes Coyne; yet they

have given a name to ours, and call it Monêash from the
English Money. Their owne is of two sorts; one white,
which they make of the stem or stocke of the Periwincle
which they call Metaûhock, when all the shell is broken
off: and of this sort six of their small Beads (which they
make with holes to string the bracelets) are currant with
the English for a peny. The second is black, inclining to
blew, which is made of the shell of a fish which some
English call Hens, Poquaûhock, and of this sort three
make an English peny. They that live upon the Sea side,
generally make of it, and as many make as will. The In-
dians bring downe all their sorts of Furs, which they take
in the Countrey, both to the Indians and to the English
for this Indian Money: this Money the English, French
and Dutch, trade to the Indians, six hundred miles in sev-
erall parts (North and South from New England) for
their Furres, and whatsoever they stand in need of from
them: as Corne, Venison, &c.

Williams correctly notes the Narraganset distinction of nomenclature—between *wompam*, the white beads, and *suck-*
àuhock, which literally translated black shell (beads); but the
latter seems also to have connoted antiquity and reverence, a
distinction that the colonist could only see as a two-for-one
deal, meaning either money or more money.

I consider making another attempt to question the curator.
I want to ask her about the present value of these beads, and
how they came to be here. While New York and Washington
quarrel over who should guard the wampum, there is growing and persuasive argument for returning them to those
stubbornly unvanishing Americans whose culture they still
belong to. But she is standing in the lobby, away from her
desk, held spellbound by the conversation of two Apaches
wearing western-cut suits and string ties. One has on a wide
red headband. They are just returned from Paris, where they
no doubt played to equally adoring audiences. Shades of
James Fenimore Cooper. I decide to let it go.

12. DON TAXAY'S SURVEY (subtitled *and Other Primitive Currencies of the Americas* [New York, 1970]) is a collaboration of the two venerable institutions sharing the corner of 155th and Broadway. Drawing on the Heye collection, published by the American Numismatic Society, the book has all the strength and weakness of that union. Describing pre-European economic life in the Americas, and to some degree its usurpation by the invaders, it is at its best in the account of wampum and the Campbell shell mint. I would more strongly emphasize, first, that the wealth of the New World was not simply appropriated but was *purchased* by the takeover of an existing economy; and second, that the economy already in place was still based on the ancient gift relation, and its tokens were not money. As a good ethno-numismatist, Taxay tries to make this clear, although it is perhaps both too deep and too obvious to be grasped by practicing monetarists.

There is one more belt in the case. About a hand's width by four feet long, it is said to have been "taken from a warrior" by a General Benjamin Bellows. Nothing of who the warrior was, who this obscure general, and under what circumstances it was "taken." Nothing said of what broken agreement it might represent. Despite elaborate workmanship, the beads themselves are comparatively cheap looking, made of glass. It must date from about a century after King Philip, and the war that wiped out his people. Along with them, the shell beads disappeared from the coastal colonies and had to be imported.

I have only to walk around a corner of the display room to see where the bead exchange had gone. On the wall are drawings and implements of wampum manufacture, undertaken by Abraham Campbell in Park Ridge, New Jersey, about 1735. A *factory*, where they turned out money in the form of beads, to be sent inland with traders and colonial agents, to a new frontier where they proceeded to reenact the cheapening of North America. It was this outrageous history, which I'd come across in a book—*Money of the American Indians*[12]—that had brought me to the museum and the one next door. Perhaps only to learn what I already knew but could not quite believe. A *factory*. How dare they even display these spoils of genocide, and beside them the enabling implements of deceit and greed.

It began as a question about money—a confession of near-total ignorance as to what money was, and what gave it value. Like the colonist, and in common with many others, I had almost none and didn't know very well how to live here without it. But after three centuries, the colonist's solution to that problem—beginning with the misvaluation of these beads—has brought this land, with all its life and wealth, to a state of spiritual and material bankruptcy. I wanted to renegotiate the contract—at least the small part of it I carry around in my pocket. So now I follow a trail of promises, made and not kept, back to these original agreements with North America. And again and again I see things the colonist missed, valuations that were in place and were ignored or misunderstood or simply betrayed. I hear voices saying things my money doesn't mention when it talks.

So while it began as a question, the note of loss and outrage will not stay down, and it comes out instead an accusation. I have to admit my reaction makes me ill-suited to this melancholy detective work. I bypass the lobby and instead wander upstairs and spend a long time looking at a raven feather cape among the Northwest carvings of wood and bone. There is a string of dentalia shells, the ancient currency of the coast and rivers I've come from. It feels closer, then the consolation passes and I feel farther from home than ever.

"Do you know about commodities?" The guy sitting next to me was several beers into his line of thought. I stared more deeply into mine. It wasn't in the budget, but I'd scrimp later. I'd subwayed down Broadway from the museum, and had sought refuge in this neocolonial tavern, full of professionals who also hadn't made it home yet. He was slight, balding, in a light gray suit, a little rumpled, his tie off. He looked distinctly unhappy.

"Futures, you mean?" I looked at him with convincing ignorance. "Not much."

He had to think about whether I was worth further conversation.

The theory of currency and commodity came to North America hand in hand with the Puritans' theories of sin and salvation. The principles brought by the colonists, had they adhered to them, still maintained a connection with ancient rules of exchange. It is no great leap from the bronze age pastoral laws of Deuteronomy—

When the Lord your God has blessed you with prosperity, and the place which he will choose to receive his name is far from you and the journey too great for you

*to be able to carry your tithe, then you may exchange it
for silver*[13]

—to the pulpit of the church at Boston, where it was declared
to the flock in unmistakable detail:

*A man may not sell above the current price, i.e., such a
price as is usual in the time and place, and as another
(who knows the worth of the commodity) would give for
it if he had occasion to use it; as that is called current
money which every man will take.*[14]

But of course the rules were subject to some interpretation,
and it was a new world. From a list of vices the archdeacon
was to search out and suppress, we can infer the forms of
usury actually in practice, as for example "whether he buys
anything for a less price than it is worth, because he pays before receiving the article, for example, standing corn." That is,
trading in futures was a serious spiritual offense. Time belonged to God.

He said his father had been a lawyer for Texaco—one of
those east coast shysters who'd recently been bullwhipped by
a Texas jury, then chainsawed by a Houston appellate judge to
the tune of 10.53 billion. All just for buying an oil company
out from under another oil company. It was only the beginning of the end of our most recent age of acquisition, and the
hostile takeover was still considered greedy and ungentle-
manly. The jury, he said, gave the judgment to Pennzoil not
because they gave a damn who got Getty Oil—but because
they saw what bastards the Texaco guys were. His father, he
said, had become increasingly mean and argumentative and
harder to take care of. He got another glass of beer. The
preacher's argument continues:

*Where a man loseth by casualty of sea, it is a loss cast
upon himself by Providence, and he may not ease himself of it by casting it upon another; . . . but where there
is a scarcity of the commodity, there men may raise their*

13. DEUT. 14:24. IT WOULD
be assumed and understood
that silver, and by extension
silver coin, represented
what did not belong to
man, but to God. Wendell
Berry distinguishes this as
The Kingdom of Heaven,
or The Great Economy, of
which human exchange
is but a small part
(*Home Economics*
[San Francisco, 1987]).

14. JOHN WINTHROP'S
sermon, cited by R. H.
Tawney, *Religion and the
Rise of Capitalism* (New
York, 1926) at the end of
his chapter on Calvin.
Tawney's book is still the
best source for the business
ethics in force at the time
of North America's first
colonization. On the
concluding article of this
sermon—"A man may
not ask any more for his
commodity than his
selling price, as Ephron
to Abraham: the land
is worth thus much"
—Tawney comments:

*It is unfortunate that the
example of Ephron was not
remembered in the case of
transactions affecting the
lands of Indians, to which
it might have appeared
peculiarly appropriate. In
negotiating with these
children of the devil,
however, the saints of God
considered the dealings
of Israel with Gideon
a more appropriate
precedent (114). . . .*

price; for now it is a hand of God upon the commodity, and not the person.

We carry in our pocket ancient contradictions. Coinage put business into the hands of the priest, in whose god one naturally trusted. But principles, placed in the care of a third party and thus divided from practice, rapidly disintegrated into text and subtext and gloss and commentary, until economic morality was taken from the priest and given to the lawyer. In whose hands the golden rule becomes so difficult of application.

He said he'd like to go back and visit the Adirondacks. He was reminded of that when I told him what I did for a living—he had worked as a carpenter once in the Adirondacks. It was a place he remembered feeling really alive. He must have dropped a bundle.

The colonists' monetary theory was fairly crude, and establishing valuations by sermon—however righteous the preacher—was not always effective in their new circumstances. In adopting wampum as their currency, they created for themselves some of the same difficulties they'd made for the inhabitants. Probably foremost was the general doubt as to whether it was really "money." But it was available and it was current—first for food and the necessaries of life, and then for beaver and peltry. And because, on one of his better days, the hatter to Elizabeth Queen of England had conceived of a use for this plentiful North American mammal—so that every head of any pretension for two centuries after had to have one—everyone knew what beaver was worth, to the exact stiver or penny. One had only to know how many beads were acceptable for a pelt of Indian-cured beaver and set the rates of exchange accordingly. At six fathom of beads (360 to a fathom) or eight guilders per skin, that's six beads to the stiver of white beads, or four of the black. This is somewhat less than clear, but what I really don't understand is, which is commodity, and where is the money? And what has happened to the price of beer?

14. (continued) The clash of Calvinist religious theory, and the entrepreneurial spirit of the Calvinist bourgeois, was similarly resolved in the case of Indian money—Winthrop's journal (*The History of New England from 1630 to 1649* [Boston, 1825], 1:112) notes with undisguised envy that Long Island "had store of the best wampum peak, both white and blue."

15. "Wampum" in Roger
Williams's *Key.* The Dutch
were at the mercy of the
same European markets and
juggled several currencies
and coin-commodities with
as little success as the English.
Beauchamp records a typical
memo from Manhattan's
Holland directors in 1656:
"We consider a change in
the value of your currency,
that is, placing the beaver
at 6 florins instead of 8,
and wampum at 8 for a
stiver instead of 6, a matter
of great importance." A
stiver was equivalent to an
English penny, a florin to
two guilders or shillings.

So here is the picture. On the eastern edge of North America we have the Colonist. He is holding beads. He is counting. Everything has a number. The year is 1637. Because of the trouble with the Pequot, the sale of guns and liquor is prohibited. Soon it will be legal again. His other hand cannot be seen.

And here, being pushed back from the edge, one transaction at a time, into the forest the Colonist feared and coveted, the Inhabitants. They are bringing from the interior the wealth of North America, now represented by the beaver that swims in its rivers and eats the flesh of its forest.

And there at the fragile margin, from the shore, they bring beads with which the Colonist can pay for the beaver and sell his brethren beer. Corn, once a currency, is no longer needed from the Inhabitants. In 1637 it is illegal in Massachusetts to purchase corn from any but the colony's plantations. The Reverend Bradford records since 1631 shipment of beaver weighing 12,530 pounds, plus another 1,000 pounds of otter to cover the freight—for total sales of £10,000 sterling. All purchased with beads.

But the New World trading companies were subject to the confusion and instability of their fledgling market system, and the value of beaver as a commodity, relative to silver as a currency, regularly rose and fell. This in turn affected the exchange rate of wampum, which was neither understood nor approved by their suppliers:

> *This one fathom of this their stringed money, now worth of the English but five shillings (sometimes more) some few yeeres since was worth nine, and sometimes ten shillings per Fathome: the fall is occasioned by the fall of Beaver in England: the Natives are very impatient, when for English commodities they pay so much more of their money, and not understanding the cause of it; and many say the English cheat and deceive them.*[15]

So the rates paid the natives could not fluctuate too radically, and some loss as well as profit had to be absorbed by the colonists, who did not yet have the considerable skill required to trap and cure and carry the beaver to market. This left the colonists hanging in the unstable breeze between European fashion and the elusive flat-tailed North American rodent.

To make matters worse, the colonies could not coordinate these values even among themselves. Beads relative to coin, coin relative to beaver, beaver to beads again—the enterprising colonists constantly struggled between the desire to undersell the competition, and the more urgent desire for gain. The first little American corporations finally came to agreement only when threats from outside became greater than their distrust of each other.

To the citizens of the colonies, the everyday muddle of exchange probably did not differ greatly from the places they'd left. People held to centuries-old devices of value, and the unquestioning assumption that gold and silver were money. But for most of those centuries, they had lived without money and were far more imaginative than modern shoppers in the old conceptual shuffle of coin and commodity. A sweetheart contract for corn between the Connecticut colony and Mr. Pynchon of Springfield sets the price at 5s. 6d. in "money"—at 6s. per bushel in wampum (at only 3 beads to the penny)—or in beaver at 9s. per pound.[16] It was a period when the dominant mode of exchange was "country pay"—that is, reimbursement in credit for merchandise at fixed prices. Commodity prices were set according to whether payment was to be in "pay," in "pay-as-money," or in "hard-money," where the price of a knife would be 12, 8 or 6 pence, depending on which medium you used and how long you could afford to wait. The "money" could be anywhere.

There was a great deal of flexibility in this monetary pluralism, and probably long-term stability. The flourishing city-states of Athens and Florence had employed such a combination of mint and commodity wealth, allowing more than

16. RECORDED BY WILLIAM B. Weeden, *Indian Money as a Factor in New England Civilization* (Baltimore, 1884). The use of multiple forms and tokens of "pay" by rural Euro-Americans is explained clearly by Alexander Del Mar's *History of Money in America* (1899; repr. Hawthorne, Calif., 1966).

one way to establish value and facilitate exchange. Now the "renaissance" nations of Europe had begun their feeding frenzy on gold and silver, and the age of monetary centralism was well under way—but outside the financial capitals the moneyless feudal society still held sway. Historians of money love to repeat the story of an English shilling found at Flushing in 1647, causing much astonishment: people from near and far coming to see it, some of them never having touched a coin before.

To function as a currency, a commodity has to be available as well as acceptable, and availability turned out to be a problem for objects other than silver coin. For beaver, because of the mercurial fashion markets and the impossibility of transacting daily business with such unwieldy bills—although ingots cast in the shape of a beaver enjoyed a brief and limited circulation. And for wampum too, there was a problem because supply and demand and quality were altogether beyond the control of the colonial councils that pretended to regulate it. Naturally, people fell back on whatever was available, especially those exchange items that had been in traditional use. Cattle, for example, probably the oldest commodity money, were readily accepted in payment of bills and taxes. The colonial councils were hardly exceptional in their problems with inflation and devaluation—the northerners probably fared no worse with wampum and beaver and silver than the southerners with roanoke and tobacco and slaves. For all of these, the problem was the perennial one—no one was minding the mint.

Anyone with manual dexterity, great patience, and a pile of shells could literally make money at home. Most of this work naturally fell to women—especially the women of the Montauk, whose proximity to the wealth of the Long Island beaches made them virtual slaves to the production of beads. As the coastal tribes were pushed out, this work fell increasingly to women of the colonies, the manufacture of beads remaining a cottage industry well into the nineteenth century.

The Campbell mint, as well as traders, farmed out piece-work to marginal households.

Those who had appointed themselves controllers of the wampum currency often found themselves controlled by forces of supply and demand they did not comprehend or were helpless to affect. One of its peculiarities, named after another of Elizabeth's clever ministers, Sir Thomas Gresham, his law, being to wit—Bad Money Drives Good Money Out Of Circulation.

> *Whereas, Very bad wampum is at present circulated here, and payment is made in nothing but rough, unpolished stuff which is brought hither from places where it is 50 per cent. cheaper than it is paid out here, and the good, polished Wampum, commonly called Manhattan Wampum, is wholly put out of sight or exported.*[17]

17. SIMON W. ROSENDALE, "The Involution of Wampum as Currency: The Story Told by the Colonial Ordinances of New-Netherland," was originally published in the *New York Times*, 1895 and reprinted as a pamphlet, 18 pp., n.d., in the Heye Foundation archive. The ordinances attempted to regulate the price charged by every tradesman, according to the form of payment.

For the thirty or so years of wampum's official currency, the confusion and deterioration of value continued. It would regularly be announced by the colonial councils that wampum was a commodity, not a currency. No one could be forced to accept it, since it was not really money. As it was declared in Rhode Island, "It cannot be judged but that it is a commodity, and that it is unreasonable that it should be forced upon any man." And then in the same declaration it would be acknowledged that it was the only available medium for the day-to-day exchange of necessaries, and its official value would be reestablished in relation to the pennies or stivers no one actually possessed.

To compensate for its rapid deterioration—"among which are circulating many without holes and half finished; also some of Stone, Bone, Glass, Muscle Shells, Horn, yea, even of Wood and Broken Beads"—a distinction would be made between good and bad, rough and polished, strung and unstrung, establishing the value of each. And then, acknowledging again that it wasn't actually money, the amount of the transaction would be limited to small purchases. Yet taxes were payable, fines were levied, and tuition at Harvard College paid in wampum beads.

This episode of colonial history, which reads like a farce of administrative ineptitude, is in other respects a tribute to the colonists' ability to keep two sets of books—one account to look after principles, another to take care of business. The devastating effect on the inhabitants was mostly ignored. The descendants of the colonist, to this day, are surprised and baffled by the consequent rise in prices and the cheapening of life.

The bar had grown noticeably louder in the hour or so we'd sat there. A joke was going around, one of those obscene analogies collected by sociologists interested in the ways we incorporate our worst losses and dislocations. It was only a few days after the fiery crash of the space shuttle, which had claimed the lives of all its astronauts, including one woman. That public cataclysm had followed hard upon the scandal of a presidential candidate's tacky affair with a young woman apparently distinguished only by her sexy looks. What the two women had in common was the joke's question, and the answer—they had both gone down on a Challenger—nearly overwhelmed the bar with its accompanying exclamations and laughter. I was shocked again by this public desperation pretending to be toughness, but pressed on with my sermon. As usual I seemed to be talking to myself.

"They had to regulate the price of beer," I explained. "Too many beads chasing too little beaver. Or too many hats and too few heads left in Europe. Made beer too expensive to drink." He was facing away from the bar now, obviously focused somewhere else. He eased away with a half-full glass, crossing to join a couple of guys that looked like they bought their suits at the same place he did. I finished my glass, left a small tip, and lurched out into the evening. I could still read by the door the proclamation of the colony's Director General, 1658:

Half a gallon of Beer—
    6 stivers in Silver
    9 stivers in Beaver
    12 stivers in Wampum

"Which just goes to show," I said to the first beggar I met. "Some people's money buys more than other people's money." I gave him the change in my pocket, which wasn't much. I didn't have to count to know I'd drunk my dinner.

By 1662 wampum had been abolished as an official currency in New England. Manhattan clung to its shell money for another quarter-century—under the English as the Dutch, as today, being perennially cash poor:

> *Whereas ye great scarcity of wampum throughout these*
> *his Royal Highness his territories, hath been taken into*
> *consideration, greate quantities thereof being yearely*
> *transported and carried away by the Indians, and little or*
> *none brought in as formerly, which is conceived to bee*
> *occasioned by the low value putt thereupon: And for that*
> *there is no certaine coyne in the Governmt, but in lieu*
> *thereof wampum is esteemed and received as current*
> *payment for goods and merchandise, as well as other-*
> *wise betwixt man and man.*[18]

18. PROCLAMATION OF the English Governor and Council, 1673, raising the rates of exchange from eight and four to the stiver, to six and three (cited by Beauchamp, *Wampum and Shell Articles*).

The value of wampum had suffered manifold devaluation, declining from 4 white beads/penny in 1641 to 8 in 1656, 16 in 1660, and 24 at the time the New England colonies discontinued its status as a legal tender. The value of beaver relative to the penny or stiver had likewise inflated, going from 8 guilders or shillings for an Indian-cured pelt to 24 before it dropped again to 6 in 1663. If this was as difficult for the colonist as it is today, one can understand their confusion and recurring sense of betrayal. The effect is unimaginable on those who brought out the product of so much natural wealth and practical skill, and went back into the forest with a diminishing handful of beads. They were declared a "mere commodity" until it was literally true. The miraculous "Indian money" had served its purpose—it had opened the door of the New World and bought the colonist time and advantage. The rest, as they say, being history.

THE INVASION OF AMERICA

"Asymmetrical prestation?" I ventured.

The waiter was setting out two steaming dishes of moussaka. My lunch partner and I hadn't seen each other in some time and were still catching up on each other's obsessions. It was my third day in town, and I was already feeling at home in this restaurant. Everyone I met in Manhattan seemed to want to eat here.

It had taken us only a few minutes to get back on the same conceptual wave—which, Paul and I agreed, the wavier the better. In literal fact, he had introduced me to the study of wave dynamics, catastrophe theory, and the laws of chaotic behavior, long before it became a trendy branch of physics. Since I'd seen him last, he'd been across the Atlantic. At the invitation of an artist friend, he'd boarded a 60-foot North Sea trawler to Bermuda, the Azores, Madeira, and Gibraltar. Every one hundred miles they dropped overboard a 460-pound block of polished stone. On each stone is inscribed some of the things we presently know—from personal anecdotes to the theory of quarks.[1] The ring of these stones will eventually circle the earth. Paul did the video, documenting this gift to the future. He was paid enough to land back here on his feet, though otherwise broke and homeless, and given the use of a hut on a mountainside of the Hudson Valley, which he still frequents.

Asymmetrical prestation, as far as I understand it, is an

1. BOB SCHULER'S *TETHYS* IS A work in progress. The project was threatened for a time by the IRS, who said that the stones were not artwork, but uncounted inventory at the bottom of the ocean.

2. THIS PARTICULAR INSIGHT
constitutes only one
aspect of Paul Ryan's
*Video Mind, Earth Mind:
Art, Communications, and
Ecology* (New York, 1993).
Witness its range: five
forewords, from the
viewpoints of ecology,
education, phenomenology,
anthropology, and art. I
find most congenial its
bioregional section, which
addresses the author's native
Passaic watershed in
relational terms, bringing to
the Great Falls a devotion
comparable to that of
William Carlos Williams's
Patterson. I first came across
these perceptions in a
journal Paul edited called
Talking Wood, after the
series of ancient pictographs
known as the Walam Olum,
but with a message of
new urgency: "that the
pictograms and the talk
must come together with
new practices, new habits.
Habits that will insure
survival as people."

economic anthropologist's term for a big spender. Not "balanced" prestation—what we do when we try to "get our money's worth." Not giving it away, either—that's "total" prestation, like love or mother's milk. It's more like Whitman's "spending for vast returns," where the sense of time and repayment are open-ended and comprehensive. What we meant by that golden rule of the late sixties: What Goes Around Comes Around. That rule had turned out to be much tougher and older than we had imagined—going way back, beyond the Diggers and the True Levelers, older than the Cynics and the Taoists—and yet was the law we had to answer every day, from whatever bed we woke up in. It was in effect on this very island as recently as a couple of centuries ago and was being celebrated at this moment at a table in one of its restaurants.

The unlikely combination of video documentary, readings in the American philosopher Charles Pierce, and four and one-half years in a monastic seminary had led Paul Ryan to a theory of relationship that I wholeheartedly agreed with, as far as I could follow it. It is based on what he calls "relational practice"[2] and argues for social and personal pluralism, something he has the nerve to call, in these days, a "community of lovers." It values the kinship relation—and here he has diagrams of triadic and dyadic combinations that are beyond me —over the state's classification, and he claims quite rightly that we will never truly settle in this land till we get our close relationships in order.

I ruefully agree. We are both reassessing relationships and renegotiating old transactions, though one calls it love and the other goes on about money. I borrow the economic anthropologists' terms, words like "prestation" cribbed from Marshal Sahlins's *Stone Age Economics*—which I take to be a direct descendant of Mauss's classic monograph, *Essay on the Gift.* So I also call it, more simply, the gift relation. Paul says that in the monastery they called it the economy of grace. To my mind, we are all—social scientists, communitarians, bioregionalists, anarchists, beaded flower children—searching the human past and the natural world for a model of relationship. Paul once spent a year documenting a waterfall. I study beads and "primitive economics," where I find the bias I am seeking:

> The bias is that of an economy in which food holds a commanding position, and in which day-to-day output does not depend on a massive technological complex nor a complex division of labor. It is the bias also of a domestic mode of production: of household producing units, division of labor by sex and age dominant, production that looks to familial requirements, and direct access by domestic groups to strategic resources.[3]

It is also the bias of kinship. We don't have a name for our tribe—I sometimes refer to it as the overextended family— but we recognize some obligation and in turn feel nourished by its web of relation. It's a chilly end-of-April day, and we both dig into our bowls of hot food. Between mouthfuls I try to explain why I've been thinking about the sixties, and how that projected book about love begins to sounds like the old book about money.

In a "stone-age" economy, all that we call "economic exchange" occurs outside the circle of family and clan and forms a wider web of relation. Within the kinship group—where today we see the final breakdown of the gift relation—all food and household goods are given and received freely. Exogenous trade, however, as in any dealing with "outsiders," is quite another matter. It could be a dangerous and delicate transaction, not unlike a negotiation of peace, usually arranged with a long-term trading partner among a friendly group within your region. But still you don't "buy" or "sell" but might give (generously) something of comparable worth to the thing you hope to receive. You probably refer to it obliquely, perhaps through a third party. People in a living or trading group are familiar with each person or region's particular gift

3. *STONE AGE ECONOMICS*, 187—another dog-eared cornerstone of my library, whose turned-down pages and scribbled margins I turn to as much for its inspiration as its professional insight, which is often refreshingly unprofessional:

From means to end "economy" is conceived as a component of culture rather than a kind of human action, the material life process of society rather than a need-satisfying process of individual behavior. . . . We reject the historically specific Business Outlook. . . . Solidarity is here affirmed with housewives the world over and Professor Malinowski (186).

Both content and attitude are appropriate to a notion of economy based on food and family.

—of wood, shell, feathers, foods—and work out in person, sometimes using tokens, all the transactions of goods and services that we enact with money.

But it isn't money—it assumes that your partner in exchange is sensitive to your wishes, as well as the value of your gift, and has an equal stake in continuing the transaction. It is not a mathematical equation, such as we define when we put money or plastic on the counter and walk out with our goods. It is a difficult long-term relationship, the exchange typically marked by a "surplus payment," so the spirit of the gift prevails. That's where the beads come in.

This is the business that was being transacted here with wampum—the ancient business of daily life on earth. The way human beings had maintained their relation to each other and to the land for millennia. A gift relation, with tokens of shell and bone and feathers, even stones too heavy to carry, to mark which way the gift was moving. And reciprocity—the return somewhere down the line—its sole and inviolable article of faith. I could almost make this better understood today if I called it karma instead of economics.

We ate as we talked, both enjoying these abstruse fields of active inquiry. A friend's obsessions become almost as dear as one's own, perhaps because we "share" them as freely as food. He envisions an eco-video network to put Manhattan more in touch with its surroundings. Video rangers roaming the parks and waterways, feeding natural data to the urban viewer. He recognizes information—especially natural facts—as one of those "strategic resources" to which the group needs better access.

Another sure sign you New Yorkers are doomed, his rural friends tell him. Nature on TV. Hopeless. He knows of course that they have their own madcap bioregionalist schemes and is undeterred. I tell him it has to be better than what we've got on TV now. His project, I can't resist adding, is like my own, an example of latter-day asymmetrical prestation. Slowly going broke. Something our tribe is famous for. An inevitable consequence, I would argue, of doing business where "negative prestation"—such as gambling or theft—is the dominant mode of economic behavior.

But the best news, to my sense of the tribe, was that my friend was with a woman his age, sharing the pleasure and confusion that comes with finding yourself on the other side of life's middle. He seemed very happy. My own life, and our collective history, had begun to remind me increasingly of the geology of home: hopelessly fractured and dangerously unstable. I had found myself in a relationship with two women, and I wasn't sure if I was stepping from one lily pad to another or slowly sinking into a swamp. For all our talk of love and community and dyads and triads, I was becoming rather gloomy on the entire subject. So his news was particularly welcome, and his present delight too rare to resist. It was spring and there was a small sign of love on this Manhattan rock.

We both cleaned our plates. Direct action. Hand to mouth. Heart to heart. To save ourselves, we seem to have to go the way we lost ourselves—one transaction at a time. The account we call home is long overdue, and our business with this great misappropriation we call America is far from settled. Get to know your trading partner. Learn to deal with family. Figure it out: who will get the check?

I plunked down most of today's meal money for my half of lunch and a generous tip. Whatever, we still agreed. And another chunk of stone, carrying all we love and the little we know, splashed and sank into the sea.

God Almightie in his most holy and wise providence hath soe disposed the Condition of mankinde, as in all times some must be rich some poore, some highe and eminent in power and dignitie; others meane and in subjection.[4]

Along with the concepts of virtue and divinely dispensed

4. THIS PASSAGE FROM THE elder John Winthrop leapt out at me from the first volume of Eduardo Galeano's brave and eccentric anthology of the Americas, *Memory of Fire*, trans. Cedrick Belfrage (New York, 1985), 221. For more of the Puritan realpolitik, of which the doctrine of divine inequality is the foundation, see Allyn Forbes, ed., *Winthrop Papers* (Boston, 1929–47).

wealth, the Puritan oligarchy—as much as the more traditional oligarchies of the southern colonies—required a class
of people to provide, along with goods and services, living
proof of their own moral and monetary status. They were the
"elect," and then there were the others. The ones we see in
the streets today. The perpetual underclass, "meane and in
subjection." The only thing they can kick is the dogs.

It was May Day in Tompkins Square Park. An old friend
was conducting me around places I hadn't seen in some years
and might not have found or recognized. She was telling me
how last time she was here she saw this junkie kick a dog in
the face. How brutal it gets. It must have been that image, or
the throng of outcast and homeless around us, that put me in
mind of the social philosophy of John Winthrop, founding father of the prosperous colony of Massachusetts. And how
within a generation his offspring had succeeded in inflicting
these principles on the New World. So great was their effi-
ciency, so thorough their ruthlessness, and the transformation
so complete, it has become in our memory like a scene change
of a miracle play—one moment a blank wilderness (what the
senior Winthrop, good Cambridge lawyer that he was, had de-
fined as a *vacuum domicilium*, meaning nobody really lives
here)—and the next moment New Canaan, full-blown and
complete, presided over by a benevolent patriarchy of Puritan
businessmen. Who also had to have a dog to kick.

The cultures that met on the eastern doorstep of North
America had each their own highly developed way of doing
business. The way of the colonist was in all basic respects the
news we read in today's paper: deficit financing supported by
inside trading of land and resource-extraction franchises. The
way of the inhabitants, older, more traditional, was based on
reciprocity and long-term relations between and within
human communities and the land. Both cultures were in flux:
partly because of their meeting, and partly because of internal changes, both were undergoing spiritual and material
adaptations, and both were involved in exogenous conflict
with neighboring nations.

The Winthrops had the indisputable edge, not so much of iron and gunpowder, but of having thrown off many of the moral restraints that had governed feudal Christian Europe. This transformation, a great step backward in human relations, was such a turning point in economic history that Karl Marx would cite it as a root cause of the miseries he denounced in *The Communist Manifesto:*

> the bourgeoisie, wherever it got the upper hand, put an
> end to all feudal, patriarchal, idyllic relations, pitilessly
> tore asunder the motley feudal ties that bound man to
> his "natural superiors," and left remaining no other
> bond between man and man than naked self-interest
> and callous cash payment.[5]

The European Middle Ages were not quite the picture of manly fealty Marx projects, but he is not far off in his description of the spirit of the Winthrops and their business associates. In throwing off the trappings of church and king— and with the additional advantage of having an ocean between the authorities and one's business—the colonists had somewhere let slip the virtue of caritas and the duty of noblesse oblige. And so brought to the New World the poorhouse and the prison, to take care of the casualties and excesses of every-man-for-himself economics. Where the natural state is presumed to be, as Thomas Hobbes put it, one of "perpetual warre."[6]

The first rule of this warfare economy—where a central authority is of course necessary to protect its investments—is that there is no rule but self-interest. This authority gives it a short-term advantage that societies based on balanced long-term exchange seem hard-pressed to overcome, despite their sometimes formidable capacity for exogenous warfare. The war economy takes its main strength from a constant of human exchange—the temptation to negative gift-giving (i.e., luck or stealth) as a means to personal enrichment. The gift economy, in this negative light, may be seen simply as a highly developed system of controls on such behavior and its

5. IN *THE COMMUNIST Manifesto* (London, 1848), Marx and Engels drew on the available models of European history and economy. It was not till Marx's discovery of Lewis Henry Morgan's *Ancient Society: Researches in the Lines of Human Progress from Savagery through Barbarism to Civilization* (1877; repr. New York, 1963) that older "new world" forms of social organization provided concrete examples of what a sustainable human economy might look like. Marx's notes on Morgan are available in *The Ethnological Notebooks of Karl Marx,* transcribed and ed. by L. Krader (Assen, Netherlands, 1972), and through their reworking by Friedrich Engels in his *Origin of the Family, Private Property and the State* (London, 1884). This connection is discussed in the next-to-last chapter of the present work.

6. THE SOCIAL THEORIES OF Hobbes's *Leviathan* are given full and lucid comparison to the gift and Mauss's theories in Marshall Sahlins's *Stone Age Economics* (New York, 1972).

destructive consequences—in the land the Winthrops had just left, for example—to both commons and commonwealth. The economy of "warre," by the same token, can be understood as a lack of these controls, a history of desperate stratagems, afterward graced with unctuous justification by the arts and sciences it subsidizes.

These economic strategies were not developed solely for the New World. By the time of the first serious conflicts with the inhabitants—skirmishes that occurred mostly in the coastal swamps—veterans of the Irish bogs were warning against the dangers of a prolonged guerrilla war against an entrenched indigenous population. But just as important as the tactics of its trade, the war economy developed a rationale for its behavior and adopted the trappings of its former morality as a pubic drapery to its deeds. Here again, the Irish had provided a convenient model. Being not only heathen, but worse—papists—they were easily relegated to the marginal status of "savage"—that is, not one of us, and so not eligible for the morality by which we claim to govern ourselves. Where there is profit to be made or advantage to gain, there in some form or another you will find a "savage." Thus the brutalization of the peasant—made into the kind of buffoon we see in Shakespeare's comedies—was a necessary accompaniment to the enclosure laws and the confiscation of the commons. They were England's own Indians, who would reemerge as the London poor. And who, delivered here by sentence or indenture or impressment, would become the "mob" that was so fatal to the colonies. And who, having won the colonies' independence, would then find themselves in the streets again, as if it were today.

The ragged revelers in the park are enacting an old tableau, of May Day in America. Readers of Nathaniel Hawthorne will recall his dark fable, "The Maypole of Merry Mount," based on the Puritans' suppression of Thomas Morton's rival colony. The New World's first entrepreneurs had as their primary duty to extinguish all that did not correspond to their idea of order—what is called today, a healthy business climate. This included not only the wild man and his wild land, but whatever "savage" remnants of the Old World had not washed off in the Atlantic crossing.

And upon Mayday they brought the Maypole to the place appointed, with guns, pistols and other fitting instruments, for that purpose; and there erected it with the help of Savages, that came thither of purpose to see the manner of our Revels. A goodly pine tree of 80 foot long was reared up, with a pair of buck's horns nailed on somewhat near unto the top of it: where it stood as a fair sea mark for directions, how to find out the way to mine Host of Merry Mount.[7]

7. THOMAS MORTON, *THE New English Canaan* (1637), ed. Adams (Boston, 1883) Bk. III, Chap. 14.

We have to marvel at the sheer audacity of Thomas Morton's revels, but like his idyllic colony, it is a hopelessly self-conscious scheme, concocted out of books, lacking the reality of the landed hospitality it reenacts. The public saints of Plymouth Colony naturally denounced him as an Idolater and a Royalist, and although he probably was neither, in the traditional sense to which he aspired, he had acted the part convincingly. Morton was rather easily tricked into surrender. They returned him to England in chains and, according to his own account, "disposed of what he had at his plantation. This they knew (in the eye of the Savages) would add to their glory, and diminish the reputation of mine honest Host." Our "honest Host," he omits to mention, had accumulated a substantial store of beaver and peltry, the trade of which now fell to the citizens of Plymouth. Who appear, no less than their neighbors the Winthrops, to have had just such an end in mind.

Morton's was not the first Maypole in the New World, nor the last. And despite their suppression by Parliament, along with the morris dance and other "pagan" rituals, they also survived in Europe. But with the pulling down of the Maypole, as in Hawthorne's story, a darkness descended on New England, a shadow that first overtook the soul of the

colonist, and then the land itself. The inhabitants, had they
been able to believe what they witnessed, had ample opportunity to see their fate.

"It says they want us to join them in the park."

I was reading from the yellow leaflet I'd been handed. The
homeless were inviting us to celebrate May Day with them.
They would have a parade, maybe a Maypole. Then we could
spend the night with them in Thompkins Square Park. *Experience homelessness,* it said.

Lori and I had walked up three narrow flights and knocked
on the door of the East Sixth Street flat. Now we were sitting
in Rosey's tiny kitchen, talking about the poor and where we
should go for lunch. I began to feel like I'd come here to research the Manhattan midday meal ceremony. I was all for it,
just no Greek food today.

Here was another old bicoastal friend, this one still working the frontline damage control we call nursing. Sprocket,
quintessential jazz bass man, is off at his day gig, repairing
the fragile structures of wood and string out of which he
makes his living and his music. It restores hope to see people
still living like this—voluntarily, stubbornly, gracefully on
the edge. You can see how it's wearing, through all the good
cheer. And you have to wonder how long it can survive the
frenzy of hunger and desperation all around. No one jumps
up and runs down to the street to join the homeless.

What is surprising again, at each stage of relations until the
final one, is how readily all parties to the New World invasion
engaged in business. The gestures of human exchange are ancient and apparently universal. The differences proved to be
so fatal in consequence, it is possible to overlook the abundant similarities. In fact, if the forms had not been outwardly

so alike, the underlying difference might have been more easily seen and avoided. As it was, tragically small distinctions
were missed—between gift and gain, exchange and tribute,
territory and ownership, and as to what was the value of a
life. Although he didn't know their source, the colonist was
quite aware of the advantage gained by these misunderstand-
ings and gave every sign to indicate that all participants were
playing the same game.

It began with beads. Then it shifted to the source of the
beads, the inlets of Long Island Sound, and then the opposite
shore, of what is now Connecticut. Both the Dutch and
English colonies wished to control this source of wealth—
typically, the Dutch for the beads, the English for beads and
an offshoot colony, and of course both for what the beads
would buy. Their competition for this strategic money supply, which they had caused to suddenly multiply to levels of
unimagined wealth, disrupted a very delicately balanced
game that had been worked out by the coastal tribes. The balance was kept by the exchange of beads, the holders of the
clam beds traditionally giving a certain number of treaty
strings (along with such delicacies as smoked clams) on an
annual basis to their neighbors north and south and inland.
Who in turn had similar diplomatic exchange with one another and the powerful inland nation of the Iroquois. But
then the stranger bought in, and the stakes went up.

Apparently the Pequot made the first move, although
they no doubt did so in response to these new valuations and
probably were aware of English interest in the Thames and
Connecticut watersheds, as well as in the clams of Gardiners
Bay, directly across from the mouth of the Connecticut—a
river access to the interior, and money to buy what it contained. The Pequot claim, based on traditional use and considerable skill at woodland conflict, was also threatened by other
parties to the bead exchange. So after suffering some setbacks
in skirmishes with both their Dutch and Narraganset neighbors (whose bead connection they were), they approached the
Winthrops with a deal. They proposed the English establish a

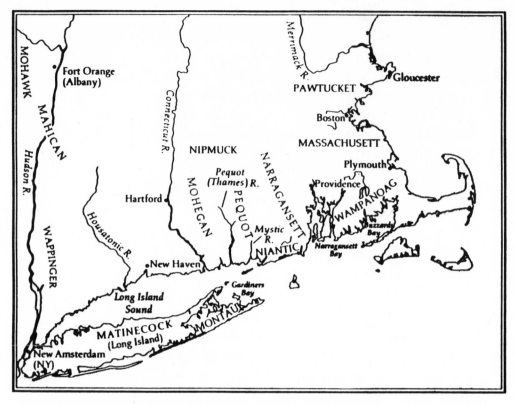

Territories of principal northeastern coastal nations with major settlements of colonial New Holland and New England in 1637, at the outbreak of the Bead Wars.

8. THE EVENTS LEADING UP TO the Pequot War are chronicled by Bradford's *Of Plymouth Plantation,* Winthrop's *Papers,* and a century later by Hutchinson's *History of the Colony and Province of Massachusetts Bay,* ed. L. S. Mayo (Cambridge, 1936). None of these official histories can be trusted as to the context of the transactions. Hutchinson, for example, is author of the "fact" that coastal and inland people had no knowledge of wampum before its introduction by the Dutch, but he sees no connection between the beads and the Indians' persistent . . .

trading post on the Connecticut and convince the Narraganset (and their Mohegan allies) to live peaceably with this new arrangement. In token of which, according to Winthrop's own account, the Pequot messenger brought to Boston "two bundles of sticks, whereby he signified how many beaver and otter skins he would give us . . . and great store of wampompeage (about two bushels), by his description."[8]

The offer to open commerce—the gift transaction that prepares the way for all the exchange to follow—was seen by the colonists as a sign of weakness, if not outright folly (Can you believe it, they want to *give* us Connecticut?). The beads were taken as a sign of vassalage, a hierarchical relation, and a form of tribute to be exacted from a dependent. The Puritans responded falsely to every term of the offer. The two bushels of wampum were not enough—400 fathom would be required. Yes, they promised to arrange a settlement with the Narraganset—but in fact they would continue to engage them in an alliance against the Pequot. And yes, they would open a trading post on the Upper Connecticut—but instead Winthrop Jr. was hastened home from London where he'd been developing their New World franchise and was installed with troops at the river mouth with orders to exclude not only the Dutch and other English colonies—Plymouth had its eye on the prize as well—but also their own antinomian dissidents who were threatening to form a splinter colony.

The Pequot had to refuse. They knew the difference between alliance and tribute and that 400 fathom of strung "manhatta grade" wampum was a considerable fortune, comparable to half of Massachusetts' annual revenue in taxes. The colony, however, considered they had a done deal, and when the Pequot failed to come up with the beads, it merely showed what savages they were, and how deserving of their impending fate. Because an even better deal, of course, was no Pequot at all between them and the bead connection.

At dawn of a May morning, 1637, four to seven hundred women, children and elders were just waking in wigwams on the banks of the Mystic River. The gang of volunteer militia and mercenaries butchered all but a handful of Pequot inhabitants. The Narraganset withdrew from the horror, only to run into the returning Pequot warriors, whose attack brought them in turn within range of the colonists' rifles. The Pequot sachem Saccacus, with about forty survivors, fled eastward and crossed the Hudson where he offered some £500 in wampum to the Mohawk in exchange for their support. But the Mohawk had a bead covenant with the Narraganset, which they honored by returning Saccacus's scalp and hands to the English. Who accepted this gift as the deed to their new colony and public mint.

This is not the story quite as Winthrop told it, and not the transaction that has come down to us in the official histories. Only recently have we been able to turn to books such as Francis Jennings's *Invasion of America* for an accurate

8. (continued) disregard for written contracts. Winthrop's account of the Pequot massacre, in a letter immediately penned to Bradford, is precise as to detail—"We send the male children to Bermuda, by Mr. William Peirce, & the women & maid children are disposed aboute in the townes"—but betrays not a clue as to the actual horror perpetrated: "Our people are all in health (the lord be praised), and all though they had marched in their armes all the day, and had been in fight all the night, yet they professed they found them selves so fresh as they could willingly have gone to such another bussines."

account of the colonists' way of doing business. The centuries of denial that have passed as American History, it turns out, have been the result of an ongoing program of official disinformation—just as we presently witness when we read the news. Here, as Jennings sets them forth, are the stages of the process:

> 1) a deliberate policy of inciting competition between natives in order, by division, to maintain control;
>
> 2) a disregard for pledges and promises to natives, no matter how solemnly made;
>
> 3) the introduction of total exterminatory war against some communities of natives in order to terrorize others; and
>
> 4) a highly developed propaganda of falsification to justify all acts and policies of the conquerors whatsoever.[9]

It is of course only the third item that we are accustomed to hearing about, under the historical headings of "Indian wars" or the back-page news of "rural pacification programs." Not only is this a false report, it obscures the fact that long before and after the violence there was a war of deception, dealing in bad faith, and betrayal of the most ancient laws of exchange. They began with a gift, and they turned it into money. This is how the New World was "conquered"—not with a bang, but one crooked deal at a time.

Begin with the gift of food, the source of all life and economy: (1) Say that corn is money. Then adopt beads as your currency, and buy corn with beads. (2) Now beaver is part of the deal, because the beads are the inhabitants' "coin," and they gladly exchange it for peltry. (3) To get more beads, sell guns. And to get more beaver, sell powder and shot on credit. (They have less time to hunt now, because they are constantly occupied in trapping and hunting for the fur trade.) (4) To get more beaver and more beads, sell them rum made of the surplus sugar of the Indies trade. (5) When the beaver is gone and the markets declining, make notes of credit your currency. The paper is redeemable in the earth you now buy

9. FRANCIS JENNINGS, *The Invasion of America* (Chapel Hill, 1975), 212–13. Through their work in institutions such as Chicago's Newberry Library, Jennings and his colleagues have let a great deal of light into the dark attic of colonial history. They show the extent to which the invasion took the form of economic exchange: "Social and political factors were involved as well, . . . but underlying all others was European domination made possible by an exchange in which Indian gifts were greater. Civilization was not brought from Europe to triumph over the Indians; rather the Indians paid a staggering price in lives, labor, goods and lands as their part in the creation of modern American society and culture" (41).

and sell. (6) When they complain the money does not feed them as the earth did, make heads and scalps a currency. (Remember, they still have the guns.) And now that the beads are devalued, except for what your own poor can manufacture for the inland trade, sell the surviving inhabitants as slaves, in exchange for the silver that follows the sugar of the Indies.[10]

Now you are rid of the savage problem, have cash in pocket, and can still keep a body of people in economic subjection, whence they may be recruited at need. The savage, the peasant, the underclass—who have bought the New World several times over, and still gather to send messages to the governor of the colony.

Shelter Now. Stop Gentrification. Homes Not Bombs.

As the waiter brought our hot curried dishes, we turned to watch the ragtag parade of desperate May Day revelers, swelling the sidewalk with their bodies and signs, spilling out into the street and stopping traffic. A motley, oddly dressed throng of life's strangers, they don't seem much different from the people I remember living in this part of town. Maybe they were less strung-out then and had homes—or at least a *shooting* gallery. Now even the walls are too expensive for anything but art. Following close behind them on horseback, uniforms and clubs and guns. The paddy wagon. Then the disinformation van, full of cameras and reporters. The parade will not make tomorrow's *Times*. We ate our Indian food and talked about the past.

It begins with beads and ends in bloodshed. Fewer than forty years later, the Narraganset, apparently now secure as brokers of the Connecticut Valley and the shell exchange, were slaughtered in their encampment much as the Pequot had been. As if they had forgotten what they had witnessed. It was an incident in the prolonged power struggle that came to crisis in what was called King Philip's War, after that

10. THE TRADE CYCLE of corn, beads, peltry, rum and guns was not sustainable, since it inevitably destroyed one party to the exchange. Fated from the first introduction of wampum as "money," lamented by every colonial authority who permitted it to continue, yet for a century they echoed Bradford's complaint, "It makes the Indians of these parts rich and powerful and also prowd thereby; and fills them with peeces, powder and shote, which no laws can restraine" and usually blamed the Dutch for the introduction of the problem. In fact the New England authorities were no more interested in restriction of trade than they were in creating a stable exchange. Colonial ordinances had no more effect on the liquor and gun business than they had on the price of beaver or the value of beads. See Francis X. Moloney, *The Fur Trade in New England* (New Haven, 1931). The inclusion of scalps in this trade cycle is usually credited to New Amsterdam's governor William Kieft, who in 1641 made them redeemable in wampum.

Wampanoag sachem, Metacom, whose beads had previously been so much admired. Again, it was not so much a war as a series of desperate schemes. It was the last stage, as the Pequot massacre was the first, of the consolidation of those North American beachfront properties known as New England. And it eliminated the Algonquin tribes as middlemen between the beads and the inland fur trade. The material and spiritual costs were enormous. By any accounting, it would prove to be not worth it.

Because he was of the second generation to deal with the colonists, Metacom had some grasp of their business methods. The hereditary chieftainship had passed to him when his brother mysteriously died after being escorted to Plymouth town by the son of Governor Winslow. For questioning, having been suspected of conveying land to outsiders. Because Plymouth had no royal charter, their land claims were partly based on the fiction that the Wampanoag (and their territory) were in the custody of the colony. This is why, each time he was "naughty," Metacom was required to put his mark to a paper in which he promised to pay a certain fine of wampum and wolves' heads—and almost as an afterthought, "not to dispose of any of the lands that I have at present, but by the approbation of the governor of Plimouth."[11] As he made his mark—in the presence of "divers of the gentlemen of the Massachusetts and Connecticut"—he surely knew, without having to read, that he was being set up. Though they called themselves "gentlemen" and "United Colonies," they were clearly neither and jealously noted each others' scheming maneuvers. For Metacom, since there was no reciprocal gift exchange, the ink on paper no doubt seemed peculiarly abstract and without reference to any obligation. In conformance to their demands, Metacom made his mark, wished them all they deserved, and disappeared into the coastal swamps.

The Narraganset, on the other hand, were engaged in diplomatic relations on several fronts, and struggled to stay on good terms with Boston. They paid their annual assess-

11. THESE AGREEMENTS ARE noted in Hutchinson's *History* with some care, since they support the colonists' justifications for war. The notes betray an undercurrent of doubt as to whether the Wampanoag understood the "subjection" to which they had agreed by affixing their marks to paper: the violation of their status as "subjects" made their acts traitorous, and therefore a capital offense, thus absolving the colonists of simple murder.

ments, the English ("to show their moderacon") requiring of them "but twoo thousand fathome of white wampum for their oune satisfaction." They delivered, when hostilities had been provoked, the heads of several of Metacom's followers. And though they never got the advertised bounty of wampum for those heads, they additionally turned over to the English for execution or deportation the Wampanoag "squaw sachem," Weetamoo, and one hundred of her people who had sought refuge as neutrals and noncombatants. But none of this, nor the fastness of a nearly impenetrable swamp, nor king's decree, nor the protest of the pacifist Rhode Islanders in whose country it occurred—none of it altered the fact that they were marginals, no longer needed, and were sitting on a very desirable business location.

And so there occurred this historical oddity: that an "Indian war" allegedly provoked by King Philip in Plymouth Colony caused the armies of Massachusetts and Connecticut to attack a friendly tribe in pacifist Rhode Island. Roger Williams, in his report to Governor Leverett, estimated casualties at the Narraganset town of up to one thousand dead or wounded. It might have been worse but for a critical blunder —the attack came at a time when the warriors were at home, and those who escaped inflicted serious losses on the colonials. The survivors hastened to join Metacom's forces, who naturally greeted their recent adversaries with musket fire before accepting them into the now widespread rebellion.

But it was too late. The generation of Winthrop Jr. had many times the demographic and economic advantages wielded by their fathers. Further, even those few pieties and scruples that had survived the Reformation and the Atlantic crossing were apparently not passed on to these Euro-American offspring. Beads and beaver were all very well, but they had simply opened the door and provided the initial capitalization for new and vaster designs. They could afford a temporary interruption of the fur trade, with the prospect of having it all to themselves. The colonial domestic economy was now better established than that of the inhabitants, with a credit and delivery system able to supply military forces in the field. "We fetch in their corn daily, and that undoes them," wrote a participant, and while this increased the price of corn to two shillings a pint, the United Colonies could afford to get food to troops in the field and let a supply-hauling contract for which they were billed £22.

The colonies would quarrel among themselves over who should pay these costs of war, but they clearly now had the means to wage it. They had other sources of revenue besides the "Indian money" they had discarded. Against the advice and rulings of their colonial directors, they were illegally issuing private coinage and public notes of credit. The growing West Indies–Atlantic trade brought new markets for fish and lumber and slaves, and a regular income of European currency as well. Soon the forest had been sufficiently cleared and the wolf population destroyed to make grazing cost-effective. Yankee manufacturing zeal began to take hold of the shipbuilding and rum industries. A lust after material gain seemed to grow exponentially, along with this new prosperity. But a spiritual blight began to set in, and an unfamiliar mildew began to attack the European wheat stock.[12] The crops never recovered. Their money would unaccountably lose value, and there would be hunting of witches.

12. BIOLOGY AND SOCIOLOGY have begun to cooperate in telling this story, following Carl Sauer's pioneer work and giving a perhaps less ethnocentric view of recent history. See, for example, William Cronon's *Changes in the Land: Colonists and the Ecology of New England* (New York, 1983).

🐾 🐾 🐾

We sat on a bench in Union Square, talking about the past and where friends had gone. The May Day afternoon air was as sweet and sad as memory itself. Lori and I had been part of that strange wild fruit of the early '70s, when small rural towns that had barely ever entertained a liberal notion suddenly blossomed with radical egalitarian bakeries and bike shops, subversive cafes and conspiratorial coffeehouses and bars. We had lived for a while on the same small farm at the edge of town. We'd worked at the same bookstore, and shared a cultural life intense enough to have permanently x-rayed a number of mutual acquaintances. We continued to admire

each other from the sensible distance of survivors. She had
come east to a culinary institute, and stayed. She'd been in
some of the best kitchens, had read her Gertrude Stein, and
was now a writer about food. She was as sharp as ever.

It was a great comfort, far from home, to find a past and
distant life still so vibrant and funny and generous. She and
Rosey had bought lunch, saying they remembered how expensive it was to leave that life to visit this one. When I explained my peculiar mission, Lori remembered my obsession
with old shells and precious commodities. She said her
boyfriend was an artist. So is the woman I've been sending
postcards to, I said. She painted crows, and I had bought one.
We talked about the po-mo scene and what a lot of crap you
had to put up with to sell art. Or anything else they gave you
money for—art being just another thing the rich had to have
to replace the souls they'd lost in the market. Something the
galleries steal from the artists, who get it from the junkies,
who must have to take it from the dogs. Everyone now having
to live at the expense of someone else.

And then one day all the bills come due, and we find that the
banks have closed. This process of bankruptcy, so familiar to
us now, was the chief weapon brought by the Europeans to
the invasion of the Americas. First they drove the inhabitants
to insolvency, and that made it possible to dispossess them of
life and land.

Retreating before superior forces, during the winter of
1675–76 Metacom set about to gather an army of his own. Its
numbers included many inland and northern people, as well
as the coastal Algonquin, drawn to the belated cause of driving
the Europeans back to the sea. They included even the "pray-
ing Indians," those converts whose souls had been bought and
sponsored by church collections, and whose bodies were employed as spies and mercenaries in the Reverend John Eliot's
holy military missions. But two factors prevented the success

of this coalition, and both of them had to do with beads. As he went about building his alliance by the traditional method of making agreement, binding warriors to the cause by gifting, Metacom's supply of wampum proved insufficient to the venture. Forty years of manufacture had devalued the beads, so that ever greater quantities were required to maintain normal social bonds, and of course even greater for the urgent diplomacy of war. And while costs remained high, the supply of wampum had been absorbed by the colonists' securing ever greater trade and tribute to their own uses, meanwhile abandoning wampum as a currency among themselves. Instead it went westward, to the Mohawk and other Iroquois nations who controlled the inland hunting and trade routes. When Metacom attempted to buy French arms with New England's paper notes of credit, he was refused.

Because the Mohawk had traditional alliances with the Narraganset and other coastal tribes, there was reason to hope they might support Metacom's proposal of war. But again, they had another deal—this with Edmund Andros, the able colonial administrator of New York, who had seen the advantage of picking up the bead agreement—the "covenant chain"—which the Dutch had let go of. He also saw, as the New Englanders apparently did not, that an Albany-Mohawk alliance would effectively put an end to any Massachusetts plans for westward expansion. He assured them that New York had "supplyed our Indians with ammunicion, armes and all they wanted" in order to put down the Algonquin uprising. Very much like the Pequot a generation earlier, Metacom and his allies were turned back toward the coast and certain defeat.

The costs to the natural and cultural wealth of North America can only be guessed at. Roughly one fourth of the coastal inhabitants died in the conflict. I find no count of those sold into slavery, although the number included Metacom's nine-year-old son, whom the Plymouth judges after solemn consultation of the Old Testament sent to the Antilles rather than hang. The head of his deposed father,

King Philip, was displayed prominently, no doubt instilling the intended terror, and presumably enriching the individual who delivered it with the offered reward of "forty trucking cloth coats"—plus the bonus that provided "in case they bring his head, they shall have twenty like good coats paid them." (Ordinary warriors were worth but two coats, with a bonus of one for the head only.) Hutchinson's *History*, perhaps squeamish by this point, has a different accounting of Metacom's fate: "Instead of his scalp, he cut off his right hand, which had a remarkable scar, well known to the English, and it produced a handsome penny, many having the curiosity to see it."

King Charles's accountant, Lord Randolph—the last person the colonists wanted to see—was sent over in 1676 to assess the damages they had brought upon themselves. Randolph put the English cost in lives at 600 (of an estimated colonial population of over 50,000) and in damages at £150,000—

> *about twelve hundred houses burnt, eight thousand head of cattle, great and small, killed, and many thousand bushels of wheat, pease and other grain burnt . . . and upward of three thousand Indians, men women and children destroyed, who if well managed would have been very serviceable to the English: which makes all manner of labour dear.*[13]

They would henceforward be dependent on an imported underclass, selecting from among themselves those destined to be "meane and in subjection."

Naturally, the new underclass would carry on the revolt. There would be widespread and violent resistance to the consolidation of territory and power, the Winthrops and their friends not meaning to stop after all the expense and trouble of removing the original inhabitants. The resistance would usually be short-lived, falling prey to the same tactics of deception and division, now accomplished with paper instead of

13. *Doc Rel Col Hist NY,* 3:243–44. As with any visit of the Crown's representatives, this investigation raised the cry of injustice and tyranny. A complaint a decade earlier, regarding the visit of royal commissioners, is typical of the poor-mouthing that came from the colonies:

For such is the poverty and meanness of the people of this country (by reason of the length and coldness of the winters, the difficulty of subduing a wildernesse, defect of a staple commodity, the want of money, &c.) that if, with hard labour, men get a subsistence for their families, tis as much as the generality are able to do, paying but very small rates toward the public charges.

In fact it was only the intervention of the Crown that prevented worse outrages, to their fellow colonists as well as the indigenous people. A 1661 letter from the king put an end to capital and corporal punishment for religious dissenters, but Hutchinson notes: "The laws were afterwards revived so far as respected vagabond quakers, whose punishment was limited to whipping, and, as a further favour, through three towns only." Poverty and meanness indeed.

beads. Its vitality would then go underground, to wait for another day, and people would continue to cling to the small ceremonies and loose change that keep us human.

For half a century after it was declared no longer legal tender, eight stivers in wampum would still get you on the Brooklyn ferry. And would still purchase, in the crossing, those "glories strung like beads," which the poet reminds us are the source of wealth and treasure. The "vast returns" for which we spend and spend.

🦪 🦪 🦪

As we sat in the bright windy afternoon, sudden gusts blowing the trees and pigeons around, through the midst of the public square—not the May Day celebration we had been waiting for, but a parade of white-eyed patriots, bedecked in their flags and regalia, utterly earnest and joyless, clanging a very loud bell and proclaiming Law Day, an occasion foisted on us by our most blatantly lawless of recent presidents. They took their brazen noisy way across the green and over to a stage, a flatbed truck trailer draped with loyalist bunting. Some ward heeler began haranguing the small but deadly serious crowd through a microphone. Such invincible idiocy, so sure it will prevail, if not by force then by rule of sheer disgust.

We got up and walked away. She had to be at her uptown office. Hey, I said. Uptown. She smiled, indulging my rural sense of humor. We said good-bye at the steps to the subway, knowing it would maybe be another ten years before we saw each other. She reached up and gave me a big kiss, we exchanged a brief look of appreciation, and she turned and descended the steps. Tasteful as ever. At heart, the gift relation is still alive.

THE HOUSE MADE OF BEADS

I should have said, when I first started out my travels in Iroquoia, that I myself was almost as much a member of a half-obsolete minority as these even more old-fashioned Americans of twenty thousand years ago.[1]

The midday commuter train picks up speed as it leaves the marginal devastation of the city, settling into a rhythmic metallic pulse against the eastern shore of the wide Hudson estuary, taking me north toward the country of the Longhouse People. Edmund Wilson's *Apologies to the Iroquois* is spread on my knee as I consider his precautionary lines and stare out at the just-budding trees bordering the great river. I had hoped that rereading the book would serve as introduction to the region I'm about to enter, but it stands now more as a warning to unwary travelers and amateur anthropologists. It says that these ancient Americans are not in the least "vanishing," as in the popular sentimentality of Fenimore Cooper and his successors, nor even in the cynical machinations of land jobbers and Indian agents. On the contrary, its point is that in the depths of the '50s and against the rising tide of benevolent authoritarianism—which declared our native brethren finally ready for full acculturation and began the aptly named program of "termination" of those few agreements not already broken—in spite of these and the

1. EDMUND WILSON, *Apologies to the Iroquois* (New York, 1959), 286. Wilson's complaint—that the government which planned to flood the Tuscarora also wanted to remove his front yard for a highway, gut the little town of Shrewsbury, and remove the elms of the town where he was writing—bears on the issue noted during King Philip's War: what does it mean to be a subject? Neither treaty nor constitution—the citizens' treaty with their government—implies the surrender of personal and collective sovereignty that is demanded by the present state. Part of the value of paying attention to the long-term inhabitants of this land, as Wilson noted, is that "by defending their rights as Indians, they remind us of our rights as citizens."

more usual forms of genocidal oppression, the Iroquois nation was experiencing a resurgence and rebirth of its traditional energies. And that the formerly dominant culture was now in serious decline.

It was characteristic of Wilson's upstate shrewdness to see this happening at New York's very back door (as the *Times* reviewer nervously put it)—to see that a foreign nation of some centuries' standing continued to exist under the impervious gridwork of our federalized bureaucracy and its security system. And with the embittered irony of *The Cold War and the Income Tax,* Wilson watched that insidious system encroaching on his own vanishing world, involving all of us in a much wider and deeper struggle:

> *I have come to believe that there are many white Americans who now have something in common with these recalcitrant Indians, that the condition of being an American, whether from A.D. or B.C., should imply a certain minimum security in the undisturbed enjoyment of our country.*

But I doubt that even Wilson's keen eye could have foreseen the suddenness and the extent of this change. Not only is that solid assumption of a "white American" identity no longer credible outside certain diminishing circles of power, the very term "security" has been appropriated from the personal and made a national prerogative, on behalf of those same diminishing circles. And if Wilson, in his stone upstate fastness, was not safe in that now quaintly evil decade, then what must be the chances of a cross-blood gyppo scholar three thousand miles from home as the "American Century" slouches toward its millennial appointments? He would have to be here seeking, at best, a note for his own time and condition, and not with any hope of recovering Wilson's embattled stance on behalf of some lost sense of mindfulness and decency in American public life. As Frederick Exley has unsparingly witnessed, the literary landscape simply would not support the weight of the gesture.[2] "I didn't know Bunny had written about the Iroquois," my ex-New Yorker friend said as I was packing books to travel. She spoke with that wistful intimacy of one who has irredeemably crossed the Hudson. There is no way back.

And it would not be the plight of the Red Man, as everyone from the Jesuits to the ethnologists had characterized it, that would justify the time and expense of this curious present mission. Wilson had called it correctly: *termination* would be the prescribed response to *any* cultural and natural life that found itself at odds with the national corporate monopoly interest—which is to say, power wielded through the control of money and information. Any organization that had held out against these forces for several centuries had something serious to teach us children of the present. Of course there would be no guarantee that the Red Man would feel any great responsibility for the White Man's salvation from himself. When Wilson's research brought him to the heart of Iroquoia, he was excluded from the longhouse at Onondaga. My own connections there were many times more distant and doubtful. What I learned would depend for the most part on what I could read as I ran. Across this land of water and flint, through the remnant of the Great Forest, by way of books and old manuscripts. A few artifacts. The wealth of North America.

The redness very gradually fades from the expectant tops of willow and sycamore as the train pulls northward and back toward winter. Across the river, every now and then the ghostly dogwood floating in the dimness of the forest. I am traveling backward in time. Following a string of beads.

Wilson was only among the more recent of a surprising number of New York writers to take up the Indian subject. Originally inspired by the dubious romances of Fenimore

2. THE REFERENCE IS TO Exley's *Pages from a Cold Island* (New York, 1975). Next to reading Wilson, this piece of work best evokes the sense of the embattled writer in his stone house, and the terrible, actual odds he works against: "Wilson's stone house, I said, was a condition of the heart, a willingly imposed isolation from the 'literary scene' or anything resembling that scene" (267).

Cooper, who retreated eastward toward Paris even faster than his savages disappeared into the sunset, later writers found the Iroquois very much a present topic. Upstate amateur scholars may even be said to have invented the subject of ethnology, using the reduced but stubbornly remnant Iroquois as their convenient subject. Parkman had to leave New England and travel to the plains, even as far as ancient Mexico in search of Indians—but New York anthropologists had an abundance of informants and materials ready to be studied. This presence, it should be noted, can be credited to the tenacity and strength of the Longhouse People, and only incidentally to the well-meaning efforts of their literary neighbors. There has been, from the beginning, a disturbing inverse correlation between the number of living Indians and the number of Indians in books.

Lewis Henry Morgan, a Rochester lawyer, met Ely S. Parker, a hereditary chief of the Tonowanda Seneca, browsing in a bookstore in Albany in 1845. Their conversation was adjourned to a downtown hotel room where for the next two days Morgan interviewed and took notes while Parker introduced him to the culture of the Longhouse. From this beginning would come, six years later, Morgan's *League of the Iroquois*.[3]

Despite all he learned from Parker, and the formidable value of all he noted and collected, the book clearly betrays its origins in the Greek revival, the initiation rites of rural men's clubs, and that passion for relics and savage chic that has followed our age of enlightenment like a shadow. Readers will cringe at Morgan's cultural paternalism as often as they are embarrassed by cloying orations that convey an image of Noble Savages in New World drapery lounging about the ruins of towns with names like Syracuse and Ithaca, Carthage and Troy. The sort of thing Emerson no doubt had in mind when he observed that Americans are not lacking for culture —lord knows their houses and museums are awash in bric-a-brac—but that they lack a culture appropriate to America.

But Morgan's legalistic methods of inquiry and the inten-

3. *LEAGUE OF THE Ho-de-no-sau-nee, or Iroquois* (Rochester, 1851). The edition currently in print (Citadel Press: Secaucus, 1962) includes a useful account of Morgan's meeting with Ely Parker and the beginnings of American ethnology, by William N. Fenton. The 1901 two-volume edition includes valuable annotations by Herbert M. Lloyd and a territorial map of the Iroquois nations by William Beauchamp.

The Five Nations—Mohawk, Oneida, Onondaga, Cayuga, Seneca—refer to their combined territory as the Longhouse and to themselves as *Hodenosaunee*, or Longhouse People, comparing their confederacy to the traditional frame dwelling of poles and bark boards, about 16 feet wide and often 100 feet long. With a door at each end, divided into double apartments with a family inhabiting each half, a shared fire between them, a typical house might accommodate ten fires, or twenty families.

The geopolitical Longhouse provided similarly generous accommodations, encompassing not only the Five Nations of what is now New York State but, by "adding rafters," extending to neighboring nations.

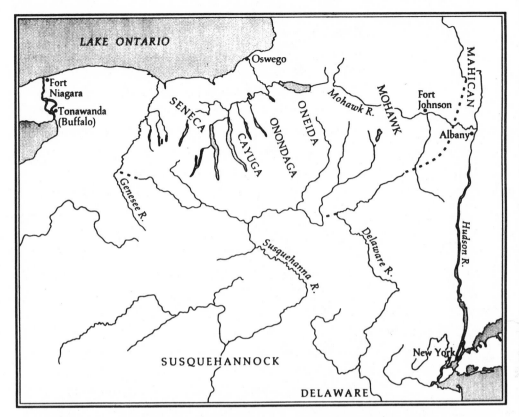

The Longhouse country. Traditional territory of the Hodenausanee or Five Nations of the Iroquois and their neighbors, about 1670. Some adjoining nations had already been incorporated into theLonghouse by forceful adoption; others would be included by voluntary treaty—and the Tuscarora (the Sixth Nation) by appeal in 1722.

sity of his amateur's passion luckily carried him beyond his intentions. The meeting with Parker drew him into the Longhouse, where he found himself in the presence of more than he had imagined. Ely S. Parker went on to remarkable achievements in white nineteenth-century society—engineer, aide to General Grant, himself promoted to general, then Commissioner of Indian Affairs—but in the Longhouse he and his family carried an even greater prominence among the largest of the Iroquois nations, the people known as the keepers of the western door, facing Niagara as the Mohawk looked out the eastern door over the valley of the Hudson. Much like Wilson a hundred years later, Morgan found himself among some very much alive and powerful people. And just as Wilson wrote of Iroquoia threatened by dam builders,

Morgan brought public attention to the rapacious moves of the Ogden Land Company, which threatened to culminate three-quarters of a century of upstate land jobbing with a final grab at the last remaining pieces of Seneca territory. Morgan's book concludes with a moving appeal to the Duty of the American People. Despite his unconscious condescension, the message still rings true: "It cannot be forgotten, that in after years our Republic must render an account, to the civilized world, for the disposal it makes of the Indian" (459–60). We shudder today at the connotations of "disposal," but Morgan's book had a long lasting and beneficial effect on the state's policies toward the Iroquois. In retrospect, it is hard to say whether Morgan found his informant or Parker his spokesman to white America.

Readers of Morgan learned—in the already familiar pattern of forgetting, marveling, and forgetting again—that there was another nation living within their borders, partly assimilated, unimaginably different and new, more ancient than their own history remembered. The Longhouse People had until several centuries ago resided in the St. Lawrence Valley and apparently moved southward under pressure from Algonquin neighbors, between whom and themselves— as well as among their own nations—there existed a state of persistent blood feud and war. The ending of this destructive cycle is the story of a remarkable agreement. Written sources, based on traditional narratives, describe the events that led to the establishment of the Law of Peace.

There appeared among the Mohawk, at about the time Europe was launching its "voyages of discovery," a prophet, Dekanawida.[4] Apparently of Huron origin, he is said to have come from the north with the warning of the white throats' imminent arrival, and laid out a plan of confederation that would enable them to withstand that event. He appeared one day at the edge of a principal Mohawk town, where he sat stringing beads. He did not reply to curious inquiries, nor to invitation to council, but kept at his task till he had finished the bead string. On the third invitation he presented the string, indicating he would speak only when his gift had been reciprocated. Nothing of equal value to his shell beads could be found, but he nevertheless accepted a lesser string of wooden beads—or some accounts have it that his beads were of eagle quill, and the return made in quill beads of partridge. He then entered the village and made his visionary announcement to the Mohawk council.

Other accounts attribute the first shell strings to a second Iroquois founder, Hayonhwatha.[5] Not Longfellow's Hiawatha, a name he cavalierly gave to an Ojibwa hero—an error that seems destined to outlast whatever truth is to be found in that lamentable epic. Confusion is further compounded by varying orthographies and national dialects, and by the fact that the names and deeds of the two founders are often interchanged, again depending where the story is told. Hayonhwatha was originally an Onondaga, who had been accepted among the Mohawk after his half brother Atodarho had brought about the loss of his family. Thus there is also a triadic relationship built upon the duality of the founders, who are often portrayed as two parts of a single sensibility: a Seer who has an unspecified impediment to speech, and the Spokesman who has already shown powers of oratory and leadership. In one retelling their doubleness is established at their first encounter. As Hayonhwatha prepares the cooking pot for a recently killed enemy, he looks into the water and sees reflected not his own face but that of Dekanawida, who is watching him from the smoke hole. His shock and subsequent dissociation prepare him to give up cannibalism and the cycle of blood feud and revenge, and hear the message of peace brought by the prophet.

In the accounts of Hayonhwatha's invention of wampum, he is said to have come in his bereaved wandering to the shore of a lake of great beauty, from which a countless flock of waterfowl suddenly fly all at once. The water being displaced by their multitudinous uplift, the floor of the lake is revealed, littered and bright with shells. Gathering them into a deerskin pouch, he then uses enough to make three strings of

5. DUAL ATTRIBUTION AND viewpoints appear to reflect the founders' origin in different nations and connection to different ceremonies (civil or religious) where wampum was used. Dekanawida establishes the Great Peace, the agreement traditionally represented by white beads, while Hayo^{n}hwat'ha seeks condolence for the loss of seven daughters—a loss of tragic proportions—and so establishes the mourning function, represented by black beads that "pay" for what has been taken. Parker translates the name Haiyo^{n}hwat'ha, given by Dekanawida in his name-renewing function, as "He has misplaced something but knows where to find it."

beads. When he is at last brought to the Mohawk village to meet Dekanawida, he has also been going from council to council with beads, hanging strings of them upon a horizontal pole, saying as he did so,

6. PARKER,
Constitution, 20.

> *"Men boast what they would do in extremity but they do not do what they say. If I should see anyone in deep grief I would remove these shell strings from the pole and console them. The strings would become words and lift away the darkness with which they are covered. Moreover what I say I would surely do."* This he repeated.[6]

But it is not until the two founders meet that his offer is accepted, and the reciprocal bead transaction is completed. Additional strings of shells are made, they are exchanged between the mourner and consoler, and grief and bereavement are put away. Now that this is done, and inner peace is restored, they can go on to the task of establishing peace among the five Iroquois nations. And that, too, would be based on beads.

Because the wampum exchange both redeemed loss and opened the way for dialogue, it was readily extended to international life as a means to eliminate the blood feud. A death was thus "paid for," the price of a life being set at the enormous price of twenty strings of shells—ten to pay for the loss of life, and if that was acceptable, ten to restore the injured feelings of the family. It was not "buying" a life, but an acknowledgment of repentance as much as guilt, and before the fact acted as a persuasive deterrent to violence. The price might be beyond the means of the offender's family, or not acceptable to the relations of the deceased—in which case the debt might be paid in other ways, such as mandatory adoption of the offender into the place of the one lost. Somewhat like the old Germanic *wer-gilt* (literally, man-gold), this assured peace by guaranteeing that in one form or another everything would be paid for. Every word must be answered, every act must have its response. The give and take had to move both ways.

But this was only the beginning of the agreement. The

ritual of "paying for death" both symbolically and literally bought the Iroquois a new lease on life. It established agreement itself, provided a currency-language to express a social contract. There must have been at that time very little of what we now know as wampum beads, and it was partly its scarcity that assured the sanctity of the words that were exchanged along with the strings. Most accounts agree that the first wampum was made of the inland lake shells found by Hayonhwatha. Only later, with the influence of the colonial wampum currency employed in the fur trade, did the coastal *Venus mercenaria* reach the Five Nations in any significant quantity. The Iroquois tale of the Wampum Bird,[7] flying from the east and shedding beads with each stroke of its wings, further suggests the early scarcity of coastal shell material. This latter story, as well as the shape of the small cylindrical beads we see in museums, confirms the accounts that say quills—probably of eagle—may have been another early form of the beads.

Like much else in indigenous culture, whether marked by beads of wood, quill or shell, the outward forms of the contract have changed with circumstance, while its substance has stayed remarkably conservative and constant. The agreement known as the Great Law Of Peace in fact grew in extent and binding power as outward conditions in this region of the New World grew ever more violent and unsettled. At the time Europeans began regular relations with them, the Longhouse People were probably at their period of highest organization and influence. By the middle of the seventeenth century the wampum contract had evolved into a great confederacy, the Longhouse into a political structure some hundreds of miles in extent, with the council fire established by Hayonhwatha at its geographical center in the Onondaga valley (near present-day Syracuse). At its two doors the Mohawk and Seneca, and to either side their "younger brothers" the Oneida and Cayuga, they comprised a nation of an estimated 25,000 souls united by a system of trails and runners and an agreement marked by strings and woven belts of beads.

7. FIRST TRANSCRIBED in Converse, *Myths and Legends* (Albany, 1908), edited and augmented by Arthur C. Parker after her death in 1903. See Tehanetorens, *Tales of the Iroquois* (Akwesasne, n.d.), who confirms this story, noting that Onondaga beads were black- or white-stained wood or porcupine quill, Mohawk beads of eagle quill, and that the mourning beads used by Hayonhwatha were freshwater shells. This same author refers to a tradition that other rare objects (a beaver skin or eagle's wing) could be tokens and describes wampum in a variety of forms and functions (*Wampum Belts* [Six Nations Indian Museum, Onchiota, 1973]). Again, while form and use varied, there is remarkable consistency and agreement as to the symbolic meaning of the beaded messages.

8. LEVI-STRAUSS HYPOTHESIZED that the Longhouse was modeled on a greater cosmic order, as any student of its balances is bound to agree. A perhaps more mundane bioregional view would suggest that this model was closer to hand, in what we call "natural systems." Thomas Berry's small monograph, *The Lower Hudson River Basin as a Bioregional Community* (San Francisco, n.d.), is a useful step toward the rediscovery of that order in the Hudson watershed.

Gliding along in the Amtrak day coach, I try to see—beneath this grid of rail and highway—another, older structure that governed here as effectively as our present states and public authorities. And that may, because it imitated even older structures and the more ancient laws of the gift,[8] outlive this idea that governs by iron lines and concrete laid across the flow of things. It seems only "natural disasters" make us aware of the impermanence of these forms and enable us to see how brief and unsettled our account with this land really is. Our history neglects to mention that as the European invasion moved inland along the rivers and lakes of North America, the new arrivals found themselves in an unexpectedly dependent relation, their lives and fortunes at the mercy of a nation as great as the one they had left. Their presence was allowed, and their offers of exchange were accepted, because of agreements already in place and very much in force. Far beyond the "walls" of the Longhouse (what we call New York State), its warriors and hunting parties ranged from the St. Lawrence to the Tennessee, and from the Atlantic coast to the valley of the Ohio. No alliances were made, no wars declared, no public agreements undertaken without it being known and approved at the Council Fire at Onondaga. And kept there as record, woven into belts. The belts now in the state museum in Albany. I would stop there to see them on the way to Onondaga.

🐚 🐚 🐚

As I get closer to where I'm going, certain doubts grow more insistent and troubling questions more difficult to ignore. Just for openers, I wonder, what hopeless romantic pilgrimage am I enacting here? And what impossibly lost wealth do I hope to find so far from home? But when I have to start writing down real questions that I can actually ask someone, the best I can come up with seems not even worth asking: was it money? No. Of course not. It was all a misunderstanding.

In fleeing the moral wreckage of the old world, the

colonists transplanted its root causes as unconsciously and in-
visibly as they transmitted smallpox, and all the newly in-
fected properties of the New World were suddenly up for sale.
The beads appeared to be the asking price. It was a tragic misunderstanding, a terrible loss to all parties to the deal—which
includes everyone present. But this was a lesson I could have
observed at home, and not have to be in a strange country,
practically vagrant, and dependent on friends and the friends
of friends. The real question, which I also haven't written
down, is probably more like Brother, can you spare a dime?

I'm perched on a sunny hillside overlooking the lovely little valley of the Housatonic, and the small town of that name
where the old Boston road crosses the river, a station on the
colonial routes of war and commerce. A party of crows is
shouting and falling about the sky. Below me, stretching
more than a hundred feet from end to end, the huge barnlike
house of my host. Morgan's been kind enough to meet me at
the Hudson station, bring me here, fix me up for the weekend
in one of its rooms. Now I'm waiting for some minor repair
to be done on his second car, which he's generously loaned me
for the two-hundred-mile trip west. I'm running up a tab that
will take some time to repay. I'm already in his debt for an old
table saw he'd given me, saying if you can get it to run, pay
me fifty bucks. It did eventually go, after some rust removal
and rewiring, but I'd never sent the fifty. I had tried to make
up part of it last night, with a number of beers all around at
the local inn, and the last of what stash I'd brought north—
but this morning, not surprisingly, I'm feeling only deeper in
the hole.

I'd worked with Morgan a couple of times before he moved
back to western Massachusetts. On our first job together we
had both carpentered for a loony liberal with a contractor's
license who'd gotten the low bid on rehabilitating some
Indian housing—probably through the BIA. The collective
profits were to have gone to an unspecified Good Cause—to
be determined by this contractor-fanatic—and that was supposed to justify the sort of gyppo work he had in mind. Both

the Yuroks and the carpenters had other ideas, and the project ended in multiple disasters. Some of the work could have been better. Some of the workers, doing extra jobs for one rancheria family, got burned for their time and materials. Long-term paybacks, they figured, and swallowed the loss. Eventually, nearly all of us walked off the job and sued for unemployment.

A few friendships survived this ordeal, both with the up-river people and among the downriver carpenters. When I had a rare design-&-build come up, I'd hired Morgan and another friend who'd been the organizer of our brief labor movement. This time it was new construction, a two-story shop and studio we all wished was ours; the actual owners were sweethearts, and everyone came out feeling enriched by the transaction. I went on to other jobs, sometimes with other participants in the great strike, usually repair and remodel, sometimes a small addition. But it's a marginal, hand-to-mouth way of living, and Morgan came back to where he had family and better credit. The enormous house, in which he took up a small niche, was a speculative venture. With a banker putting up capital, he supported himself installing the cabinets he sold to the steady influx of yuppies restoring old houses into second homes—and with his "spare" time and some of his own "spare" money he had undertaken the Herculean task of single-handedly rescuing this sagging leviathan from the past.

Apparently all this did not sufficiently overextend his life's economy, since he also maintained a relationship with a single mother who shared his east coast intensity (what must they think is expected of them?) and also still worked at his real vocation, which lay in the recent paintings he brought out to show me, huge and vividly colored flowers contending with abstract geometrical forms. Nevertheless, with all this going on, he had not hesitated to offer me a room and a car, to take time to smoke and drink beer and listen to me trying to explain the mission that grew more questionable the nearer it came to accomplishment—whatever that would mean. And it further comforted me to suppose that there was mutual recognition at the heart of our visit—of another neoromantic artist-carpenter, whose tangled economic and emotional priorities were hopelessly out of step with what passed for present-day reality.

9. FROM THE TEXT ADAPTED by John Bierhorst in *Four Masterworks of American Indian Literature* (Tucson, 1974). The ritual is discussed further in chap. 8, but even in more detailed studies what is being described is a generalized ceremony, collated from various sources into a "typical" enactment. There is of course no such thing.

The genius of the Iroquois contract lay not simply in its rituals of repayment, but in its vision of the exchange as a ceremony of rebirth and renewal. Not just the establishment of the blood price, but the use that was made of the beads now invested with such power. More than simply a recompense to the families of "victims," the beaded strings were incorporated by the Iroquois into a ceremony by which their collective life was literally redeemed from death. The Ritual of Condolence[9] is performed whenever there is a death, by whatever cause, among the fifty chiefs of the League. By its enactment, according to the ceremony prescribed by Dekanawida and set forth by his spokesman, a new chief nominated by the clan mothers is "raised up" in the place of the fallen, and assumes both the hereditary title and name of that position. While the names of the Prophet and the Founder are left vacant, each of the remaining names of the original Council of Chiefs remains literally present. And by this same reenactment, just as the political fabric is restored, the mourning family, clan, and nation are brought back from the darkness and despair of the house of death.

At the heart of the ceremony, in what is known as the Requickening, successive strings of beads are presented to the mourners by the "clear-minded" who have journeyed through the Great Forest to bring consolation and renewal. Each string "holds" a "chapter" of the ceremony and so functions as a mnemonic device for the recitations of comfort and healing. The first three—the "three rare strings"—represent the essence of recovery: restoring the vision, hearing, and speech that have been obstructed by tears and grief and ashes.

Each successive string is taken from a horizontal pole before
one of the two moieties; it is "spoken" and then carried across
the fire to a similar pole before the mourners. In response,
their speaker lifts each string and repeats the message. Thus
the beads act out as well as describe the steps of consolation.
The bereaved see, hear, and then repeat the stages of recovery.

The healing bead-verses continue through a series of such
gestures and responses, bringing back the mourners to their
right person and place, cleansing the scene of death from
their minds, placing the sun back in their sky, burying with
the deceased all the insanities and animosities that threaten
the personal and social order. But the Condolence Ceremony
is obviously much more than a recitation of sermons and
stage directions, which is the effect left by the ethnographic
transcripts. It is the ritual *enactment*, the actual *exchange* of
encoded objects, that constitutes the substance of the ceremony and provides a model of reciprocity that can be found
in every aspect of the Longhouse culture. The message of
death and summoning, answered by the message of arrival at
the wood's edge, the Council seated by nation and clan, facing
across the Longhouse, speaking and responding, presenting
and accepting beaded messages—all this expresses a profound
social architecture of dualisms and triads, a structure that—
again both literally and metaphorically—supports the house
within house of family, clan, nation and confederacy, a geometry that no doubt antedates the Prophet and Founder and extends to the house of the stars.

Down here, however, on the ground of the two-hundredth
year of its constitution, there is serious reason to believe that
our house is not in order. This region's recent boom in land
and housing may have gone as far as it's going. The New
England Miracle (as it was billed by the region's boosters),
being but a short-term side effect of the more general epicycle

of speculation and inflation—in other words, being no miracle
at all—may pull my friend and his backers down into that
worst nightmare of the small-time "spec" contractor. Not
only is the huge old wavy-roofed barn of a house unheatable
and hence probably unlivable for anyone but an oil baron, but
it was designed for the life of another century, with the rooms
and conveniences of this century thrown on as an afterthought. At best, it was probably never worth what it would
cost to fix it. And at worst, as the market falls back toward
whatever reality will be "bottom" for now, you desperately
throw in time and materials faster than its value can depreci-
ate out from under you. Typically, you end up helping someone else do the same to their house and take their money
home and pour it into yours. And all the houses eventually
make one great ramshackle hopeless fixer-upper, which one
day collapses because nothing but empty promises held it up.

As I walk down the hill to meet Morgan and the car, the
world appears as substantial and solvent as it ever has on a
midday in May. The little village below is the very one that
used to come with model railroad sets. The snow is all gone,
the crows are calling from far away now, the bell is pealing in
the Congregational noontide, and I hear the voices of children
echoing from Pleasant Street. Somewhere in the background,
a jackhammer suddenly stops its digging into the Berkshire
rock. For a moment in the widening silence I hear voices
speaking of bills that are due.

It was both irony and prophecy that the Longhouse People
received the Ritual of Condolence as they were about to have
greatest need of it. The principles of reciprocity and balanced
exchange, no doubt much older than the wampum ritual,
were given objective reality by the physical gestures of offering and receiving, of palpably "paying" for personal and
collective loss, and "marking" words as they were spoken,

heard, received, and returned. The beads enacted a structure of recovery and renewal that would see them through the cataclysmic changes of the ensuing centuries.

By the mid-1600s, after fewer than forty years of contact, it is estimated that roughly half the Iroquois people had died by the agency of invisible microbes bred in the urban host populations of Europe. Also by this time, the beaver had been effectively exterminated as an "economic animal" within the bounds of present-day New York. All the wampum that could not be kept as currency in New England and New Amsterdam had flowed inland and upriver to Fort Orange, to return as beaver. And to continue up the Hudson and the Mohawk to condole the loss of those who succumbed to smallpox or lost their lives in the hundred years of frontier violence required to maintain access to the materials and markets and routes of trade that delivered these beaver to the maddened hat makers of Europe. So much to mourn. So much to pay for.

☙ ☙ ☙

"Let me put it this way: for one party to the transaction, the beads were a ritual language, and for the other they were ready cash. It was a question of meaning." I'm trying to explain this yet again, seated in the comfortable living room of my next evening's host, somewhere in suburban Albany, drinking tea and talking. It's been a relatively light day of travel, and I'd even had time to stop at a diner and take in a solid meal after the short westward crossing from Stockbridge. Somehow I'd eaten fifteen dollars' worth of liver and onions and mashed potatoes and coffee and pie—as if to somehow make myself substantial again. I'm trying to place myself, and my questions, back at some origin—some place where words and meaning, body and spirit, unaccountably parted company and then met again in the New World. Where the money went one way, and the ghosts went the other.

My host for the night is a teaching scholar and working

poet, so he's delighted that I see these "economic" issues as a
question of crosscultural semantics. As if we American scrib-
blers might yet vindicate the crackpot fiscal theories of Ezra
Pound—or show that his insights were unerring, even if (as
Pound had to admit at last) his western suburban prejudices
had led him to look for causes in all the wrong places. But the
theory—that a culture cannot exist where its public language,
which also means where it puts its money, is not in touch
with the root facts of life—this is so clearly in evidence everywhere that we now have to ask ourselves what such a rooted
culture and language might be like, and whether they can be
salvaged from the utter breakdown of everything from the
wealth of nations to the walls of our cells.

10. FRANÇOIS DU CREUX'S history of Canada, quoted extensively by Carl Sauer in his chapter on the destruction of Indian nations by feud and disease (*Seventeenth-Century North America* [Berkeley, 1980], 118). Sauer insists that the surge of Iroquois power did not have economic motivations: "The confederation of the Five Nations was not concerned with profit of furs or other goods but was a body politic established to serve the common weal."

Precisely here is where the ironic twist of culture and history enters the story. At just this point in their development,
when halved in numbers and under deadly pressure from
both recent and traditional enemies, the Iroquois unaccountably reached out and, one after another, overwhelmed and incorporated their neighbors. Where statistics would indicate
they were on the path to extinction, they actually expanded
the influence and power of their Confederacy to its greatest
extent. By the French account, who along with their allies felt
the force of this expansion, it was attributable to the ferocity
that was already legendary throughout the northeastern
woodlands.

> *The fierce Iroquois seeing that they had all but finished
> the Hurons turned their rage and their weapons upon
> the neighboring nation [the Neutrals]. . . . There was a
> general massacre in which old men and children were
> the chief victims; the younger women were carried off so
> that there might be more little Iroquois.*[10]

The Hurons, the Neutrals with whom they sought refuge, the
Erie, Algonquin—all had ceased to exist as independent nations by the end of the 1650s. This astonishing outburst has
been regarded by later and more objective historians as an

early episode of the Beaver Wars, on the grounds that by this action the Iroquois eliminated all obstacles between themselves and the remaining trapping grounds to the north and west. And there is no question that these are early episodes of a war that would be given that same name by Pontiac, some 120 years later and 500 miles west. Involving most of the indigenous people of eastern North America, as well as the French and the English and Dutch, along with many of their other colonial investments, it was also the early stages of that war for the control of global markets that continues to appear in our daily news and stock quotations.

It was, however, as Du Creux rather lasciviously suggests, also a way to make more Iroquois. But it was not primarily by procreation—rather, it was an act of incorporation, adoption, and replacement of those lost. It was the rationale of the Condolence Ceremony, but now that paradigm of internal relations was extended outward. Thus, more recent historians have come to call this period the Mourning Wars. The ceremony of loss and the gesture of the wampum exchange—with the coincidental arrival of freshly minted beads from the English and Dutch, and the glass and Mediterranean *porcelaine* beads employed by the French—enabled the Iroquois to so effectively counteract their losses that it led to an otherwise inexplicable expansion of their confederate influence and power.

If we suppose the Five Nations clear-minded enough to see their own several interests—there is no evidence that this outburst of energy was a concerted plan by the unified Confederacy—then it is not difficult to suppose that economic and political as well as demographic interests were being pursued. To acquire beaver—and as much would be seized by raiding parties as trapped by hunters, probably but a slight distinction—to be in possession of the peltry was to be the holder of the wampum trade, and of the European goods that followed. As the nations expanded their control of the woodlands and its diminishing resources, they made moves eastward, displacing the neighboring Mahican and securing from the coastal Algonquin, both by trade and tribute, direct access to wampum. But more than "economics" was at stake here. To hold the wampum beads was to possess the language by which the Confederacy talked to itself, renewed itself, and dealt with its friends and enemies. If we are to attribute these conflicts to some central operative agency, other than simple conquest and dispossession—the Iroquois made no move to occupy the territories of their former neighbors—then they should be considered the first inland stage of the North American Bead Wars.

There was property, and on the property a house. Around the house the colonist saw roads and lines of ownership and utility, and in front of the house a sign that said For Sale. The price was a few beads. As the poets would say, it was a war of language, of competing descriptions for the life and soul of this continent. They sit in the house in the gathering dark, sharing words of consolation. The war goes on.

THE OPENING OF THE FIVE-AND-TEN

I'm sorting through books, unpacking a few things for the night. As I brought my bags in from the car, I'd noticed the sky had clouded over. Not a star to give a clue as to direction. I'm somewhere in the southern suburbs of Albany, the cot in the poet's study has been made up for me, the curtains are drawn against the night, and for now it is the center of the world. While Don is in the kitchen making tea, I leave my portable library and begin to look through his shelves.

My Albany host has situated himself—as poets will frequently do, contrary to their reputation for aimlessness—at the very heart of his subject, where the matter of his poem is bound to show up. Or say it has placed him exactly in the way. And brought me here to read.

Fort Orange was built at the lower end of the short overland portage from the Hudson to the Mohawk. It quickly overshadowed the original trading outpost of Beverwyck, located at the site of a Mohawk town for convenience of trade and security. With its cannon trained on the Hudson, it now guarded both openings into the interior, and maintained a rival avenue of competition with the French voyageurs. So Beverwyck gave way to Fort Orange, and so to Albany in the colonial advance toward inland market sources. Meagerly supported by the feudal *patroon* system and the legendary Dutch skill at shaving the coin of commerce, the strategic outpost came into the hands of the English at a highly convenient time. It opened a new front in their New World contest with France, which would continue for another century, and it offered a means to pay its costs. Moreover, it could absorb the cost of other revenue-producing ventures, such as the devastation of Ireland and Scotland. Their lands enclosed for cash crops, their forests used to build a Royal Navy, those farmers not lucky enough to be recruited into it had to be disposed of somewhere.

"Whatever occasions their going," reported the Bishop of London by 1728, "it is certain that above 4000 men, women, and children have been shipped off from hence for the West Indies. . . . Of these, possibly one in ten may be a man of substance, and may do well enough abroad; but the case of the rest is deplorable."[1] Within a generation, those one in ten who came to the New World as overseers and administrators and agents had inextricably woven their interests into the trade and politics of this city's unacknowledged history. "Half shame," the poet declares it,

the city's history, built on trade
skins, timber and government, not legitimate production.
Henry James wrote fine sentences
on the hides of beavers, an animal,
to my memory, not mentioned in his thirty volumes.[2]

The indictment rings with the truth of a great cash register, part of the poet's function being to locate and post these debts to the appropriate accounts. Henry's grandfather was but a comparative latecomer to the trade at Albany, arriving more than a century after the first Irish governor was installed by the duke of York. But even then, still in time to make all that money—underwrite all those words. Written installments on promises to pay, inscribed on the skin of the New World.

The Great Dimestore Centennial takes its title and format from this great cheapening of the continent. Upriver and out into that earliest West, delivered by the dispossessed, navvy and bargeman and trader, laid out before savage shoppers as in Frank Woolworth's five-and-ten, the products of Europe's

1. *LETTERS WRITTEN BY HIS Excellency Hugh Boulter, Lord Primate of Ireland,* quoted in the valuable anthology, Martin Ridge and Ray Allen Billington, eds., *America's Frontier Story: A Documentary History of Westward Expansion* (New York, 1969).

2. DON BYRD, *THE GREAT Dimestore Centennial* (Barrytown, 1986), 52— in the copy given me and inscribed by the poet, 5 May 1987, in exchange for a chapbook of my poems I carried as a kind of currency to acknowledge hospitality. Here, as throughout, the exchange was heavily one-sided, to the advantage of the traveler.

plantations and mines and domestic mills: guns and powder and lead, knives and scissors and axes and awls, steel traps and woolen blankets, vermilion and tweezers and combs, mirrors and glass beads and ready-made shirts, rings and bracelets and silver bells—and always, always a deal on rum.

The poets stay up drinking tea and reciting the names, weaving pleasure and sorrow in the litany of objects as they cross the counters of the trading houses of Albany. Voices making deals in the taverns and back rooms of the city beneath the city. Hearing the speech of the underworld, the traffic of the river, the slang of the market, the whispered commerce in hallways, the names of the dead. Names to recite over beads. Don tells me that William Kennedy, whose novels like the city itself are built on this river of exchange, has turned some of his literary profits back into a foundation that aids local poets and writers. Paying back interest on Henry James's literary indebtedness, I imagine, as I lie waiting for sleep on the cot in the poet's study.

And downriver, downriver came the beaver hides, the peltry of marten and mink and otter, skin of raccoon and doe and the original American buck. Also hardwood logs and timber, tar and turpentine, honey and wax, the apparently endless bounty of the Great Forest. The money could be anywhere. For a time the Albany traders had the inhabitants, and their own poor among them, scouring the forest for the native ginseng root, a valuable item in the budding China trade. As with the four-cornered Atlantic slave-sugar-rum-beaver cycle, probably no more than a handful of mercantilists saw or even cared where these commodities came from or went. The market would govern, and the ginseng find its way with the tea and opium of the Indian plantations to the newly addicted client population of China, with enough left over for domestic use. The world had become a discount store, just opened for business. Everything was on sale, and Europe was shopping. The governor of New York saw beyond his colony only as far as the Lords of Trade at Whitehall, who ran things according to the prevailing laws of bookkeeping.

The Crown needed cash commodities to pay its bills.[3] There had been no working revenue since 1672, when Charles II stopped payment of interest on tax warrants. King William's War (to Europeans, the war of the League of Augsburg) had required a means to finance it. War profiteers subscribed £1,200,000 to establish the Bank of England. Now its payments had to be met. Bills were due, and those who had patents and concessions on colonial properties were told to kick in additional rent. They raised the taxes on the fledgling corporations of North America, who sent even more beads inland, making such attractive profits they eventually went into business for themselves. We can do it cheaper, their revolution said. And we can do it for ourselves.

So the Iroquois met the wandering traders and spiritual emissaries of Europe during a period of national expansion similar to their own. Except for some critical differences: metallurgy, money, and the Law of Peace. The European wars of succession, named in North America for one crowned head after another—King William's War, Queen Anne's War, King George's War, and so on through the Seven Years' War when they apparently ran short of monarchs and could account for nothing but the length of it—all of these found expression here as the colonial bead wars. The far-off excuse was church or nation, the arguments about whose family idiot should rule, but the motive was short-term profit, and the expense and income became the engine of enormous monetary expansion, creating by the early 1700s an international system of credit and banking essentially like today's—with many of today's effects.

Modern democratic capitalism began with the ability of the bourgeoisie to buy into this new world order of making money with leveraged money. The period saw the beginning of those speculative bubbles and panics that we experience today as hyperinflation and double-digit recession. Oddly enough it was the Dutch, their legendary acquisitiveness overwhelming their legendary parsimony, who first experienced this modern financial phenomenon during

3. THIS EARLY BANKING CRISIS was but one of a series in the growth of centralized finance, funded consistently by expropriation of wealth elsewhere. The first example may be the classic: Bank of Barcelona, established 1401, by 1468 had defaulted due to civil war, famine, and recurrent devaluations, thus establishing the desperate conditions under which Cristóbal Colón could find underwriting for his shortcut to wealth, at a generous 10 percent finder's fee.

the Great Tulip Bubble, a frenzied buying and selling of options and futures in hybrid tulip bulbs. Fortunes in Dutch
dollars were accumulated on paper and then as suddenly
vanished when nature and common sense once more took
hold. But this new plague of speculation seemed only to
breed more speculators, and as soon as the bubble had burst
all memory of its causes seemed to disappear, along with
everything but the bills.

It was while in Holland, with his experience in North
American land bank ventures, that the Scotsman William
Law came up with an investment scheme, which he even-
tually sold to the cash-poor regent of France, whereby the
Banque royale issued *billets d'état* based on the credit of the
Crown—and when that eroded, on the promissory notes of
the *Compagnie des Indes occidentes*, best known as the
Mississippi Scheme, after that half-legendary river in the
Province of Louisiana, and the entirely legendary gold and
silver said to lie therein. Law's erratic and wandering career
was as representative of this commercial renaissance as his
monetary schemes, and even the feeblest financial memory
would predict that its brilliance would come to ruin. At one
point hailed as the *duc d'Arkansas,* and as powerful as any of
Europe's monarchs, Law died in poverty and ignominy, reduced at last to pursuing a lottery scheme in Venice. The government of France was left indebted to an amount it had not
previously needed a name for, many *millions* of francs that
were to be repaid by the labor of those least able to afford it—
again with the revolutionary results that from our present
vantage seem so predictable.

So short had the collective memory become—and so de-
fenseless even the marginally prosperous, against this new
medium of paper credit—that in the very year Law's scheme
exploded, London fell into a similar frenzy of bogus wealth. It
was the age of the coffee house and journalism, and you can
hear the breathless frenzy of his characters in Smollett's account of the South Sea Bubble:

All distinctions of party, religion, sex, character and cir-
cumstance were swallowed up in this universal concern,
or in some such pecuniary project. Exchange Alley was
filled with a strange concourse of statesmen and clergy-
men, churchmen and dissenters, Whigs and Tories,
physicians, lawyers, trades-men, and even with multi-
tudes of females. All other professions and employments
were neglected, and the people's attention wholly
engrossed by this and other chimerical schemes, which
were known by the denomination of bubbles. The sums
proposed to be raised by these expedients amounted to
£300,000,000 sterling, which exceeded the value of all
the lands in England.[4]

4. Tobias Smollett's
novels— *The Expedition of
Humphry Clinker, Peregrine
Pickle, Roderick Random,
History and Adventures of
an Atom*—are the epitome
of the economic hurly-burly
of his volatile time, as was
his own career. *A Complete
History of England* (1757,
with a continuation, 1765)
chronicles the "bubbles"
of the years before his birth
and, along with novels, plays,
poems, and periodicals,
exemplifies the literary
side of his speculative age.

When the bills piled up until they collapsed—as they were
still doing, even as I slept, in what would be called the Savings
& Loan Scandal—then a period of restraint would set in, and
money and life in general would be more tightly controlled.
The Bank of England picked up some of the pieces of the
burst bubbles and established itself as the conservative "little
old lady of Threadneedle Street." But each time around, there
were bills left over; everything remaining seemed to cost
more, and a life to be worth that much less.

It had showered heavily during the night. The grass in my
hosts' backyard still held much of the downpour, thoroughly
wetting my recently bought traveling shoes. The downstairs
bath being occupied with the family's morning preparations, I
had walked outside to the bushes and was standing under an
occasionally dripping, just-leafing maple, taking in my first
coffee and tobacco and impressions of the day. My head still a
procession of dream images, it slowly came to me that I was
standing in the midst of a rather well dressed audience of
high-windowed suburban homes. I tried not to look like a

transient who'd slept in the bushes. After all, I reminded myself, I had an appointment today in the treasure house of the
Empire State. I wondered if I would feel any less an intruder
there than in these bushes.

I gratefully drank more of my hosts' coffee, ate oatmeal
with their daughter Ann, and as she went off to school I
pointed the borrowed Subaru into the morning commute like
any downtown Albany civil servant.

Renamed for the duke of York's principal residence, the
city became a piece of England's map, and a name on the floor
of the London exchange. The British Isles might be taxed and
tithed entirely, but in Albany there lay opportunity—or at
least the patents from the Lords of Trade to claim it, or the
name of the person to talk to. The prime farmland and trade
of the Hudson were held as tightly as the Dutch could hold
them, and the signing of treaties in Europe had little effect on
their grip. But long-term access to the inland wealth, the
speculator's dream, depended on treaties with the Iroquois,
and that depended on a chain of beads through the forest. The
governor, as the duke's representative, held one end of that
chain. And in New York, an Irishman—especially if he'd
served the Crown well in its wars—could become that
governor.

2nd August 1684

*A speech of the Onnandoges & Cayouga Sachems
made in the Court House at Albany to Colonel Thomas
Dongan Governor of New York in the Presence of Lord
Effingham Howard Governor of Virginia. . . .*

*When the English first came to New York to Virginia
& Maryland, they were but a small People & we a large
Nation; & we finding they were good People gave them
Land & dealt Civilly by them; Now that you are grown
Numerous & we decreased, you must protect us from the
French, which if you dont we shall loose al our Hunting
& Bevers: The French want all the Bevers & are Angry
that we bring any to the English. . . .*

*We have submitted our Selves to the Great Sachem
Charles who liveth on the other side of the Great Lake,
And we now give you in token thereof Two white Buck-
skins to be sent to him, that He may write & put a great
Red Seal thereto, that we put under the Protection of the
Great Duke of York, the Susquahanna River above the
Wasaghta or Falls together with all the rest of our Lands
& to no one else. . . .*

*And we will neither give up our Selves nor our Lands
to any other Government than this. And We desire that
Corlaer (the Governor) will transmit these our Resolu-
tions to the Great Sachem Charles who lives over the
Great Lake, with this Belt of Wampum & this Smaller one
to the Duke of York his Brother, & we present you Corlaer
with a Bever Skin that you may fulfill our request.*⁵

5. From INDIAN SECRETARY
Peter Wraxall's account of
a meeting at Albany, August
1684 (Charles H. McIlain,
ed., *An Abridgment of the
Indian affairs contained in
4 folio volumes, transacted
in the colony of New York,
from the year 1678 to
the year 1751, by Peter
Wraxall* [Cambridge, Mass.,
1915], 10ff).

Here, then, roughly two centuries later, is Dekanawida's
invention, the wampum belts now a compact of trade and
mutual defense—a beaded memorandum of understanding
between the Iroquois Confederacy and the invading nations
of Europe. With a parallel memo to be endorsed in the in-
vader's own language and record-keeping system—and a
beaver thrown in for the messenger, Thomas Dongan, the
Irish overseer given the customary "hereditary" name of
Arent von Curler, a minor Dutch official whom the Mohawk
distinguished as the first European honest enough to deal
with, and in traditional Iroquois fashion gave the title to all
the ensuing governors of New York.

Dongan had the shrewdness to see that New York's future
lay upriver in Albany, where the Mohawk had opened a new
diplomatic center for the Confederacy's dealings with the
English. The Five Nations, he said, "are a better defence to us,
than if they were so many Christians." And it was at Albany
that this compact of trade and mutual assistance, which became known as the Covenant Chain, would be held and renewed for a hundred years. It was of course not a "chain" at
all, but a wampum belt—again an adoption of the European

technical vocabulary—and its end could be grasped for purposes of commerce as well as diplomacy. Though the Dutch
traders' hold on the Hudson traffic would not be loosened by
decree of kings or moralists—where they dealt indifferently
with France's Indians as with England's Indians, furnishing
powder and shot, rifles, rum, hatchets, whatever brought in
peltry—there was still a handsome living to be got by a trader
with a little venture capital, a willingness to risk doing business a little farther upriver, and an understanding of the bead
exchange. Such a trader might also be an Irishman.

William Johnson arrived in Albany in 1738, along with
twelve families of County Meath contracted to accompany
him to North America. After the journey overland from
Boston they continued upriver to a tract of land on the
Mohawk belonging to his uncle, Peter Warren, then a captain
in the Royal Navy but well on his way to becoming an admi-
ral, a war hero, and the wealthiest commoner in the realm.
Uncle Peter had secured a patent extending some three and a
half miles along the river at the mouth of Schoharie Creek.
The plantation, with its indentured Irish augmented by impoverished survivors of the Pallatine German exodus, was
soon producing maize and staples and milled timber from the
dense forest that was cleared to make way for their improvements. Much of the timber went into the construction of
Peter Warren's own home and the surrounding developments
that would become Greenwich Village.

But this enterprise, solid and profitable though it might
be, was not bringing the sort of returns hoped for by uncle
and nephew, and it was soon agreed they should branch out
into trade. The nephew established an estate of his own, Fort
Johnson, across the river from the uncle's Warrensburg. He
was a quick observer and lost no time in adapting to what he
saw of Albany and the river trade. He no doubt found it, as
had his brother Warren, "a fine River, And but a Nasty dirty
Town." And he cannot have failed to note—so that Uncle
Peter's old-world advice and conventional wisdom were of little help—that trade was carried on by barter and credit and

was in some way facilitated by one of the raw new town's few industries: "Many people at Albany," reported the traveler Peter Kalm, "make wampum for the Indians, which is their ornament and money, by grinding and finishing certain kinds of shells and mussels. This is of considerable profit to the inhabitants."[6]

Johnson was also quick to appreciate the advantage, from his estate on the Mohawk, of locating upriver from the jealous Dutch traders at Albany. And he saw the even greater advantage of carrying on business even farther upriver and deeper into the forest, at the recently established trading outpost at Oswego, where one might also intercept peltry on its way to Montreal and Quebec. Aside from this strategic insight and about £200 of "Indian truck" advanced by his uncle, Johnson apparently also had an unnamed mentor who introduced him to the ways of doing business in the forest, "haveing a fellow here who I would take wth. me that Understands their tongue and way of dealing."[7] And while he was being tutored in wilderness commerce, he can scarcely have escaped the essential lesson in diplomacy taught by his compatriot, the now-retired Governor Dongan, whose renewal of the Covenant had not only cemented trade relations with the Iroquois but committed them to the defense of those routes and outposts essential to their mutual business interests.

But Johnson's ensuing career isn't accounted for solely by the influence of supporters and advisers. His prosperous activity as a trader for twenty-five years on the Mohawk was due in part to the remarkably bold military ventures that also won him the rank of colonel in the state militia. But his fortunes in the military were in turn due partly to his career as a diplomat among the Five Nations—now Six, after the "adoption" of their dispossessed southern cousins the Tuscarora—such that he eventually became the Crown's first Superintendent of Indian Affairs. On all of these counts, he was no doubt aided by the Iroquois' predisposition toward the English, who apparently seemed more open-handed than the Dutch and less guileful than the Jesuits and their agents. And

6. ADOLPH B. BERGSON, ed., *The America of 1750: Peter Kalm's Travels in North America*, 2 vols. (New York, 1937), 1:243.

7. *THE PAPERS OF SIR WILLIAM Johnson*, 13 vols. (Albany, 1921–62), 1:7. The history of wampum beads in trade and forest diplomacy is laid out in these volumes, thanks to Johnson's obsessive accounting, one transaction after another. It is essentially the business that preceded —and made way for—the history of "discovery" and had been transacted a century earlier by the traders who first carried beads of wampum and roanoke into the interior. It would be carried on a century later by the trappers of the intermountain West who learned to compete for the supply end of the trade. It represented the first intercultural contact and for better or worse was usually the most direct. Not until the anthropologists arrived would indigenous economics be taken seriously again.

perhaps they shared with the English a certain reserve of demeanor and strict adherence to forms and—as Edmund
Wilson pointed out—a similarity of speech that allows either
language to be pronounced without perceptible facial expression. But most likely, Johnson succeeded in New York and
was accepted by the Mohawk because he was a willing student of Iroquois custom and readily adopted their ways of
doing business. Like his Pennsylvania German–Mohawk contemporary Conrad Weiser, or his French opposite, the legendary Jean Couer (Joncaire) who lived among the Seneca at
the other end of the Longhouse, and in common with his
Dutch assistant and translator (also Albany's official secretary) Peter Wraxall, he was taken up as an apt pupil and
shown how to carry on trade and war and diplomacy after the
Iroquois fashion.

In rereading Johnson's journals and papers, I come to
sense that as much as Lewis Henry Morgan he deserves
credit for the first Euro-American insights into the ethnology of the Longhouse people. Not in the way of sorting and
codifying, at which Morgan excelled, but for actively incorporating and living the principles at the heart of their culture.
The quintessentially Scots-Irish Johnson by no means "went
native," but probably his own native conviviality—remnant
of his own not-so-long-buried tribal manners—made it possible for him to adopt and observe Iroquois customs of dress
and dance, warfare and feasting. And deeper, underlying these
outward habits, a thorough understanding and acceptance of
the Ritual of Condolence and the principle of gift exchange.
"It is obvious," he wrote, in a passage footnoted by Morgan
and later scholars, "to all who are the least acquainted with
Indian affairs, that they regard no message or invitation, be it
of what consequence it will, unless attended or confirmed by
strings or belts of wampum, which they look upon as we our
letters, or rather bonds." Not money, and not mere ornament
—letters, or rather bonds. Yet for all this, Johnson was a
trader, and while profit lay in keeping these bonds intact, it
began to alter the meaning of the contract.

In the winter of 1746–47 the French and their Ottawa allies raided and destroyed the hamlet of Schenectady, almost on Albany's doorstep. Albany itself was under siege by smallpox and the usual hardships of cold and hunger. New York's governor and assembly, between incompetence and corruption, could do no more than renew the usual bounty offer of £10 for scalps and £20 for prisoners. Perceiving this as a distant and ineffectual gesture, Johnson proceeded to organize raiding parties that prevented a complete rout of the English from the upper Hudson Valley. His methods of organizing, and the complex transactions required of the forest diplomat, are reflected in the many pages of expense account forwarded to the sympathetic but notoriously incompetent Irishman then in office, the Honorable George Clinton. The bill was never paid, but excerpts from that winter's books will convey some belated account of the diplomatic and economic complexity that was lost on the governor and assembly. As they must have supposed, Johnson was acting in his own best business interest—but it is clear to us that his priorities have changed considerably from those of the speculative young adventurer who had landed in the New World less than a decade before. It is an account, not simply of commerce, but of ritual and spiritual transactions. And while it strives to honor both, the effect is to blur their differences. Instead of renewing and renaming, it is cheapening the price of North America.

1 *Belt of Wampum to Moses, for one he gave
   the Caghnawagas to stop their mouths when
   he was at Canada* _____3.....5.....9
14 *Ells Black Strouds for to wipe of the tears of
   both the next Castles being their Custom 'ere
   they can be spoke with at 12/pr* _____8.....8.......
*To 3 Strings Wampum to Speak wth. Contg.
   300 @ 6/pr* _____18...........
2 *Gallns. Rum to each Castle at Meeting* _____1..............
*Cash to Sundry Indians for mending Guns*_____2....12......

Provisions to Sundry Do: _____5....10......

To 2 pair Womens Hose to Hance the Wilts
    Wife 8s; Cash & Rum to Buy Corn for 20s _____1.....8.......

Cash to Young Brant for Encouragement to go Out _5....12......

To 3 Strings and 1 Belt of Wampum thrown to the 5
    Nations to Insist upon their steadfastness that
    this Delay might make no Change in them _____3.............

1   Black stroud 30s Stockgs. & Shirt to Clean
    Brants House after the Decase of his Son before
    he could keep Council in his House _____2....10......

Provisions for 32 Outscouts 10 days at 6d a man
    pr day _____8.............

A Treat at the Castle before they went Out_____2..18......

30 lb Powder & Lead 90 lb, 60 flints _____6...17....6

Tobacco & pipes 5s & 30 lb Shott 22/6 _____1.....7.....6

To a Belt of Wampum to David a Conajee. who
    went out a fighting a Treat & a Cagg of Rum ___2....15......

A Black Stroud for Nickus of Conajohees Child ____1....10......

25 Ells Red Ribbon @ 12d _____1.....5.......

7   Belts Wampum to Condole the Deaths of the
    Nations 8400 Wampum that is 7000 Black at
    6s pr 1400 White at 4s pr _____23..16......

Making each Belt at 6/ _____2.....2.......

2   Long strings Wampum 2s: 500 white at 4s _____1.............

Cash paid Sundry Fighters Wives for
    Subsistance Dureing their mens Absence _____15...........

6   Razors 6 Combs_____16...6.......

15 Ells Black Strouds, sent with the Belts
    of Wampum to the 5 Nations to Condole
    their Loss _____9.............

To a Feast or Treat to Lt. Walter Butlars party
    when they returned with 6 scalps from
    Crown point_____5.............

14 Ells Ribbon to the 6 Scalps @12d _____1.....4.......

Presents to 2 Oghquaga Sachems in
    our Interrest_____14...........

Provs. on their Journey home with Rum &ca _____2....10......

A large Belt Black Wampum to call them to

   Warr Immediately _____7.....5 ....* [8]

Through all this mingling of Indian truck and beads, dry goods and wet, pound notes and colonial paper, it does not appear that wampum is regarded as money. The beads themselves—as well as the "treats" of food and kegs of rum—are used after the manner of the Iroquois (even "cash" is not used here as money is commonly employed) and more nearly accords with ethnographic descriptions of a tribal chiefdom economy. Most of the items in his account are not for the necessities of life on the warpath—as we would expect, say, of a commander merely "hiring" and outfitting mercenaries—but are of a symbolic, gestural, and ceremonial value, binding receiver and giver to a covenant chain of personal and tribal agreement. Nevertheless, loose beads are exchanged for English money—"I told them," Johnson confides to a correspondent, "to keep their wampum, as it had cost them money"—and the values of the belts are quoted at the current price of loose manufactured beads, between four and six shillings per hundred. He even notes the labor cost of stringing and weaving the belts, payable in the available currency. And precisely here, in the cheap money that is the engine of war and material abundance, is the weak link in the chain of agreement. In the loss of distinction between money and gift, profit and politics. How appropriate this was to the diplomacy of the forest—but how like the ways business was also done in Albany, in the back rooms and corridors of government. Where they have another name for it.

8. FROM "AN ACCOUNT OF Expenses wth Receipt to His Excellency The Hon. George Clinton Governor of New York for Sundry Disbursements made to the Six Nations of Indians who were Engaged on the Expedition Intended against Canada," 13 December 1746 et seq. (Johnson, *Papers*, 9:16ff.).

🙿 🙿 🙿

About a mile back from the Hudson, up State Street, standing amid the great cultural expanse of the Rockefeller Empire State Plaza, the imposing new museum whose archives I've been digging in all morning. By a skyway, the museum attaches to the old state buildings across the street. But by an-

9. FROM BEAUCHAMP'S papers (ten volumes of paginated holograph manuscripts in two boxes) in the library of the State Museum, Albany (*Antiquities of Onondaga,* 1:248). The two boxes reflect years of historical devotion by the pastor of Onondaga's Church of the Good Shepherd. With Morgan's encouragement he read and noted every available history for its Iroquoian facts, particularly those pertaining to wampum. He acquired two belts, *Tatadaho* and *Wing* (or *Dust Fan*), which were purchased by the State Museum in 1898. A third, known as *Beauchamp "Path,"* went to the museum in 1949.

10. ALTHOUGH IT DOES NOT specify a covenant, the 1613 Iroquois-Dutch exchange noted earlier— which included a silver chain—may have marked the beginning of this agreement between the Five Nations and the nations of Europe.

other route, less traveled, an elevator takes you down from the dioramas and imperial vacancies of Lewis Henry Morgan Hall, to a wide underground corridor leading to the lower levels of the seat of government. There, in a vault beneath the capitol dome, is where the State of New York has been keeping its wampum. I'm to be taken there today after lunch, which I've skipped in order to get my work done. Frantic as a billing clerk, I'm copying from the two boxes of papers of the Reverend William Beauchamp, pastor to the Onondaga at the turn of the century, and a collector of objects and ethnographic data as well as souls. My own goes wandering in the current of history and profit and loss, like a loose penny or an unstrung bead. I'm looking for an old contract, lost and apparently forgotten.

The five Nations received a hank of zewant (wampum) to bind a treaty at Albany, 1682, and gave three belts of peak, or zewant, 16 deep. These were from the Senecas. The Mohawks gave one, the Onandagas two, the Cayugas one. These were a pledge of their answer. The agents gave 50 guilders zewant to each nation.[9]

Beauchamp does not note the source of this exchange, but it appears to be the renewal of an already existing agreement between the Iroquois and the Dutch, who were doing business as if Albany were still Beverwyck. It is the oldest reference I've found to the Covenant Chain, the agreement between the Five Nations and the Europeans, held and renewed at Albany for more than a century.[10] But it reads more like a business transaction—the Dutch are dispensing "zewant" by the careful measure of hank and guilder, while the symbolic sense of the belt exchange is not even referred to. It contrasts sharply with the highly metaphorical exchange two years later between the Iroquois and the English governor Dongan, where figurative terms underlie and confirm agreement. The Covenant required, like the Iroquois social contract, that the meaning of those symbols be ritually repeated and reconfirmed with each successive administration. Here they are addressed to Dongan's successor, Col. Henry Slaughter:

> *We have been informed by our Forefathers, that in former times a Ship arrived here in this Country, which was matter of Great Admiration to us, especially our desire was to know what should be within her Belly. In that ship were Christians & amongst the rest One Jaques with whom we made a Covenant of Friendship, which Covenant hath since been tyed together with a Chain, & always been kept inviolable both by the Brethren & us, in which Covenant it was agreed, that whosoever should hurt or prejudice the One, should be guilty of injuring the Other, all of us being comprehended in One Common League.*
>
> *(In testimony here of they gave a Bever Skin)*[11]

11. ANSWER OF THE ONEIDA, Onondaga, Cayuga and Seneca, to a speech by His Excellency Col. Henry Slaughter, Albany, 2 June 1691 (Wraxall's *Abridgement*, 10).

12. CADWALLADER COLDEN'S account of negotiations following the Treaty of Ryswick, which in 1697 restored France and England's New World property boundaries, undoing (on paper) the victories and losses of King William's War (*The History of the Five Indian Nations dependent on the province of New-York in America* [repr. New York, 1904], 253–62).

Both Beauchamp's and Wraxall's transcripts tell us that the Covenant Chain required regular renewal, that it may have originally been a silver chain but was represented by belts and strings of wampum, and that a "fire" was kept at Albany where this ceremony was to take place. The Iroquois were as famous for holding to their contracts as for enforcing them, and this appears to be a consequence of their fidelity to symbolic forms, whose meaning was frequently restated and renewed. The beaver skin token here is functioning with the same force as wampum belts, suggesting that beads may have simply been the prototype of all such contracts. They "kept their word," that is, not by a signature, but by constantly repeating and polishing its meaning. The exactness with which they observed the covenant was frequently noted, and this too was by design.

A contemporary historian, Cadwallader Colden, recorded a wampum exchange with the French at the end of King William's War.[12] He attended the meeting as a commissioner from Albany, the Six Nations saying they would not otherwise talk with the French, the Treaty of Ryswick notwith-

standing. Decanesora welcomed Joncaire, a Monsieur Mari-
cour, and the Jesuit Bruyas to Onondaga, greeting them with
three strings of mourning wampum: to wipe away the tears
of their losses, to open their mouths that they might speak
freely, and to cleanse the blood from the place where they
were to meet. The Jesuit returned the gesture and in his address gave three consecutive belts: offering condolence, requesting a prisoner exchange, and offering to come live with
them. The first two were accepted, but despite a great deal of
figurative reference—planting the Tree of Peace, overturning
the War Kettle, and brightening the Chain—his third belt was
rejected out of hand. The terms of his proposal are as laden
with spiritual symbol as the Dutch contract is notable for its
material plainness—but the overtures of both European parties achieve only partial acceptance, both being known for
their failure to match these two halves of the equation. They
were poor keepers of their word. The Iroquois, on the other
hand, submitted their account of these speeches by recitation
to the earl of Ballamont, and Colden copied that transcript for
his history, being more accurate than what he could provide.

It would appear that the English idea of a contract, combined with the social intelligence of their Scots and Irish
agents, came very close to making and keeping successful
agreement with the Six Nations. But here again, where understanding seems most complete, a subtle difference will
prove fatal. And again, it is in the beads. I read and reread
these agreements, asking wherein is the flaw that allowed
them to unravel. It is ultimately in the betrayal of the words,
of course—sheer duplicity, lies, and theft. But something had
to fail before the words, something in the bonds themselves.
And precisely there, at the bottom line, is the fatal misunderstanding: in that double sense of "bonds," where the very
symbols that marked and kept the agreement—the beaver,
the beads, even the handshake, our original five-and-ten—
were convertible to money, and as good as ready cash. The
promise was for sale.

It was not only the trader, then, but the maker of treaties

who changed the value of things in North America. Money and language are but the body and soul of our agreements, and when they do not agree, the effect is to cheapen life, no less for personal and social than for investment bonds. The causes may be subtle of discernment, but the effects are un-mistakable. Here is the covenant at Albany half a century later, an appeal from its former inhabitants:

> *Fathers, . . . the white people . . . came as far up the River,*
> *as where the old Fort stood; Our Forefathers invited*
> *them ashore, and said to them, here we will give you a*
> *place too make you a Town, it shall be from this place up*
> *to such a stream, (meaning where the Patroons Mill now*
> *stands) and from the River back up to the Hill, our Fore-*
> *fathers told them they were now a small people, they*
> *would in time multiply and fill up the land they had*
> *given them.*
>
> *Gave a Belt.*

> *Fathers, You see how early we made friendship with you,*
> *we tied each other in a very strong chain, that chain has*
> *never yet been broken, we now clean and Rub that chain,*
> *to make it brighter and stronger, and we determine on*
> *our part, that it never shall be broken, and we hope you*
> *will take care that neither you, nor any one else shall*
> *break it. . . .*
>
> *Gave a Belt.*

> *Fathers, Don't think strange at what we are about to say;*
> *we would say something respecting our lands. . . .* [13]

And gave yet another belt, although it proved of little use. The residents of an expanding Albany replied that these lands belonged to King George. This was following the war named after him, during one of those lulls when Albany did not need its Indians, and had little memory of the belts that had been exchanged there. Those received were either converted to money, like the beaver, or restrung for some more urgent

13. RECORDED AS PART of the preliminary unfinished business between New York and its Indians at the Albany Congress, 1754 (*Doc Rel Col Hist NY*, 6:881).

purpose. Their devaluation is evident in the quantity required, as in this case, just to get to what you had to say. And they carried no assurance you would be heard. Real promises were kept on paper, and the paper kept where you couldn't see it.

I was still a little early for my appointment when I abandoned the day's researches. As usual, I'd come away with a few clues, and a sense I hadn't found some truth I was looking for. I paid the office to xerox some things I couldn't find elsewhere, put the Reverend's papers back in order, and came down the elevator to Morgan Hall. I browsed in the museum's gift shop a while, among real or simulated artifacts of the indigenous cultures of other far-off colonies, most of them as expensive as the glossy photo books in which they were portrayed again. I bought three postcards and a card for my sister's birthday, only two days away. The clerk left another customer browsing among silver work, put my cards in a small bag, and rang up my $1.84. I was directed back to the elevator, third floor. Ask for Historical Services.

KEEPERS OF THE
NAMES

The state of New York, knowing that governments must appear to keep their word, has created in Albany a dual repository where two sets of books are kept. It is hard to imagine how much of the city had to be razed to create the great mall, across which the new museum and the old state house appear to be keeping an eye on each other. It's hard to say which most bears watching.

My audit of these old accounts had hardly begun when I had to leave the archives. I'd made little progress through the two boxes of papers the librarian had set before me this morning but would just have time to view the museum's wampum collection before departing. I calculated I'd have to be on the turnpike soon if I was going to get to my next investigation by nightfall. I couldn't avoid recognizing again how poorly I'd budgeted time and money for this expedition. Not to mention heart. No one mentions to aspiring scholars the considerable costs of working outside the centers of letters and finance, and what it's like to enter these temples and be regarded much as the Athenians must have Diogenes when he said, "I have come to debase your coinage."[1]

Fortunately, after some shuffling between secretaries and higher-ups, I'd been referred to the museum's Historical Services Department. The man who greeted me introduced himself as Ray Gonyea, and I supposed by his appearance and

1. DIOGENES OF SINOPE, THE "dog philosopher," or cynic, was speaking partly in jest, at his own expense; his father was a mint official who had been convicted of debasing coinage and thus disgraced his family. Without property, kin, or citizenship, Diogenes highly valued his position as slave to Xeniades: "Sell me to that man," he said. "He needs a master" (*Herakleitos and Diogenes,* trans. Guy Davenport [San Francisco, 1976]).

demeanor that he was representing more than a department of the museum. I explained my mission here and mentioned that I was next on my way to Onondaga, and the name of the man I was hoping to see. "Oh yeah," he said, "he lives just over the hill from me." I wondered if this wasn't a quiet joke, Onondaga being named for its hills, but at this point I was deeply grateful for any connection. We talked about how I knew of the person, and where I was from. At a conference. The local college. Northern California. His manner was impeccably direct and clear, and he scheduled the appointment as if it were an everyday gesture of well-bred hospitality.

When I returned to Ray's office that afternoon, he explained that we would be joined by some other visitors to the vault. One was a young man presently bent over a drawing table working on a pencil sketch. We looked at some of his finished drawings—one in particular, of an ancient stone pipe of Seneca origin, as palpably present as if it held the touch of the artist's eye and hand. I would have supposed such work outmoded by cameras and electronic gadgetry, digital enhancements, and virtual realities. The museum, I was having to admit, seemed more sensitive to its mission than some of its history had led me to expect.

We would also be joined by his director, my guide informed me. Having read of the museum in its early days, when it had but one Director and one Indian, I assumed this meant the head of the museum. Hardly prepared for such illustrious company, I felt myself becoming the occasion for a group cultural tour. I could see I'd deluded myself yet again, this time into supposing I'd just quietly duck into the vault, check out the wampum belts, then head on over to Onondaga and see what's happening with the keepers of the names. And get home again with at least half a basket of facts and enough change to call someone to come get me out of the bus station.

I couldn't really claim total ignorance of what I was doing, though it might sometimes seem both uninformed and deliberately provocative. I knew that the belts were a major treasure of the museum, and that the movement for repatriation of artifacts had made their possession a very sensitive issue. I also knew that "He Carries the Names" is a title inscribed, not in wampum at Onondaga, but on a sheepskin in Albany, and bestowed not on a traditional chief, but on the director of the museum. It was officially given in 1908 as a final gesture of admission that the wampum belts of the Iroquois Nation were best left in the keeping of the regents of the University of the State of New York. Because anyway, they had the wampum and were not about to turn it over to an impoverished people of unregistered ancestry who had kept these priceless treasures in kettles and sacks in the back rooms of board houses and had moreover according to the best ethnographic testimony lost the ability to "read" them. They had—according to one Albany judge—even ceased to exist as a nation. The wampum belts, he had ruled, "are curiosities and relics of a time and condition and confederation which has ceased to exist."[2] So why are they locked in a vault beneath the capitol building?

Ray has handed me an unsigned museum bulletin—"Information Sheet on Wampum"—which briefly and lucidly outlines this story. It generously skirts the issues of money and power that are at the heart of this astonishing misappropriation. The amount of five hundred dollars is mentioned with some frequency, as if it were the token by which "big money" was offered to Indians. It was the price of a horse and wagon in the 1890s, paid to Thomas Webster, described as an Onondaga wampum-keeper, for a number of belts in his possession, by a General Henry Beebee Carrington, a veteran of the western Indian wars now appointed census taker to the Iroquois. By his own testimony, Webster did not hold the traditional Longhouse title and although able to read the belts declined to do so before a legislative committee, saying they did not belong to him.

When Thomas Webster handed Carrington the battered valise tied with rope, both parties seem to have been concerned primarily with the safekeeping of its contents. It was a gesture the general could apparently ill afford, because when

2. THIS WAS PART OF THE legal justification for allowing Albany's mayor, John Boyd Thacher, to retain custody of his personal collection of four wampum belts, later bequeathed to the State Museum by his widow. The belts were *Hiawatha, Washington Covenant, First Palefaces,* and *Champlain* ("Information Sheet on Wampum," New York State Museum and Science Service [Albany, 1971], 10).

the Smithsonian declined to buy them, in order to pay for the publication of a book about the Iroquois (*The Six Nations*, 1892), he sold the belts—again for five hundred—to a Reverend Crane of Boston, who—still at five—in turn conveyed them to John Boyd Thacher, a longtime mayor of Albany. The mayor paid Crane with a personal check and, after loaning the belts to the Empire State exhibit at the Chicago Columbian Exposition of '94, would not part with them at any price during his lifetime. Oh, and another five to the chiefs and clan mothers who showed up at the 1898 Convocation—described by the Albany *Argus* as the finest display of pomp and glory since colonial days—to ratify the bestowal of these and all Iroquois wampum, along with the title of wampum-keeper, upon the regents of the State University.

As grossly appropriative as these transactions now appear, they indicate only the petty theft. Many of the purchases were made with a genuine concern for precious relics. The deeper spiritual and cultural crime was that of the state and its hireling anthropologists, whose 1971 letter to the Honorable Nelson Rockefeller expresses the essence of several decades of self-serving professionalism:

> As political documents of an earlier period the belts belong in Albany. We urge their retention by the state for its new cultural center in the South Mall....
>
> As scholars whose researches depend on the great ethnographic collections of now largely vanished primitive peoples of the world we urge the preservation of such mementos of culture in museums. We deplore the principle of returning such treasures to the acculturated descendants of their original owners lest a precedent be established that would require logically returning Ibo carvings to Nigeria, Asmat art to New Guinea, and the works of Florentine painters to Italy.
>
> That the wampum collection of New York has now an appreciated value of one quarter of a million dollars is a

further footnote to inflation. Nevertheless, state proper-
ty should not be legislated away lightly in the illusion of
religiosity or as capital in the civil rights movement.... [3]

I don't mention these issues to Ray, as he is in a traditionally difficult position. The library bulletin (which refrains
from mentioning this letter, for example) probably says as
much as can be discreetly said on the matter. Part of the
legacy of New York's ethnographic pioneering has been a
deep but unspoken difference, quite evident to outsiders, between white professionals and native representatives and informants. Much of the conflict has been acted out within the
walls of this museum—or of its predecessor, destroyed by a
disastrous fire in 1911, another of the colorful spectacles of
the city's history, which took with it the greater part of its
Iroquois collection, a fact seldom noted in the pious assurances of safekeeping.

I think especially of Arthur C. Parker, great-nephew of
Morgan's informant, whose talent for ethnographic collecting was consistently thwarted by the traditional archaeologi-
cal bent of the museum's then-director. Like his predecessors,
John M. Clarke was not above adding a good amount of senti-
ment to his excavations, and one of Parker's first diplomatic
errands as a museum employee was to secure for his superior
a Seneca name and the official title of wampum-keeper. [4] And
while his director presided over these treasures, Parker was
set to work editing the papers of Harriet Maxwell Converse.

Daughter of an Elmira trading post proprietor, turn-of-
the-century poet, and prominent Manhattan hostess, Harriet
Converse carried on in Morgan's footsteps the work of ad-
vancing Iroquois causes. She also did considerable collecting
among the Onondaga and Seneca—of ten belts of wampum
among other objects, and many myths and tales that she
rather inexactly translated into the prevailing mode of romantic prose. Parker edited, rechecked, augmented, and recast
the work of this woman whose Indianesque affectations—
reminiscent of Morgan's pretensions to savage fraternity—

3. THIS LETTER, SIGNED BY
five anthropologists and
directors of prestigious
museums—including
the Smithsonian and the
University of New York,
Albany—is reprinted in
*The American Indian
Reader* (San Francisco,
1972), 224f. It is followed
by a response to both
the letter and the 1909
Wampum Law. The letter
is dated February 1970,
the response dated Spring.

4. PARKER'S SUPERVISOR IS
easily confused with Noah
T. Clarke, museum
archaeologist, who was
apparently the next
wampum-keeper, and
author of "The Wampum
Belt Collection of the
New York State Museum"
(Report of the Director,
New York State Museum
bulletin no. 288, 1931).
With a photo of each, the
descriptions are a useful
census of the twenty-six
belts then in the museum's
possession. In keeping with
the dynastic names and
titles, and like the mayors
of both Albany and New
York, these descriptions
suggest a ritual display
of appropriated wealth.

5. *MYTHS AND LEGENDS OF the New York Iroquois,* cited above. Between 1882 and 1899 Converse acquired and turned over to the State Museum ten wampum belts. Most of them are memorials of alliance and diplomacy. Parker re-collected the stories she had assembled, doubling the size of the book; the introduction sets out his method of re-creating these myths, which put to good purpose some of the doubleness he perhaps felt, being matrilineally of European descent:

> By this method the transcriber attempts to assimilate the ideas of the myth tale as he hears it, seeks to become imbued with the spirit of its characters, and, shutting out from his mind all thought of his own culture, and momentarily transforming himself into the culture of the myth teller, records his impressions as he recalls the story. His object is to produce the same emotions in the mind of civilized man which is produced in the primitive mind . . . without destroying the native style or warping the facts of the narrative.

could be overlooked in view of her sincere friendship and genuine aid. She was instrumental in getting Parker his job as museum anthropologist, in creating the museum's mission of preserving New York's indigenous culture, and along with the Reverend Beauchamp, in transferring to it the major part of its wampum collection. She was given a Seneca name (apparently without the necessity of lobbying) and made an honorary chief of the Longhouse. Her book was published posthumously, after many months of Parker's labor.[5] The Director of the Museum, signing his own new Iroquois name, provided the book's preface. One can only wonder at the diplomacy, restraint, and strength of identity this work must have required of Parker. I imagine those qualifications still go with the job.

"Ah. Here she is," Ray said. He introduced me to a pleasant, businesslike woman, much younger than I'd expected, whose title turned out to be Deputy Commissioner for Cultural Education. Obviously, something new had replaced the dynastic professionalism of the good old directors of the past. She said almost immediately that she was glad of the opportunity to visit the vault, as she hadn't yet seen the museum's famous wampum collection. I wondered if she knew she had been remiss in her duty as name-keeper, but refrained from asking. She as kindly did not inquire into the exact nature of my mission. I was not at all sure why this custodian of the belts had consented to my strange visit, and these people brought along to witness. Perhaps because each of us, for very different reasons, needed to see what we were attempting to represent. We were on sensitive and unknown ground here, and deferred to Ray with exaggerated solemnity.

As we descended through the museum floors and began our walk through the subterranean corridor, he directed the conversation to the young man's drawings and his plans for future work. He seemed full of promise. Parker's own groundbreaking studies of maize and culture were graced by the drawings of Jesse Cornplanter, a young man whose work he had encouraged. I wondered if the habitual Iroquois conservatism was at work here, this young artist being "raised up" in the other's place. Or maybe I was simply feeling the strain of more historical reverberation than most of us recent Americans can bear.

We came out into the windy afternoon with the skyway above us, crossed what I guessed was Madison Street, then reentered and continued down a wide corridor extending beneath the Empire Plaza. As we traversed the underground passage it grew narrower and darker and older. Soon we were passing through high hallways, dim and quiet but for the occasional sound of our talking. We were somewhere beneath the capitol building, and the air was almost palpable with lobbying and cigar smoke—what the Iroquois councillors referred to as "talk in the bushes." At a junction where we had to turn, a tall and very thin man in a dark suit was waiting for us. He was the one, we were told, who knew the combination to the vault. He escorted us to the left, down an even dimmer hallway, somehow evoking the combined manner of banker, undertaker, and CIA operative—a being conjured by this subterranean passage between museum and state house, as if the words inked onto paper and voices talked into beads, like relics beneath the Vatican, were a living dead from which the Empire State might draw its otherwise doubtful title to land and wealth. We all self-consciously looked away as he turned the dial on the massive steel door. Maybe, I thought, I'm not a culture thief but some kind of fool detective whose job is to stumble upon the scene of a crime. Where they keep the symbols, and where they hide the true wealth of North America. It was an agreement. It was never money.

The keeper of the combination pulled the great door slowly back on its hinges. Now it was money.

A broad belt of wampum of thirty-eight rows, having a
white heart in the center, on either side of which are two

white squares all connected with the heart by white rows of beads shall be the emblem of unity of the Five Nations.[6]

6. ARTICLE 60 OF *THE Great Law of Peace of the Longhouse People,* in the edition published by *Akwesasne Notes* Rooseveltown, 4th printing, 1975). The belt being referred to is the one that lay before us, in a glass case in the vault beneath Albany.

These are the words spoken by the prophet Dekanawida, as confirmed by Hayonhwatha, co-founders of the League of the Iroquois, some half a millennium ago. The words were woven into a belt of wampum, a constitution made of beads. The *Hiawatha Belt,* by act of the legislature, was now kept here along with two dozen others by the state of New York—which, as it declared in 1909, as if this too were prophecy,

7. FROM THE NEW YORK State law relating to custody of wampum (L. 1909, Ch. 31 pp. 3725–3726) Section 27. It continues in much the same tone, further authorizing the state "to secure by purchase, suit, *or otherwise any* wampums which have *ever* been in the possession of *any* of the Ho-de-no-sau-nee," and so on (the italics I've had to add).

shall hereafter be recognized in all courts and places, as having every power which has ever, at any time, been exercised by any wampum-keeper of the Onondaga nation, or of any of the Ho-de-no-sau-nee, otherwise known as the Five Nations, or the Six Nations, or the Iroquois, and shall keep such wampums in a fireproof building, as public records, forever.[7]

As if the state itself is awed by the boldness of this claim of precedence and duration, and no doubt in the interest of security, the belts rest in this dimly lit vault beneath the state building. But even here, and even by the incandescent glow of a low-watt bulb, it is apparent that we are in the presence of a great treasure. It is one of the original documents of human agreement in North America. Considerably older and more basic in pattern than the belt known as *First Palefaces,* its age and authority are equaled by its great beauty. It is intrinsic wealth, "rich" in itself, in a sense only faintly indicated by what we call money. Nevertheless, I had to ask the vault-keeper what he thought it was worth. He nearly smiled, as if I were trying to bait him into supposing this might be some bizarre heist. He had no idea. It had not recently been appraised. He spoke as if from a text. Not money—a map.

The first of the squares on the left represents the Mohawk Nation and its territory, the second square on the left and near the heart represents the Oneida Nation and its territory, and the white heart in the middle represents the Onondaga Nation and its territory. It also means that the heart of the Five Nations is single in its loyalty to the Great Peace, and that the Great Peace is lodged in the heart (meaning with the Onondaga League chiefs) and that the Council Fire is to burn there for the Five Nations. Further it means that the authority is given to advance the cause of peace whereby hostile nations out of the League shall cease warfare. The white square to the right of the heart represents the Cayuga Nation and its territory and the fourth and last square represents the Seneca Nation and its territory.

White here symbolizes that no evil or jealous thought shall creep into the minds of the chiefs while in Council under the Great Peace. White, the emblem of peace, love, charity, and equity surrounds and guards the Five Nations.[8]

These are the words, as spoken and confirmed by the founders, passed on for generations, and early in this century transcribed by Arthur C. Parker. They were to be repeated as the Onondaga speaker held the strings of the articles of law, and recited the belt's "contents." This "reading" of the Great Law Of Peace to the assembled delegates of the League would be performed only at specified times and under certain conditions—for example at midsummer, under a cloudless sky. It was customarily recited in conjunction with the installation of a new representative to the council of fifty sachems, just as if it were the beginning of the League.

Now Dekanawida addressed the council and he said, "I am Dekanawida and with me is my younger brother. We two lay before you the laws by which to frame the Ka-ya-neh-rehn-ko-wa. The emblems of the chief rulers shall be the antlers of deer. The titles shall be vested in certain women and the names shall be held in their maternal families forever." All the laws were then recited and Hayonhwatha confirmed them.[9]

8. THIS CONTINUES THE reading of article 60. In Parker's *Constitution of the Five Nations,* it is article 61. The "map" has the eastern nations on its left and so sees North America from another perspective than the Automobile Association's.

9. PARKER, *Constitution,* 27.

10. From article 27
(Parker, *Constitution*, 38).

The repetition of the terms of the Law, as set forth by the Mohawk prophet and confirmed by the Onondaga speaker, was both a reenactment and a renewal of the original covenant of loss and recovery by which the Longhouse was established and extended. The purple beads into which the white are woven, these are the "dark and bloody ground" that the northeastern woodlands had become—and with the arrival of the Europeans would become again. If not heeded, the Great Peace would be enforced and extended by arms—but it was not the war club or the rifle that gave it the power that it continues to wield among the Iroquois today, even when the document itself has been sold into captivity—into this vault, where its words are held by the power of words on paper. Its law was embodied by acts, of which our guide was perhaps offering us example.

> You shall now become a mentor of the people of the 5 Nations. The thickness of your skin shall be proof against anger, offensive actions and criticism. Your heart shall be filled with peace and good will and your mind filled with a yearning for the welfare of the people of the Confederacy.[10]

The operative symbols of the *Hiawatha Belt*—the meanings that must be *enacted* if the Great Peace is to be maintained—are the lines by which the several nations are united —"all connected with the heart by white rows of beads." Where "heart" is of course a place (the Onondaga valley), but also the fire at the center of the Longhouse (kept by the Onondaga fire-keeper), as well as the Great Peace itself (turned 180°, the heart shape is the great White Pine by which Dekanawida rooted peace in the Confederacy). But "heart" must also mean exactly what it says: the human heart. And "connected" means literally the open path, unrestricted use of the system of trails that united the northeastern woodlands, and a freedom of access that characterized the Longhouse itself—as a multifamily residence, a council house, and a passage with doors at both ends. The white beads, the broad lines outlining and connecting the Five

Nations, are then the heart's path, the way itself—the acceptance, the land and soil in the custody of the women, the titles
to chieftainship in the keeping of the female line, the clans—
Turtle, Bear, Wolf, and all the rest—in the power of the clan
mothers. This is the Great Peace, of which the League was
custodian.

This is how the accounts were kept and valuations maintained in North America. Not by the iron law, and not even
the golden rule. A peace that came from the heart's will to
peace. The keepers of its word answerable to the keepers of
the earth.

Each of us thanked the guardian of the door on our way out
and left him to lock the vault behind us. With the sound of its
closing, history collapsed and we were back in subterranean
Albany. The social contract expressed in brick and mortar,
concrete and marble, hallway and archive, one beneath another, department and bureau and drawer and file, record of
who knows what. We walked through the corridor in silence,
the air palpable with things forgotten.

In 1754 the English colonial representatives assembled at
Albany presented to the Longhouse People a wampum belt
which they'd had made for the occasion. It appears at first to
replicate the format of the traditional "covenant chain" of
linked shapes or figures. Here, however, the "reading" was
first composed as a speech committed to paper—"settled,
Read and unanimously approved of" by the commissioners of
the several colonies, and then read to the assembled nations
by the Lieutenant Governor of New York:

> Brethren. This represents the king our common Father—
> this line represents his arms extended, embracing all us
> the English and all the Six Nations—These represents
> the Colonies which are here present and those who
> desire to be thought present—These represents the Six

*Nations, and there is a space left to draw in the other
Indians—And there in the middle is the line represented
which draws us all in under the king our common
Father*[11]

11. *Doc Rel Col Hist
NY* 6:861. This volume
contains the minutes of
the Albany Congress, and
verbatim record of the
speeches that follow. See
also Beverly McAnear,
"Personal Aspects of the
Albany Congress of 1754,"
*Mississippi Valley Historical
Review* 39 (March 1953).

This belt has not made its way into the vault beneath the
state buildings. It apparently survives only on paper, a sign of
a new set of agreements come to North America, and a new
way of making and keeping agreement itself. As to the meaning of both "king" and "common Father"—to take only the
most obvious terms—but also as to the force of abstract representation, in both the visual and political sense of the words.
The picturing of those only thought to be present, the blank
space where "other Indians" might go—these do not appear
to conform to the way business was previously done in the
Longhouse. And the all-embracing arms, the line "which
draws us all in," do not appear to represent Iroquois notions
of paternity nor their feelings on the issue of personal and
national sovereignty. Between the lines of beads, another way
of doing business.

Not only was there more than one form of agreement
going forward that summer of the Albany Congress, there
were a number of conflicting agendas. It is doubtful, in the first
place, that the colonies had authority to make treaty with an
autonomous nation. So far as the Lords of Trade in London
were concerned, the business of the congress was to buttress
colonial frontiers against renewed incursions by the neighboring French and their Indian allies. In the five years of "peace"
since the stalemate of King George's War, the Covenant Chain
between the English and the Six Nations had been seriously
neglected, and increasing colonial encroachment on the latter's
traditional hunting grounds had brought the former
"brethren" near to conflict. The year before, the Mohawk chief
Hendrick had walked out of a conference in New York City,
disgusted at the ineffectual governor and the assembly controlled by upriver land and peltry interests. Now once again
the French were almost literally at the door, and a general al-

liance between the colonies and the Iroquois was of the utmost urgency. The Lords of Trade pressed the colonists to set aside short-term self-interest long enough to save themselves.

Representatives of the several colonies, however, had other reasons for uniting. More than one brought a draft of a plan, the most influential being Franklin's "Short Hints Toward a Scheme for Uniting the Northern Colonies."[12] While it touched on the issue of Indian Affairs long enough to put them in the hands of a Crown-appointed President General, it placed the acquisition and allotment of Indian lands in the care of the Grand Council of representatives of the several colonies—that is, safely in the hands of those most interested in their "development" (that is, buying and selling without the expense of an Indian war). A deed, in this new way of talking about North America, could mean these marks on paper. These words that captured territory, and not the imitation covenant belt, were the more urgent agenda of the Albany Congress.

The English colonies, however, were still more threatened by one another than by far-away despots and gift-hungry savages. There is little likelihood that the Albany plan of union would have worked, even had it been adopted by the separate colonial assemblies. Franklin's scheme would have to wait thirty years, and the plan would have to be a confederacy of independent colonies who could not reach agreement. At present, they could not even decide how to seat themselves, let alone how to provide for their common defense (i.e., how to pay for forts and Indians). In the end it was the Crown that came up with most of the troops and money. New York was quarreling with New Jersey over boundaries; Virginia, not in attendance, was peeved because New York had failed to send militia to maintain its incursions upon the Shawnee; Connecticut claimed a large chunk of the Susquehanna, on which Pennsylvania considered it held an option, its delegates having come to Albany with large amounts of cash to cut a deal with the Six Nations.

Within the colonies, the situation was hardly better—in

12. A. H. SMITH, ED., *The Writings of Benjamin Franklin* (New York, 1905), 197–226. Some sources attribute his idea of confederation to the cantons of Switzerland, which seems rather distant. The Iroquois were hardly unknown, and their political forms were familiar to anyone who did business in that part of the world. According to their own accounts: "In 1755 . . . at the 'Albany Congress,' we suggested to twelve British colonies that they should form a union, for strength and peace" (*Akwesasne Notes* 3, no. 3 [Midwinter 1992]).

New York, the governor had at last resigned, but his replacement, within two days of his arrival from England, was found
at breakfast-time to have piteously hanged himself by his
kerchief. The lieutenant governor who had attacked his superior's Indian policies was now left to carry them out. The assembly, under the influence of Albany, would do nothing to
restrict the trade in arms for peltry brought in by French-
allied tribes. Nor would they support or even reimburse
William Johnson, their most effective diplomat among the
Iroquois, because his Mohawk and Oswego trade was cutting
into theirs. And at Albany the Indian Commissioners carried
out the policies of Albany, which was to do nothing, except
insist the Iroquois become more centralized for better trading
access and more convenient defense.

Johnson had given up on the expense and trouble of representing colonial interests to the Iroquois some three years
earlier, so even if they'd had a policy toward the nations that
surrounded them, the colonies had no way to express it. So
out of touch were they with their own boundaries, and so
much preoccupied with their imagined prospects of expanding those boundary lands, that it would come as a great surprise to them a few months later that Virginia's young
George Washington had been rather ignominiously defeated
by French forces in the Ohio, where he and a number of other
gentlemen had some interest in land. Speculation in that
commodity meanwhile moved along briskly. The lieutenant
governor (now acting as governor) who chaired the congress
had to be reminded that sales of Mohawk lands, in which his
family had some interest, were to be included on the agenda
for discussion. The meaning of agreement changing, one forgotten deal at a time.

But the colonists' lapse of memory had not yet overwhelmed the Six Nations. While parties of Iroquois arrived at
intervals during that stormy June, Hendrick and the upriver
Mohawk rather pointedly kept the colonial delegates waiting
in Albany for two weeks. Franklin, though it provided oppor-

tunity to develop and lobby for his scheme, was furious over the lost time and business. For a fortnight, thrown upon the hospitality of residents (the town was still too small to have an inn), reduced to touring the battlements of the ill-prepared Fort Frederick, the commissioners waited out the thunderstorms and monotony of midsummer in Albany. To their great consternation, and then entertainment, an enormous flood brought down the accumulated debris of decades of upstream land-clearing—slash and mud along with logs and milled timber, uprooted trees and drowned animals, all roiling and churning as high as the palisades of the town—and then within a day subsiding. Between people, and between people and land, the agreements changing.

When he arrived, Hendrick gracefully made his apologies to the New York delegation, who had no choice but to accept them. But the next day in addressing the council, he spared no brotherly feelings in his complaint about the traffic in rum and land, and the need for an adequate and organized defense against the war that the English had brought upon them all. As to the root causes of the conflict, he called upon the delegates seated before the Albany courthouse to look around them:

> Brethren. You desire us to speak from the bottom of our
> hearts, and we shall do it. Look about you and you see all
> these houses full of Beaver, and the money is all gone to
> Canada, likewise powder, lead and guns, which the
> French now make use of at Ohio.

This piece of blunt political economy was saved for the ending of a speech that had begun with all the usual formality of Iroquois diplomacy. Hendrick had repeated, with customary exactness, the terms that had been read from paper into wampum by Lieutenant Governor Delancey. Virginia and Carolina would be considered to be "present," the Six United Nations would endeavor to fill the "vacancies" in the chain, and the belt of covenant would be taken to Onondaga, "where our Council Fire always burns." More than accommodating, the speech simply incorporates the terms of abstract representation—terms that again subtly changed the nature of agreement. Nothing was said, however, of the all-embracing arms of King George, except to repeat the expression, "our common Father."

In all respects, the speech had proceeded as its listeners probably expected. Anyone involved in frontier politics, trade, or land sales—usually all three—was accustomed to the indigenous tradition of oratory, and though they missed many nuances and so found it repetitive and tedious, they also knew they had better watch and listen closely. They would have expected the belt given in return for the one they had presented. The three strings of dark beads, given to condole all who had died since the last meeting—they knew this "paying for the dead" had to be done before any business could go forward. What they did not expect was for Hendrick to call attention to the real business of Albany and to then pick up a stick and throw it behind him, to indicate the way the Six Nations had been treated during the recent years of colonial peace and prosperity. Nor could they have failed to note that his words were underscored by a belt of wampum, as were his next remarks—

> The Govr of Virginia, and the Govr of Canada are both quarreling about lands which belong to us, and such a quarrel as this may end in our destruction—

whereas at the conclusion of his speech, he sat down and made no offering of beads. It was also noted that a belt given with the request to reinstate William Johnson as ambassador to the Longhouse was as large as that given to renew the covenant. And one acute observer noted that the voiced approval of that agreement was given simultaneously, rather than severally, nation by nation, as was customary. It was upon such points as these—and again the quantity of beads required to make them—that agreement can be seen breaking down. Despite outward signs of cooperation, the British colonists and the Iroquois went into the final decade of conflict with France on very shaky terms. When this marriage of necessity was ended, the true nature of their commitments would emerge. Even now, their deeper conflict was barely submerged. The congress was hardly ended when John Lydius, Massachusetts's Indian agent, went among the chiefs with rum and £2,000 New York currency, securing deeds to the land they had already sold to the Pennsylvanians.

The Albany Congress appears now, in more than two centuries of retrospect, like a faded tableau of misrepresentation. While the Six Nations attempted to renew their ancient covenant, they made every gesture short of outright violence to indicate their displeasure and distrust of the colonies— who, on the other hand, used this defense compact as a screen to cover their true interests. Giving a wampum belt to Indians was one thing, but to restrain growth and trade was simply contrary to colonial purpose—which was to run a profitable colony. So in those terms—that is, rum and land sales—their reassurances were a promise to pay what was not forthcoming. The Six Nations must have knowingly accepted this bad check of beads. Despite oratory and gesture and wampum belts, there was no other bank they could take it to.

What we witness in this birthing of "union" for the colonies, besides outright chicanery, is a form of appropriation not unlike the colonial adoption of wampum as a currency, and strikingly similar to its later usurpation by anthropologists. It appropriates to the makers of written contracts a natural proprietorship over the land and its inhabitants, who lack the permanence of books and the house of state in which to keep them. The secretary to the Lords of Trade explained this defect as arising from their way of life:

The Indians Therefore would consequently be as they were, in fact not Landworkers but Hunters, not Settlers but Wanderers; they would consequently never have, as

in fact they never had any idea of property in Land. They
would consequently never have, as in fact they never had
any common fixed interest, any one communion of
Rights and actions, one Civil union, and consequently
not any Govern^t. They know no such thing as an admin-
istrative or executive power properly so called.[13]

13. *Doc Rel Col Hist NY*, 6:896. It is impossible to say how much of this popular ethnography was only conveniently ignorant, and how much was outright disinformation. For five centuries such "explanations" accompanied expropriation and provided the rationale still popular today.

This is not the outright denial of the previous century, which maintained that North America was technically "vacant," but a more insidious form of expropriation. In good "Enlightenment" fashion, it sees private property as the only basis of the social contract, and was used to argue that the Iroquois might be ripe for "development." They might finally, that is, be ready for a president general to direct them toward this higher stage of society—and, incidentally, preside over land sales. The person chosen for the job, William Johnson, had married from among the Mohawk and so knew that the Longhouse subsisted principally on maize, cultivated by the women, adjacent to long-term settlements—and that the gifts of the earth and human affairs were managed only by their consent. The idea of a central male authority was as foreign to the Iroquois as the matrilineal clan was to the lapsed memory of the Europeans. The colonists' plan would have to wait for a president general of their own, and a Bureau of Indian Affairs.

The delegates of the colonies, holding out the belt of wampum as their fathers had held out strings of "Indian gold," made a contract in what was essentially a counterfeit currency. While it attempted to be meticulous as to form, it masked other agreements, which ran directly contrary to prevailing valuations. Even among the colonists it was something of a bogus document; between them and the Iroquois it was little more than a clumsy attempt to buy Indians to defend them from other white men. But between its lines was another contract, which would, like bad money, drive wealth out of circulation and into museums.

We came back up into the high-ceilinged light of Morgan Hall, and it was as if we'd never been in that other, ulterior hall, wherein lay the words that supported all its grandeur. I was disoriented and tried to remember the way to the parking garage. My museum hosts gave me directions and assured me I would reach Onondaga before dark. I said good-bye, expressing to Ray my heartfelt thanks. Thanks a million, I said. He never even blinked.

A MAP OF THE HEART

1. SAHLINS MAKES INSIGHTFUL comparison of Hobbes's state of "warre" and Mauss's gift relation, showing that they in fact find similar ground for the social contract, in that both propose a "law of peace" to enforce it. The distinction, as I read Sahlins, is that Hobbes's state of nature—in which life is "solitary, poor, nasty, brutish, and short"—leads to the necessity of a coercive central authority; whereas Mauss points to "primitive" societies which maintain long-term peace by reciprocal exchange—trade and festivals, and the sort of balance implied by the Maori *hau,* or in North America by the ritual of bead exchange and the social architecture of the Longhouse. The balance is still enforced, since refusing to participate in the exchange is an insult, and would in theory return the parties to a "warre" relation. The beads that maintain the gift relationship, such as the Iroquois used them, were not what is called "primitive money" but appear to . . .

Book in hand, as if clinging to memory, I'm sitting in a motel room just south of Syracuse, at the edge of the Onondaga valley. The proprietor, who is Indian but not of this continent, has extracted from me thirty-five dollars for the night—including tax of 10 percent, but not the dollar deposit for the key, which he also got. After some fruitless discussion as to our location, the time of year, and the value of lodging I slipped the money under the bulletproof glass between us. Beside the window was a small picture of a Hindu temple, above which was emblazoned on a banner in the sky: Temple of Understanding. "Hey—no vacancy," I ventured, indicating the picture. He smiled and looked through me and slid my receipt and the key under the glass. It's now very late at night, I've been to a beer joint just down the road, and I think I've come upon a passage that describes the agreement at the heart of the Iroquois Confederacy. An agreement we've lost and like amnesiacs on the edge of the bed late at night struggle to recall.

As a corrective to the loss of social memory—so that traditional society is remembered as a headless and imperfect version of the state in which I'm a traveler—I carry with me a copy of Marshall Sahlins's *Stone Age Economics,*[1] which reminds us of our oldest human agreements. All social contracts, he recalls for us, are "an agreement of incorporation," whose purpose is "to put an end to the strife born of private justice." This was part of the function of the Ritual of Condolence, the ceremony that brought the several Iroquois nations together. But their union was neither a monarchy nor a republic, because the exchange of power was *reciprocal*. "The gift," we have to be told again,

> *would not organize society in a corporate sense, only in a segmentary sense. Reciprocity is a "between" relation. It does not dissolve the separate parties within a higher unity, but on the contrary, in correlating their opposition, perpetuates it. Neither does the gift specify a third party standing over and above the separate interests of those who contract. Most important, it does not withdraw their force, for the gift affects only will and not right.*

Here is the critical point, which goes directly to the heart of the thing that presently governs our lives in the name of peace and security:

> *Except for the honor accorded to generosity, the gift is no sacrifice of equality and never of liberty. The groups allied by exchange each retain their strength, if not the inclination to use it.*

After studying the matter for ten years and crossing the continent to get here, it now seems so simple: *the heart*. The lines all connected to the heart. The *will* to peace. That is the intent of the gift and the foundation of the Great Law. That I have had to come all this way to read, that heart may understand.

> *Then Dekanawida taught the people the Hymn of Peace and the other songs. He stood before the door of the Longhouse and walked before it singing the new songs. Many came and learned them so that many were strong by the magic of them when it was time to carry the Great Peace to Onondaga.*[2]

The original journey to the heart of the Longhouse, as the

1. (continued) define a chiefdom society in which all are incorporated as family members. Even though there is no buying and selling among them, the beads function as a supraeconomic form of trade, and conform to Mauss's description of the peace-making function of exchange. In Sahlins's words: "All the exchanges, that is to say, bear in their material design some political burden of reconciliation" (170).

2. FROM PARKER'S *Constitution*, 27. The language of Parker's rendition has a remarkable way of moving to its point. It is in one sense a "translation" of an oral reading. But it came to Parker already in English, transcribed and translated by Seth Newhouse, an Onondaga of the Six Nations Reserve who had been laboring to record the "Law of Peace and War" for twenty years. It was apparently not the first such transcript, and Newhouse's version provoked another official document to be made by the Council of Chiefs, said to be "set over into flawless English." Earlier, Parker and Newhouse had cooperated to recover the *Pledge* belt, which marked the agreements made between George III and the Longhouse, and their relation on his project seems to . . .

2. (continued) have been
partly that of collaborators.
The transcript was also
submitted to Albert Cusick,
an Onondaga-Tuscarora
who had worked with
ethnologists studying
Iroquois history. Parker's
editing of the result,
although questioned as
soon as it appeared in
1916, carries great energy
and clarity. But it should
be noted that it carries
no sanction of the Six
Nations council.

3. LIKE THE NAMES OF THE
Founders, this Onondaga
name would vary in its
pronunciation from one
nation to the next and in
orthography from one
transcriber to another.
Here the name is close to
Morgan's apparently
Onondaga transcription,
whereas the Mohawk
would write it as *Atotarho*,
and Parker uses the
Seneca *Adodarhoh*. For
consistency I follow Parker's
usage, but see also the
reworking of his sources
that yields the Onondaga
names *Hayónwentha*,
Deganawídah, and
Tadodáho (William N.
Fenton, "Seth Newhouse's
Traditional History and
Constitution of the Iroquois
Confederacy," *Proceedings
of the American
Philosophical Society* 93
[1949]: 141–58).

Seneca scholar Arthur Parker has related it, is characterized by a pervading sense of grace mixed with foreboding. After five years, and then five successive midsummer days of working to establish agreement among the Five Nations, there was still one major obstacle to the Great Peace. Adodarhoh, whose intransigence had led to the death of Hayonhwatha's seven daughters and his subsequent grief and wandering, still held to the old principles of chaos and darkness. This demigod of the Onondaga valley was reported by spies to be suffering under several terrible afflictions: his body was crooked in seven places, his hair was filled with snakes, and he was still practicing cannibalism. This multiple curse was eventually lifted by Dekanawida's song, by his healing touch, and the combing of snakes out of Adodarhoh's hair with wampum, apparently in its early quill form. That these acts are sometimes attributed to Hayonhwatha, who might otherwise have come seeking revenge upon this powerful shaman half brother, is a first example of the new principles in action. But the new peace was a negotiated one, and Adodarhoh accepted it only with very favorable conditions. The Onondaga were granted a numerical and administrative superiority in the League, and he and his successors assumed an office as close to "presidential" as anything allowed by the Iroquois Confederacy.

The *To-ta-da-ho*[3] Belt, or *Presidentia* as the museums prefer, is forty-five rows of beads strung and wefted together with buckskin to portray a chain of sixteen diamonds, a covenant that must reflect the Confederacy at its greatest extent. The only wider belt is its companion, the *Wing* or *Dust Fan* of Council President. Both of these substantial pieces are the symbols of office of Adodarho, Fire-keeper of the Longhouse. He is charged with the humble task and great honor of seeing that the fire burns brightly and the hearth is kept clean. He opens the council of the assembled nations. No decision can be issued without the assent of Adodarho and his fellow Onondaga statesmen. Their duty, however, is to bring about agreement. All decisions had to be unanimous, all obstructions overcome. It was a task to match the powers of a potent magician.

As Dekanawida and Hayonhwatha traveled the long route I'd driven this afternoon, Parker's account says that they passed old villages and camps and "the names were lifted to give the clan name holders." When the Confederacy was established at Onondaga, each of the forty-eight chiefs nominated by the clan matrons gave Dekanawida a string of lake shell as a pledge. He in turn said, "I disrobe you and you are not now covered by your old names. I now give you names much greater." This power to bestow names was not transferred exclusively to the Onondaga statesmen—anyone might, with a string of beads, hang a new name about your neck as a heartfelt gesture of love or friendship—but like the job of fire keeping, the Onondaga name-keeper carried an honor and a tedious responsibility. On the one hand Orphic and bardlike, the words of the Great Law, the roll call of the chiefs, the founding agreements—all were committed into his keeping, to be brought out of memory with the reading of woven beads. They are the essence of the social fabric, and their reading was a highly developed and exacting mode of performance.

> On the manner in which the belts or strings of wampum
> are handled by the speaker, much depends; the turning of
> the belt which takes place when he has finished one half
> of his speech, is a material point, though this is not
> common in all speeches with belts; but when it is the
> case, and is done properly, it may be as well known by it
> how far the speaker has advanced in his speech, as with
> us on taking a glance at the page of a book or pamphlet
> while reading; and a good speaker will be able to point
> out the exact place on a belt which is to answer to each
> particular sentence, the same as we can point out a pas-
> sage in a book.[4]

Most accounts, such as this, were given long after the Confederacy had ceased its civil functions and wampum itself

4. J.G.E. HECKWELDER, *History, Manners, and Customs of the Indian Nations who once inhabited Pennsylvania* (Pennsylvania Historical Society Memoirs, vol. 12, 1876). This early Dutch observer was one of Fenimore Cooper's more reliable sources.

had fallen into disuse. But even in this decline, a late nineteenth-century researcher found that the Canadian Onondaga, after a separation of a hundred years, gave "substantially the same narrative" of the history of their founding as the Onondaga remaining in New York.[5]

So it was also a demanding skill. And not only did the wampum-keeper function as secretary and note taker and archivist, he was also an active facilitator in a highly complex decision-making process, which required him always to find the words of agreement arising from conflict. Here, for example, is article 10 of the Great Law:

> In all cases, the procedure must be as follows: when the Mohawk and Seneca statesmen have unanimously agreed upon a question, they shall report their decision to the Cayuga and Oneida statesmen, who shall deliberate upon the question and report a unanimous decision to the Mohawk statesmen. The Mohawk statesmen will then report the standing of the case to the Firekeepers, who shall render a decision as they see fit in case of a disagreement by the two bodies, or confirm the decisions of the two bodies if they are identical. The Firekeepers shall then report their decisions to the Mohawk statesmen who shall announce it to the open Council.[6]

There are many further extenuations of this deeply conservative process. Previous to the agreement of the two Elder Brothers (Mohawk and Seneca) and the two Younger Brothers (Cayuga and Oneida), each Nation comes to terms within itself. For example, the nine Mohawk councillors are divided into three groups (corresponding to the Turtle, Wolf, and Bear clans), and the first triad listens to the discussion of the second and third and confirms the decision as it is to be referred to the Seneca, whose eight chiefs put the issue to a similar process, but now employing dualities. Moreover, when the decision is in turn finally referred to them, the fourteen Onondaga deliberate in two bodies, with one mem-

5. A CONTEMPORARY OF Lewis Henry Morgan, Horatio Hale consulted with Six Nations chiefs in his native Ontario as well as making several trips to Onondaga and publishing *The Iroquois Book of Rites* (1883; repr. Toronto, 1963).

6. *THE GREAT LAW OF Peace of the Longhouse People,* in the edition published by *Akwesasne Notes,* "as a starting point for discussion until a sanctioned translation is available."

ber set aside to listen and confirm the agreement as it is to be announced by Adodarhoh.

The consensual process and the elaborate geometry of decision making seemed to outsiders like impediments rather than aids to agreement. It is hardly surprising that the English colonists kept wishing the Iroquois had a George Washington to make and execute policy. Adding even more complexity was the kinship structure underlying the Longhouse, making the Six Nations also a confederacy of eight clans, in which the titles of the chiefs followed matrilineal descent. The titles were revocable and subject to the continued approval of the clan matrons. The sachems also shared public power with hereditary and elected war chiefs, as well as individuals who might sprout up and be nominated "pine tree" chiefs. Anyone able to generate sufficient public interest could bring their business from clan to nation to Council of Chiefs. Before a council could begin, all the rules of notification had to be followed and the notice had to be confirmed, as every piece of business was "returned" across the fire.

The civil councils thus followed procedures established by the mourning council, and every formality of statement and response, agreement and confirmation had to be attended to. And finally, consider again that every participant, though strictly bound to these formalities, was in every other respect utterly and inalienably at perfect liberty. As Morgan put it, after comparing the Iroquois favorably to the only democracies he knew of, "It would be difficult to describe any political society, in which there was less of oppression and discontent, more of individual independence and boundless freedom."[7] Small wonder that when not in the forest or the field, the Iroquois could be found at a funeral or a meeting. Only the willingness to agree, boundless patience, and devotion to the process of agreement, allowed the Confederacy to function. That, the sufferance of the women, and the path to the heart.

7. *LEAGUE OF THE IROQUOIS*, 139. Much of the working of this freedom is opaque to Morgan, as it must be to anyone not experiencing it. He observes, without seeing its pertinence to this issue, the "curious fact" that every Iroquois transaction began or ended in a council. And that a "singular trait in the character of the red man" is his seeming not to feel the "power of gain." In both cases Morgan fails to recognize the working of reciprocity, the desire to come to agreement: every decision required unanimity, and majority and minority made no sense to them.

Late into the night, in a motel room a continent away from home, I do my daily travel accounts. Expressed as a column of debits, I retrace a journey toward the gift, the source of all wealth. I reconcile this with the diminishing balance in my pocket and commit the rest to the peculiar agreements made by our lives.

By the tollway that follows the ancient track, west along the Mohawk, occasional thunder clouds had crossed my afternoon path, now and then showering the granite hills across the river. At Schoharie Creek the bridge had apparently washed out, and I traveled many miles on the old highway past farms and hamlets all but abandoned. Somewhere I missed the detour signs and went many miles out of my way. Stopping for a late lunch at a lone roadside diner, I got directions and found the Thruway again but then impulsively left it and spent much longer than I meant to wandering trails and sitting on rocky overlooks. The landscape felt comfortably familiar, reminiscent of a place I'd been before.

But then I arrived here too late to make the calls and connections I had hoped for. As every day made more clear, too little money and planning had gone into this strange pilgrimage masquerading as research. I couldn't afford another night in this establishment—I couldn't even afford this one. It seemed, Columbus-like, I'd found the wrong passage to the wrong Indies. I had come to what I thought was the heart of my journey but in the crookedness of the way there had lost the path. In the night of the soul of this continent, a reader in the dark, I had somewhere missed the message I thought I had come here to receive.

As I lay on the bed feeling failure as palpable as the motel mattress spring, books and papers in disorder beside me, an old memory for some reason came through the confusion. I remembered being told that about the time I was born, my father, who was in the movie business and would be known to us for the most part by his absence, had been on location making *Drums Along the Mohawk*. Along the path today, in the granite hills, I must have thought I was seeing the land-

scape of that old movie. This was hardly possible, since that
John Ford frontier spectacle had been shot in northern Utah,
which bears little resemblance to the Mohawk Valley. But
what I recalled was something more palpable—through our
family's subsequent wanderings, for many years my mother
had somehow held onto a pair of baby's moccasins that must
have been among my first gifts. They had been given by the
Iroquois who worked as consultants and extras, outfitted by
my father as the villains of this frontier melodrama. The
moccasins were white doeskin, lined with rabbit fur, and deco-
rated with tiny beads, pink and white and blue. My sister
found one of them in a cedar chest many years later. The fine
work is impeccable.

How long, and how indirect, the path to the heart. I've
said I was looking for the source of wealth and the origin of
all our failed contracts. What is money but a way to repay a
gift—and the gift a way to compensate for loss.

🐚 🐚 🐚

"Then this shall be done.
"We will suspend a pouch upon a pole, and
will place in it some mourning wampum—some
short strings—to be taken to the place where the
loss was suffered. The bearer will enter, and will
stand by the hearth, and will speak a few words to
comfort those who will be mourning; and then
they will be comfortable, and will conform to the
great law."[8]

These are the words prescribing the use of the Short
Wampum, to be repeated following the Hymn of Condolence;
they describe an action that comes in response to the string of
beads sent out with a death notice, called "the black strand of
notification." Also called "tears," it goes out as a cry of loss
and comes back as this word of comfort. And following it, the
ceremony of consolation goes on to another exchange, of

8. THE RITUAL OF
Condolence, in John
Bierhorst's version (Four
Masterworks of American
Indian Literature [Tucson,
1974], 143), which is
collated from the text
derived by Horatio Hale,
from ritual manuscripts
kept at the Six Nations
Reserve, Ontario, and
published as The Iroquois
Book of Rites; from the
Requickening Address
recited by Chief John
Arthur Gibson in 1912;
and with program notes
from William Fenton's
observation of a Cayuga
Condolence Council in
1945. None of this should
be taken to indicate that
these are sanctioned texts.
What is of interest is the
early transition from beads
to writing, apparently using
orthography suggested
by missionaries in the
mid-eighteenth century.

attesting bead strings that accompany each of the several "matters" that restore the mourners' body and soul. At each of these enactments—what the linguistic anthropologists call "speech events"[9]—a message is given, of which the beads are the palpable sign. The ceremony may be enacted, in full or in miniature, for the loss of the noblest chief or clan mother, or for the loss of a child. What we might take to be repetition is rather an insistence that every loss, each particular sorrow, have its answer and consolation. At any time the dark message —the notification, the short strings, the attesting beads— might go the other way. It sends a message to all, including the truly "other side." Here a curtain is hung between the two moieties, then removed, and through it the speaker addresses the dead and those yet unborn. It is a democratic medium—as egalitarian as life and death—and it is owned by all.

9. MICHAEL K. FOSTER, "When Words Become Deeds: An Analysis of Three Iroquois Longhouse Speech Events," *Explorations in the Ethnography of Speaking,* ed. Richard Bauman, Joel Scherzer (Cambridge, 1974), 354–67.

I'm parked in the middle of the green expanse of the Syracuse cemetery, late afternoon of my second day here. I've come here rather than seeking out the site of the first Great Council, and the first enactment of the Ritual of Condolence —said to have occurred near the corner of Genesee and Warren Streets, near the shore of Onondaga Lake. About an hour early for tonight's dinner invitation, I'm seriously in need of what I've been told is the most peaceful place in town. I've been altogether unsuccessful in my daylong quest for information and shelter. I've forked over another thirty-five at the Passage to India Motel and after feeding quarters into phones all day will make one last try in the morning to reach my Onondaga connection. I've had to remind myself that these difficulties might have been anticipated. I'd had no reply to my letter of inquiry some weeks back, and no real invitation but a brief conversation years ago. I said I had been studying the indigenous bead economy of the Northwest coast and had come by that route into the study of wampum and would like to talk to him about it some time. And he had replied, politely but offhandedly, "You bet. Wampum. That's our business."

Considering that my appointment might be as much with the place as the person, I'd driven the trusty borrowed Subaru out to the reservation that morning. The Onondaga valley and its surrounding hills appeared much more stable, soft, and ancient than the cracked and thrust-up landscape I'm used to. It was as beautiful, this first week of May, as any of the accounts of the place I'd read. But no one had remarked—and maybe only a visitor from a younger part of this continent's crust would notice—how astonishingly *solid* the place seemed. It truly looked and felt like the center of something as great as the Law of Peace, the foundation of the Iroquois Confederacy. The hearthstone of the Longhouse. Of course it also looked and felt like our rural communities in general, and reservations particularly—isolated, depressed, run down, but somehow surviving with some redeeming strength and grace.

Among the laws of the League it is stated that a stick against the door indicates that a person is not at home and no one should enter. When a visiting party—even a condolence bearer or a messenger—entered the clearing around a town, or when a hunting group entered the territory of another nation—they were obliged to stop and kindle a fire or otherwise give notice of their presence. Although I hadn't approached anyone's dwelling, I nevertheless had the distinct feeling that on State Highway 11 I was driving through the middle of the Longhouse. On the return trip, like the tourist that I was, I stopped at a small unpainted house beside the road with a sign that said GIFTS.

I stayed half an hour or so in the two small rooms inside, browsing among the woven and leather goods, objects of fur and feather, glass and shell and bone. I looked for a while at a book, *The White Roots of Peace*, in which the Great Law was written out.[10] Like most of the objects on the shelves, although a bargain by any standard, it was out of my price range. A couple of women had come in and were selecting loose beads from bins in the front room. There was a third

10. BY PAUL A. WALLACE, a reissue by Kahiones/John Fadden of the University of Pennsylvania Press 1946 edition. A gloss on Chief Gibson's rendering of the League's founding and laws, translated from the Onondaga by J. N. B. Hewitt, its presence in the gift shop would seem to lend it some authority.

room off to the side, where some food was served and sold. I
picked out a couple of oranges for the road and paid a young
woman for them and the things I'd selected from the gift
shop. A card and a beaded feather. It came to $8.50.

When I left the shop, stepping out into the breezy cloudless morning, a couple of men were sitting on a bench facing
the road. One of them remarked on the leather vest I was
wearing. I said a friend had had it made for me as a gift. The
other fellow asked what kind of buttons those were. They
were made from old buffalo nickels. I showed them the buffalo still embossed on the surface, between UNITED STATES
OF AMERICA and FIVE CENTS. They complimented the workmanship. We said nothing of the Indian who had been on the
other side of the coin. When I told them who I was looking
for, one of them mentioned that he was a very busy man. "I
think he's at a funeral," said the other. "Yes," I told him.
"That's what I'd heard."

In all the material importance attached to large wampum
belts by traders and the custodians of other people's culture, it
is easy to lose sight of the small strings of beads and the fact
that they are part of a *symbolic* system. They were by no
means the only objects used in this fashion. The condolence
ritual, for example, also employs the Water of Pity, a spirit
elixir that cleans and reorders the inner organs of the grieving
party. The Little Water ceremony in turn has become an entire ritual in its own sphere, from the cleansing of the newborn to reviving the mourners at death's door. Likewise the
spotted fawnskin, used to "wipe away the blood" from the
mat where the deceased knelt, is called *words of pity and
comfort.* In a sense, the Europeans were right in thinking that
wampum, in its symbolic exchange function, was a kind of
money. What they were unable to see was a system of representation that allowed a single currency to be redeemable in
mourning councils and in councils of government, that could
function as a language of trade as well as of treaties, and that
opened communication between friends, between nations,
and between this world and the world on the other side. The

symbol had a life even beyond its vehicle, an anthropologist reporting in the '50s that although none of his informants had used the bead strings during their lifetime, nevertheless *"the words remain."*[11]

🐚 🐚 🐚

From the outset, the colonists' manufacture of wampum and its use as currency had a destabilizing effect on the shell bead message system. The process was slow at first, because the making of beads was such an extremely tedious process. It took so much time, as one contemporary Virginian put it,

> *an Englishman could not afford to make so much of this wampum for five or ten times the value; for it is made out of a vast great shell, of which that country affords plenty, and is ground smaller than the small end of a tobacco pipe or a large wheat straw; the Indians grind these on stones and other things until they make them current, but the drilling is the most difficult to the Englishman, which the Indians manage with a nail stuck in a cane or reed. Thus they roll it continually on their thighs with their right hand, holding the bit of shell with their left; so, in time, they drill a hole quite through it which is very tedious work, but the Indians are a people that never value their time, so they can afford to make them, and never need to fear the English will take the trade out of their hands. This, being their money entices and persuades them to do anything and part with everything they possess and with which you may buy skins, furs or any other thing except their children for slaves.*[12]

Among the number of things invisible to the European interested in profit, the iron nail is probably not the first thing we would point to. But it had already had its effect on production, the awl itself having become such a valuable tool that it sometimes served as a currency—one hundred "muxes," as

11. GEORGE S. SNYDERMAN, "The Function of Wampum in Iroquois Religion," *Proceedings of the American Philosophical Society* 105 (1961): 571–608. Snyderman's piece describes a 1951 Tonowanda ceremony, recited by Isaac Lyons, whose traditional name was Ha-no-sah-das, wampum keeper.

12. ATTRIBUTED TO Lawson, author of a 1714 history of North Carolina, in Converse, *Myths and Legends*, 144—a gem Parker may have supplied in rewriting the book.

13. REV. WILLIAM
Beauchamp's manuscript
notes, recording Barber, a
historian writing in New
Jersey in the 1840s. The
Campbell Brothers' business
picked up briskly a century
after its founding, with the
far western fur trade of
1820–75. Even with
ingenious methods to
speed production and with
shells from the Fulton fish
market or conch that came
in as ballast on ships from
the Caribbean or clams
brought over from Jamaica
Bay, bead making was
a tedious and difficult
process. The quahog clams
became less plentiful and
smaller, the purple "heart"
much diminished. This was
of no great consequence,
since beads of purple mixed
with white would do as well
for their market. Apparently
no beads went to the Six
Nations during this period.
So far as they retained the
use of wampum, they
unstrung old belts to supply
mourning strings and
condolence belts. See
again Taxay, Money of the
American Indians, and
William C. Orchard,
Beads and Beadwork of the
American Indians (Heye
Foundation, New York, 975).

they were called, said to have been the price of East Hampton. In conjunction with the bow drill, it turned out that an Englishman (usually a poor one, and usually a woman) might indeed eke out a living. But it was only after the use of wampum as a currency had declined, along with the indigenous coastal people and the New Englanders' need for either, that the manufacture was reinvented on a new scale for the unimaginable store of inland resources that had begun to be accessible. The most notable example was the factory of the Campbell Brothers, who had taken over the company founded by their father Abraham. Essentially a mechanization of methods originated by piece-working immigrants—a holding stick, for example, and a specially grooved grinding wheel— the Campbells' factory was so efficient that during the peak years of the far western fur trade, they could wholesale finished wampum beads for about five dollars a thousand.

It was still not enough to meet demand, and much of the work continued to be farmed out to women and adolescents, who would drill and polish blanks purchased from the company, which would then buy back the finished product. They could be traded at country stores—where in-kind "country pay" for beads remained a staple of home industry until Astor closed his last trading house hardly a century ago.

They are strung on hempen strings about a foot in length. From five to ten strings are a day's work for a female. They are sold to the country merchants for 12½ cents a string, always command cash, and constitute the support of many poor and worthy families.[13]

The first wave of cheapened beads flowed into the Longhouse in the mid-1600s, and from the outset the demand was fueled more by the needs of ritual and diplomacy than by the convenience of trade. Reverend Beauchamp, researching the early use of wampum belts, by the year 1687 notes: "After this, belts are so numerous that it will suffice to notice the most remarkable." During a century of playing off French against English, the colonies against the western tribes, struggling to postpone the inevitable and fatal conflict that would find them at its center, the Iroquois gave and received many hundreds of belts and countless fathoms of strings of wampum. Millions of beads changed hands. By the time of the actual outbreak of the French and Indian war, not long after the Albany Congress, there was so much wampum circulating diplomatically that traders sometimes complained they had none with which to pay for peltry.

The result of this outpouring of a medium of exchange was a predictable cycle of inflation—but here, instead of affecting an isolated "monetary system," it alters every aspect of social exchange. The effect, although we like to imagine that one medium does not inflate another, is predictable and familiar—to make a message effective began to require more and more beads. Where a string once sufficed, now a belt was used. New York State's wampum collection includes a summoning belt, a call to council that had previously been announced by strings. Also a condolence belt that once belonged to Cornplanter, the Seneca leader who played a great role in the wars and treaties that finally broke the Confederacy, and who may have sent out so many death announcements that the old string of "tears" no longer sufficed. Ceremonies that had once been used to raise up new leaders were also thereby cheapened, and leadership itself devalued by the use of a belt of nomination rather than the traditional strings.

This process of inflation and devaluation appears to have been for the most part invisible to those who were caught up in it, although they were aware of some of the effects. William Johnson's letters record an increasing pace and intensity of exchange, subtly raising the price of trade and diplomacy, both in money and blood. Beads are referred to as if they were diplomatic memos, such as in "my wampum of the 14th May." It is as if the quantity of beads were trying vainly to keep up with the urgency of public affairs—a widening war of colonial rivalry, overseen by bureaucrats and advisers and generals, employing whenever possible the inhabitants and His Majesty's unfortunate Irish footsoldiers, all

14. JOHNSON, PAPERS,
1:531, 631. Johnson was
keenly aware of the
value of "early intelligence"
in his trading enterprise,
which to a great degree
was also a political
enterprise. His
correspondence supplies
as many of these forest
transactions as the
accounts kept at Albany.

to shore up a colony that would soon break all covenants and ties. Things were coming apart faster than they could be strung back together. "I dispatched a belt," writes Johnson, but then adds, "I thought best to dispatch one of the Interpreters thither with another belt." In that same year, as the Seven Years War (as it was known in Europe) got well under way, "I did send a string of wampum with this Message on my coming home, but lest that should not be sufficient I now send this Belt."[14]

To whatever degree possible, the competing powers chose to negotiate, even spend a little, to achieve their goals—and whenever possible to employ Indians rather than Irish to fight. The Lords of Trade were practical administrators. They were supposed to see that their North American interests stayed profitable, but they were not so shortsighted as the colonial legislatures who would not appropriate even the costs of doing business. While the Albany Congress waffled on expenditures for militia and forts, the English administrators promised the colonies £800 with which to buy Indians— 500 for the Iroquois, 300 for the western tribes. Not that great a price, considering the wealth of a continent. The French, at the other end of the Longhouse, were not backward in meeting the English ante. At one treaty exchange, the Seneca sent twelve belts to the French, nine of them "as long as a man," and the French returned to the Six Nations the amount of 500 crowns.

These colonial business methods had the effect that is familiar now around the world, wherever investor nations compete for hearts and minds and markets. And naturally this had its usual effect on the price of everything. By the end of the Anglo-French Beaver Wars, the value of wampum had sunk by a third in relation to the price of gunpowder and peltry. But another effect was that wampum itself began to fall into disuse as an article of trade among the Iroquois, who this time fought the French for cash and the articles cash would buy. The bead trade began to move west, where the beaver still could be found and the inhabitants had little use for colonial coin and even less for their bills of credit. As diplomacy moved so fast that belts were unstrung and restrung with some frequency, the value of everyday exchange was left without the ceremonial belief system that had attached to beads. The price of a life could be expressed now in dollars, and the amount was negotiable—"If the French go on so," complains Johnson, ignoring the English policy of under-selling at any cost, "there is no man can be Safe in his own house, for I can at any time get an Indian to kill a man for paying of him a Small matter."[15]

15. *PAPERS,* 1:303.
The year was 1750.

16. *DOC REL COL HIST
NY,* 6:848.

The colonists, on the other hand, were feeling the strain within their own cycles of exchange. As a way to finance their share of the frontier defense budget, since the assembly would not vote taxes on any account, New York's lieutenant governor (still acting as governor) wrote the Lords of Trade asking permission to issue £2,000 of paper bills of credit, to be put out for ten years at 6 percent. This would, he said, bring the paper currency then in circulation to £115,000—"from the best information I can obtain." The English administrators responded with great restraint and clarity:

> *We are inclined to believe from the Nature of paper currency in General, that a moderate quantity issued upon proper security and having a proper fund for its redemption within a reasonable time may operate to the advantage of a Colony and may also be the least burthensome method of levying money for the supply and support of Government.*[16]

They went on to add, however, that these notes should by no means circulate as a medium of exchange. This injunction had already been enforced upon New England, where by the mid-1700s about two and one-half million pounds in unsecured legal-tender bills of credit were in circulation, with a resulting inflation of prices by a factor of ten to fifteen times. A general ordinance, the Paper Money Act, was put into effect at the end of the Beaver Wars—an attempt to restrain the colonies which, along with the Sugar Act of the same year,

17. FRANKLIN'S COMPLAINT, and the account that follows, are recorded by Norman Angell, *The Story of Money* (Garden City, 1929), 254ff. He also records some of the result of the new nation's hyperinflation: *Barber shops were papered in fact with the bills, and sailors, on returning from their cruises, being paid off in bundles of this worthless paper money, had suits of clothes made of it, and with characteristic lightheartedness turned their loss into frolic by parading through the streets in decayed finery.* Angell's history and warning of the fate of unsecured paper make his book a particularly poignant reference, published in 1929 on the eve of the Great Depression.

and the Stamp Act of the year following, would lead to rebellion and the next phase of war and the next economy. Now ink stamped by screw press onto rag and hemp would be the mark of agreement. The colonists—strictly speaking, the colonial business interests—favored what they favor today: cheap money secured (if at all) by cheap land and raw resources.

"On the slight complaint of a few Virginia merchants,"[17] wrote the aggrieved Franklin, "nine Colonies have been restrained from making paper money, become absolutely necessary to their internal commerce, from the constant remittance of their gold and silver to Europe." This was an old complaint, a half-truth holding up half a lie, since the colonists had no intention of giving up their habits of deficit finance. By the outbreak of the war of "independence," some ten to fifteen million dollars in paper currency was in circulation. A week after Bunker Hill, another two million was authorized. Within four years the provisional government would issue another two hundred forty million. A paper dollar would be worth two or three cents in specie.

All of this sounds so familiar, today's news account of some third-world colony: impoverishment by war and unchecked avarice, the collapse of inflated value, disappointed faith, the cheapness of land and life. The absence of spirit, the inability to read and remember. We are still that colony.

🦋 🦋 🦋

I had spent the rest of that afternoon on a quiet side street of Syracuse, sitting on the curbside in front of the East/West Center, talking to its proprietor. David's was more a temple-keeper's function, really. He lived in the back of the large open building, but this was hardly apparent—a bed, a sink, and a hot plate on which he made us an herb tea. The front was a meeting place, a literature table, and on shelves various leaflets and newsletters, a few books and periodicals for sale. Plants in the window.

The writings included a range of concerns that are usually now summed up as New Age: health, organic foods, alternative energy, Eastern mysticism, ecology, peace. The center's own newsletter covered local manifestations of these topics, including issues affecting native sovereignty. Hundreds of little storefronts such as this evolved out of the peace centers that sprang up during our most unpopular of recent colonial wars, eventually becoming environmental or spiritual centers when the war came home and it appeared that peace would be a long time coming. The scale of exchange here was about the same as the Onondaga gift shop, and obviously didn't afford the luxury of accommodating wandering scholars, which is why I'd phoned David in the first place. Now, as seemed to be a general rule of this journey, I was finding out what I was supposed to be finding out.

We sipped tea in the afternoon sun, out on the curb where I'd gone for a cigarette. David joined me when the smoke had subsided, and I'd continued my story about money and beads and Onondaga. He agreed with my feeling about the place and had verified its power. He was a geomancer, it seemed, who by dowsing and measuring electromagnetic and hydraulic currents could actually map out lines and centers of energy in the landscape. I loved this sort of inquiry, and we talked about the rediscovery of this ancient earth science, the nineteenth-century fervor that became the Old Straight Track Society, uncovering ancient "roads" that connected such sites as Stonehenge and Canterbury for some unknown magical purposes. I wasn't sure I agreed with all its theoretical extenuations—remember how a pyramid, aligned correctly with terrestrial forces, would sharpen dull razor blades left in it overnight?—but there seemed a great deal of plain fact on the side of geological harmonics and centers of power. If that's what you were looking for.

Many of these locations of great geological energy, David had found, turned out to be the present-day site of a cemetery —as if people had found the natural location of ceremonial or sanctified ground—and they would often be marked by stones

18. FROM A SPEECH BY the Delaware leader Teedyuscung, on the eve of the western "conspiracy," in Anthony F. C. Wallace, *King of the Delawares: Teedyuscung* (Philadelphia, 1949), 111–13.

more ancient than those on graves. Naturally these investigations required some circumspection, as well as timing. He said he was often accompanied by his friend Sara, who I noticed had written a very lucid account of their findings for the newsletter. Usually they worked at night. He described one trip, timed to coincide with an eclipse of the moon, which had offered perfect conditions for both secrecy and intense geomagnetic activity. They had worked feverishly through the entire period of intense cold and darkness, mapping and marking and stringing lines and when the moon reemerged they had marked a great circle intersected by lines of perfect geometry. I was moved by the beauty and intensity of their research, and the purity of their devotion to it.

Later in the afternoon, sitting in the car in the Syracuse cemetery, I wondered if this had been the site of David and Sara's witching for lost meanings in the earth. I wondered if they were in love, as I imagined. And if all lines, truly followed, no matter through what darkness, are connected to the heart. The only map I have, and the only path left to follow.

You see a Square in the Middle, meaning the Lands of the Indians, and at one End the figure of a Man, indicating the English; and at the other end another, meaning the French; our Uncles told us that both these coveted our lands; but let us join together to defend our Lands against both, you shall be partakers with us of our Lands.[18]

This is the message and the map now, as read by the Delaware, sent to them by the Six Nations (their "uncles"), at the end of the Anglo-French Beaver Wars. But the Six Nations also had maps and agreements with the Man at either door of the Longhouse. Their policy of play-offs, which perhaps coincided too well with a habitual balance of oppositions, was now being complicated by the rise of a new confederacy, formed in response to the westward expansion of the colonies. A great deal of wampum began to be exchanged between hands that did not always care to know what the other hand was doing. The system appeared to stay in balance as long as messages could be moved fast enough, but when the French let go of their end of the Covenant Chain, and when they and their ancient adversaries no longer had need of their New World allies, the connections rapidly deteriorated. The Six Nations, by the Treaty of Paris, were now only one of many nations in a new Anglo-American empire that extended south to the Floridas, and from Nova Scotia to the Great Lakes. A greater house now surrounded the Longhouse, and the options at either door were rapidly dwindling. At the eastern end, in the now English town of Montreal, former allies were forgotten in the rush to recolonize:

> The Inhabitants, seeing themselves free from their former Yoke are disregarding the Indians and won't let them come into their houses so that they often come to me for Lodging and Victuals the former I am Obliged to refuse them having but a small Room and put them off with a little Money to buy themselves Bread, the paper money wch some of them have being of no Value which they regret much.[19]

19. A letter from Daniel Claus to William Johnson (*Papers*, 10:189).

At the western door, on the other hand, new indigenous allies were being actively sought, as the English bead exchange hastened to occupy the territories and markets vacated by the French. The result, once again, was high prices and scarcity.

> Understanding shortly after my taking command of the post [at Green Bay, Wisconsin], that there was a vast number of Indians dependant on it, more than was ever thought of, I found that I should send to Detroit for belts to give them on their arrival in the spring. . . . As I could not get any from Detroit, and could not do without it, I

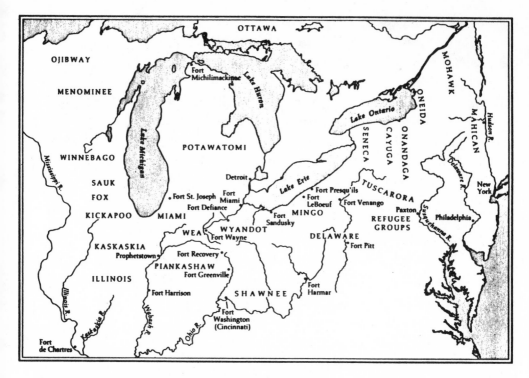

Indigenous nations of the "Frontier" and the "Old Northwest" in the early 1760s. Scene of the French and Indian Wars (1754-63), Pontiac's Conspiracy (1763), the Paxton Riots (1764), Little Turtle's War (1790–94), Tecumseh's Rebellion (1809–11), and the Blackhawk War (1832)—three quarters of a century of resistance to the second invasion of North America.

20. THE NEW INDIAN AGENT had received instructions from William Johnson, as well as verbal advice "that unless I did my best to please the Indians I had better not go there" (*Papers*, 10:698).

was obliged after getting what Mr. Goddard had, to borrow of the Indian squaws, and pay them some twelve hundred for a thousand. I also made use of some I had from Lieut. Brehm, which was for his own use. That borrowed from the Indians, I was obliged to repay on the arrival of the first trader that brought wampum. So that I had six belts made, one for each nation that visited that place, but I found that some required two, some three, and some four, as they had towns. The French, in their time, always gave them belts, rum and money, presents by which they renewed their peace annually.[20]

With the English attempting to pick up the far end of the Covenant Chain and deal directly with the western tribes, the

Six Nations were no longer at the center of affairs and lost some of their traditional powers of middlemen. They could still make a deal with both parties for collective support or neutrality, and warriors and diplomats of the separate nations could then make whatever arrangements they had to. This policy would eventually prove impossible, but even in the short term it must have further eroded the diplomatic credibility of Six Nations wampum. The Delaware, along with the Shawnee and other confederates, learned to be extremely wary of their neighbors the Seneca, whose loyalties they knew also extended eastward. When the red-painted Seneca belts arrived, saying, the French are gone, let us also remove the Redcoats, the Delaware forwarded the message from their "uncles" to English authorities.

21. JOHNSON, *PAPERS*, 10:769.

Increasingly, paper began to be preferred over beads, the messages not always penned by willing scribes. The following account describes the written message that announced the frontier uprising that would be called Pontiac's Conspiracy. The note was simply dropped at Fort Pitt where soldiers would find it.

> *After putting ye whole Garrison (Wh consisted of 18 Men) to Death, they made ye Officer write ye reason wh they gave for wt they had done, vizt the scarcity & dearness of Powder for these two Years past, being oblidged to pay two Deer Skins for a gill of powder, & so in proportion for everything else, that when they complained of ye dearness thereof, they were Ill treated, and told to go where they could get it cheaper.*[21]

The outbreak of another cycle of war—the last of the Beaver Wars, still being fought out in the west, partly by the instigation of French traders who were not taking their losses lightly—occasioned a number of belts to be exchanged within the Longhouse: from the Seneca warriors and women, urging the other nations to join them in the uprising, and from the Mohawk and Onondaga in response, a large black belt

22. Letter from Amherst
to William Johnson (*Papers*,
10:284). It should be noted
that while his means were
consistent with the laws
of forest diplomacy,
Johnson was a colonial
administrator carrying out
colonial policy, which
despite his Mohawk
alliances put him at war
with the western Seneca
during this period. The
Mohawk of course also had
more than one interest,
apparently reassuring
Johnson of peace while
their western brothers
prepared for war.

condemning the action and affirming ties to the English. But outside the Longhouse, the bond of wampum exchange was being rapidly eroded by high-priced trade goods, inflated currencies, and the very literal obstacles to the traditional routes of trade—military forts, lawless backwoods settlers, and the heavy traffic to and from the now-distant hunting and trapping grounds. Outside the Longhouse, such a world was better described by ephemeral marks on paper. Even as early as the Albany Congress, Hendrick had complained that there were "writings for our land" for which there was no wampum record or memory. Bills of credit and letters patent, endorsed by the agents of colony and king, were fast becoming the prevailing currencies. Coupled with this, of course, was the usual colonial arrogance, which was only too happy to dispense with traditional ways. "It is not my intention," announced the insufferable Jeffrey Amherst, commander of His Majesty's army of North America, "ever to Attempt to gain the Friendship of Indians by presents."[22]

It is hardly surprising that the western "conspiracy" was not successful. Only desperation and Pontiac's tactical genius enabled it to get as far as it did. Although his alliance was depicted on a belt showing more than forty Indian towns, it could only be maintained finally by his personal IOUs inscribed on birch bark. It is tragically reminiscent of the fate of King Philip's uprising less than a century before. Despite last-minute promises by French traders, the western confederacy soon found it had destroyed its own sources of supply—of powder and lead, not to mention the goods and services and bead currency it had come to depend on. The cry for rum and gunsmiths was already a constant note on the frontier, and it would grow to be a long last wail.

It is hardly coincidence that at this time a prophet arose among the Delaware, preaching the expulsion of the English and a return to a somewhat Christianized version of the old ways. And it is no surprise that in Neolin's vision the Master of Life should manifest his word not in beads but in writing.

Here is a written prayer that I give thee; learn it by heart, and teach it to all the Indians and children. It must be repeated morning and evening.[23]

The prophet was unable to read this document and was instructed to take the prayer to the headman of his village, who would be able to teach it to him. In a subsequent vision, he was directed to create another document that he was able to read and interpret. He went among the western tribes carrying a folio-size deerskin parchment, on which was mapped out the progress of the soul through the world, showing how the way to heaven had been blocked by the intruders. He called the map the Great Book of Writing. Saying every family should own one, he sold copies for two doeskins or one buck each. He pointed to places on the map as he preached, and as he preached he wept.

23. NEOLIN'S PRAYER AND the account of his teaching are included in Anthony F. C. Wallace, *Death and Rebirth of the Seneca* (New York, 1969), 118–19.

I sat in the car in the Oakwood cemetery for about an hour. When it was time to go to dinner I put away my travel and expense journals, feeling somewhat more reconciled, in mind if not in pocket. If I was missing my intended connection, at least I was making others, even if they didn't seem at first to fit into what I called the Money Book. It was less consoling, though, to find my own life so inextricably bound into its pages, and my own heart a place on its map.

I'd been sending postcards home to an old friend, an acquaintance recently rekindled among the ashes of my personal life. I'd thought of her more than I would have expected and had found myself visiting a cafe in the center of Syracuse that was still owned by her relations. The place had the feeling of family, and a menu close to home. I'd had pie and coffee for a dollar and while paying the check said to the proprietors that his niece had said to tell them hello. He was surprisingly affected and seemed quite pleased—Hey Mary, did you hear that? he said to the kitchen. They were delighted to get news of family gone so far west.

So at least that much message, I told myself, I had been able to deliver. But the lines of communication weren't done with their messenger. As I closed the car door to leave the cemetery, I glanced at a wide and massive grave marker at the intersecting paths where I'd parked. It was her name—in all these acres of stone, her name. Of course. Where her grandparents were buried. I sat for a few more minutes before starting the car. It was a simple coincidence, one of those tricks of the subconscious guidance system—those winks of the fates we call weirdness. A crow flew down and chased some small birds from the graves, then returned to its corbie's posture, high up in an overhanging pine.

Our path must be chosen by what the heart chooses. From beginning to end, no other intention matters. My errand is from the present to the past, and from the living to the dead. And back, I had to suppose.

So I said hello. Your granddaughter says hello. Hey, Anna, did you hear that?

I found my map, started the borrowed car, and went to the family dinner I'd been invited to share.

WORDS AND DEEDS

As I traveled back from Onondaga, east along the Mohawk, southward down the Hudson Valley, I tried to picture these wooded hills and green valleys as the scene of a prolonged and devastating guerrilla war. The accounts of our "revolution" are comparatively recent and unsettled like ourselves, but the conflict is coming to be viewed less as a war of independence than a definitive stage of a larger struggle: the invasion of North America, and the appropriation of its wealth. The methods and effectiveness of the combatants appear remarkably modern, magnifying many times over the comparatively antique war with the French less than two decades before. Better supply lines, immensely more weaponry, and the education by crisis of both the Euro-Americans who had crossed into the interior and survived there, and the inhabitants who had first welcomed and then resisted those advances—all these combined to create a deadly new conflict that took place not just on great plains overseen by generals, in that eighteenth-century garden of warfare, but within and upon the land itself, and for and against the minds and hearts of its inhabitants.

As the Continental Congress met to consider their economic grievances and initiate a boycott of British imports, the Iroquois and western tribes had more pressing business at hand, trying to absorb the damages of the escalating invasion from the east, and negotiating an end to one of its bloodier consequences—called Lord Dunmore's War, after the Virginia governor who declared it. In two senseless acts of racist violence, a company of land jobbers and a band of backwoods hooligans massacred the entire family of Captain John Logan, a Seneca become Shawnee by marriage. When Logan, known as the Great Mingo, assembled a war party and took revenge, the governor of Virginia sent thousands of militia against them, incidentally allowing the colony to confirm some of the land acquisitions of its more ambitious citizens. Logan, among the survivors, delivered a speech later reproduced by Thomas Jefferson as an example of native abilities, calling into question the prevailing theory of natural white superiority. Its point, however, was the radical and widening inequity between the two races, and between the gift relation and the economics of desperation. The speech, included in nineteenth-century children's readers, should be taught as an accounting of the latter's refusal to pay damages or make condolence for what has been lost. An account that has grown beyond numbers and remains outstanding.

1. FROM QUERY 6 OF Jefferson's *Notes on the State of Virginia*, 1782, an early venture into the still meta-sciences of geology and ethnology that presents Logan's speech as an example of the power of indigenous oratory, one of several evidences used to refute the prevailing "scientific" view of native inferiority.

> *I appeal to any white man to say if he ever entered Logan's cabin hungry, and he gave him not meat; if ever he came cold and naked, and he clothed him not. During the course of the last long and bloody war, Logan remained idle in his cabin, an advocate for peace. Such was my love for the whites, that my countrymen pointed, as they passed, and said, "Logan is the friend of the white men. . . ."*
>
> *Who is there to mourn for Logan? Not one.*[1]

Within the contending parties, in this age of betrayals and the breaking of social contracts, the divisions were also widening. The Six Nations Council refused to take sides in Lord Dunmore's War, even though many of its warriors had aided and encouraged Logan's settling of scores. As had been the case in Pontiac's uprising a decade earlier, the confederate chiefs were unable to disengage themselves from the role of middlemen and were sometimes forced to leave dependents and allies hanging in the wind. Within less than a lifetime, the doors of the Longhouse had been forced to open and close to the competing demands of the French and the English, the English and the western confederacy, and now of the Redcoats and the American rebels. That the Longhouse survived at all is remarkable.

The councillors of the Six Nations, bound to ancient procedures and the law of unanimity, prohibited from themselves taking up arms in an age of nearly constant warfare, and no doubt feeling the general erosion of credit and credibility, found themselves swept aside by the rising torrent of events. The breakdown of the political process—again inseparable from economic, social, and biological process—was completed by an epidemic that took the lives of ninety people at Onondaga during the winter of 1776–77. Unable to proceed until the completion of the Ritual of Condolence and the replacement of deceased councillors, this loss threw the final handful of dirt and extinguished the council fire at the heart of the Longhouse. In the subsequent war, Onondaga was burned to the ground. The Six Nations were left to act according to their separate interests, in whatever way they thought might get them through the impossible choices at hand.

The American commissioners had come to Albany in '75, employing the traditional forms of treaty, offering wampum and urging neutrality in the coming conflict. But in the winter of the Onondaga's great loss, no doubt preoccupied by their own crises, the Americans sent no offer of condolence. The following May of '77 found the Iroquois warriors gathered at Oswego to hear a British appeal for their continued loyalty. Two of the Six Nations, the Christianized Oneida and the Tuscarora, were not in attendance, having been persuaded to the cause of the Boston men. The remainder were divided between neutrality and adherence to their old agreements. "Now here is your father," the British commissioner reminded them, holding out the weapons of war. He encouraged them, as a Seneca participant later recalled it,

to take his axe and Tomahawk to hold against American
and here is the Buckenknife and Bowisknife that you will
also take for take the American lock and scalps and my
father will pay much Each one scalps in money.[2]

2. BLACKSNAKE'S ACCOUNT
of the Oswego conference
is reproduced in Wallace,
*Death and Rebirth of the
Seneca,* 132, from papers in
the Draper collection,
State Historical Society of
Wisconsin. Note that this
meeting was not of the
sachems of the League but,
as was customary, of the
warriors who would
do the fighting.

At one end of the Longhouse the Mohawk war chief Joseph Brant urged the cause of William Johnson and the Loyalists, who faced exile or "revolutionary" mobs only too willing to confiscate their property. And who would also not hesitate to appropriate the land that still remained to the Mohawk. At the other door, beyond the line of demarcation drawn by the Crown at 77° west—impeding the sale of Indian lands, if not actually slowing the tide of westward immigrants, who seemed to squat wherever on the road their wagons broke down—the Seneca war chief Cornplanter urged the wisdom of continued neutrality. This was in line with historic policy and common sense—involvement with either party to this white man's quarrel had only led to misfortune thus far. Brant's reply of cowardice, British gifts, and the display of a covenant belt carried the warriors' decision, to which the clan mothers assented. Adhering to the rule of unanimity, Cornplanter urged the diminished Confederacy to wholehearted engagement.

In the terms of this war, the land itself was now a prize to be won, with each combatant willing to lay waste all possibility of the other's habitation. This now serene springtime valley was a place of ruin—after five years of war it and the southern watershed of the Mohawk, much of the Allegheny and Susquehanna, from the Ohio to the Delaware—fire and devastation. The Loyalists, contrary to the movie version, are cast in the defensive role of guerrilla woodsmen. In a regular seasonal rhythm, with each spring a force of up to five hundred Tory rangers and a thousand Iroquois would sweep down on backwoods forts and settlements, burning houses and barns, destroying crops and any livestock they could not carry off. Huge agricultural holdings, the legacy of the feudal patroon system, worked by tens of thousands of immigrant tenant farmers, were left in barren ruin. In one raid, at German Flats, sixty-three houses, fifty-seven barns, three grist mills, and two sawmills were destroyed along with one hundred square miles of farmland and more than eight hundred horses, cattle, sheep, and oxen taken. Five years of this sort of destruction effectively reversed the settlement of rural New York and Pennsylvania and kept the western immigrants largely confined to their walled forts.

The colonials were not long in mounting their own campaign of economic warfare. Washington's strategy—which would earn him the enduring new name of Town Burner—and Lawyer-turned-General Sullivan's thorough tactics, soon created a program of counterinsurgency that mirrored those of their opponents, and the skies grew even darker with smoke. Our best ethnographic data on Iroquois agricultural practice and use of maize is to be gathered from Sullivan's accounts of his campaign:

> *Colonel Butler destroyed in the Cayuga country five principal towns and a number of scattering houses, the whole making about one hundred in number exceedingly large and well built. He also destroyed two hundred acres of excellent corn with a number of orchards one of which had in it 1,500 fruit trees. Another Indian settlement was discovered near Newtown by a party, consisting of 39 houses, which were also destroyed. The number of towns destroyed by this army amounted to 40 besides scattering houses. The quantity of corn destroyed, at a modest computation, must amount to 160,000 bushels, with a vast quantity of vegetables of every kind . . . I flatter myself that the orders with which I was entrusted are fully executed, as we have not left a single settlement or a field of corn in the country of the Five Nations.*[3]

This fiery exchange of attack and retaliation left the land nearly uninhabitable for indigenous as well as colonial populations—a literal no-man's land. Probably the suffering of the

3. *ARTHUR C. PARKER'S first (and most traditional) ethnographic bulletin for the New York State Museum was Iroquois Uses of Maize, 1910. His study showed the extent to which indigenous people drew on available plants and how the colonist used maize as a bridge to the New World. The toll at that bridge of course was wampum.*

Iroquois was more harsh, since their losses were relatively greater, and they had no way to replace lost staples by import. Hunting and gathering now occupied most of their winter days. But the Continental army, some regiments reduced by two-thirds, also frequently went hungry. What food there was could oftentimes not be bought by their officers, since the rural population was itself half starved. And when food was for sale, the paper money the army had been issued was considered worthless—"not worth a continental," went the saying for more than a hundred years, as if to announce not a new nation but a notoriously bad investment in real estate. The new land already burdened by unspoken debts.

On my last evening in Syracuse, the failure of my mission to the Longhouse all but certain, the loss had been partly compensated by the kindness of an invitation to dinner. Doug and I had been put in touch by his editor, and in his office on campus that afternoon I had repeated the unlikely story of selling our mutual friend a treatment of a book that would get me an advance to write a book, which would buy the time to write the Money Book. Only it wasn't really about money. After this pitiful tale, we had of course eventually discussed accommodations. He and his wife generously invited me to partake of roast beef dinner that evening but had both her mother and his brother already staying at their house. The dinner was something of a family occasion, and I felt deeply grateful to be included.

I knew Doug Unger by his novel *Leaving the Land,* and both him and Amy by a couple of West Coast friends. In retrospect, perhaps because in little more than a year both these friends would be lost, our dinner that evening holds in memory an air of love and sadness. Of course it was partly my mood at the time, the weirdness of recent gains and losses, and maybe as well my sense of Doug's writing—about the

fate of the American land and the people whose lives are tied
to its terrible betrayals. We shared some of that history of
rural people and their broken cars and bad credit and hopeless
jokes. We also shared some suspicion that the landless and
alienated writer's life might not be much different. And that
the problem had been around for a long time.

The enduring insight of *Leaving the Land* is not a new
one—it takes another and deeper look at the knot of people
and place that has preoccupied the vision of most of our poets
and novelists. Set off apart now in libraries and universities,
packaged as American Literature, or when that would not
contain it, American Civilization—and now incorporating the
"oral lit" of our less than willing co-inhabitants—it will be
seen in the light of history to be the belated outcry and after-
shock of half a millennium of invasion and misappropriation,
first of this continent and now of the entire planet. The writing that is distinctly American acknowledges and mourns
that rupture and displacement, both for those cultures
brought here and the host culture that received the visitors
and treated them according to the laws of the gift. It sees that
the relations of people are not separable from their relation to
the land—that the contracts they make are part and parcel of
their agreements with the earth. From which all gifts come,
and to which they all return. The books that we call American
are a condolence, and essentially elegiac.

The primary difficulty of the new American confederacy,
which claimed to include the Six Nations as well as thirteen
states, was the perennial one of a shortage of ready money.
And the solution, once the bead and raw resource exchange
had established a new class of merchants and landed patri-
cians—the ones who had resigned from all that remained of
their oldest agreements—the revolutionary answer to the
cash flow problem was the monetization of the land itself.

4. ALEXANDER HAMILTON'S
*Report on the Subject
of Manufactures* was
presented to the House
of Representatives,
5 December 1791.

*This idea of an extensive domestic market for the surplus
produce of the soil, is of the first consequence. It is, of all
things, that which most effectually conduces to a flourishing state of agriculture. If the effect of manufactories
should be to detach a portion of the hands which would
otherwise be engaged in tillage, it might possibly cause a
smaller quantity of lands to be under cultivation; but, by
their tendency to procure a more certain demand for the
surplus produce of the soil, they would, at the same time,
cause the lands which were in cultivation to be better
improved and more productive.*[4]

Hamilton's *Report* exemplifies that wonderful tendency of
eighteenth-century Euro-Americans to outreason and outen-
lighten and by all means be more practical than their Atlantic
cousins. Who were not slow, by any means, to adopt these
revolutionary business methods. Alexander Hamilton might
be a paternalistic Dickens character, finding a practical use for
those hands now detached from the earth:

> *The husbandman himself experiences a new source of
> profit and support from the increased industry of his
> wife and daughters, invited and stimulated by the
> demands of the neighboring manufactories.*
>
> *It is worthy of particular remark that, in general,
> women and children are rendered more useful, and the
> latter more early useful, by manufacturing establish-
> ments, than they would otherwise be.*

Thus manufactured wealth is divorced from the natural
wealth of the land, just as natural wealth had become divorced from the spirit of wealth itself—from the gift relationship. Connections that were then replaced by "money" and
the profit motive. It is only a few adjustments of economic
machinery to get from this monetization of land and the in-
dustrialization of husbandry—that is, take the factory to the
farm—to the present-day vertically integrated agribusiness

that Doug's novels call Safebuy. Somewhere on the way, something has been terribly lost.

> ... like my father, I believed it was right that way. Now-ell-Safebuy wheat farms were so much more efficient than what I was doing. The point was food, quantities of food. It all looked so easy, that tractor driver in his air-conditioned cab, that wonderful machine crawling across the face of the same earth it would have taken my ancestors forty years to plow. What matter if a whole style of life was gone? What matter if the earth no longer served a single family, a small parcel of immortality for the common man? All that was lost to me, as lost as a cherry orchard in which people no longer knew the meaning of cherries, as lost as the unwritten language of a long-expired race of men. All that mattered was food, the wheat on the hill, the hay in the meadow, the mutton under my boot. Whatever method could raise them best and most efficiently would win the prizes of the earth.[5]

5. DOUGLAS UNGER, *LEAVING the Land* (New York, 1984).

Driving to the market to get a six-pack before dinner, sitting between these brothers still rooted in family if not land, I felt once again in the congenial company of survivors, of those who had been close enough to the heart of the gift to know that something was missing here. Live-in exiles, veterans of wars both foreign and domestic, the essential war still against the land and the hearts and minds of its inhabitants. Doug's brother had taken some serious damage in Vietnam and had developed the grim good humor of those who've looked over the edge and come back. Who can say, Call me Ishmael, and mean it.

The Safebuy was full of midweek dinner shoppers, and the parking lot crowded with cars. The only convenient space left was between the blue-painted lines reserved for the disabled, directly in front of the automatic supermarket doors. "Hey. I'm paranoid schizophrenic. Park here," he said, and we wheeled into it. I offered money for beer, but it was refused.

While they went in, I waited in the car. If anybody asked, I could explain that I was here to demonetize their food.

🦁 🦁 🦁

Because the War of Independence was fought in the modern way—on borrowed money and shaky credit—peace brought the new nation's first depression. The newly independent states' immediate problem was the old colonial one: how to raise money for men and arms from a group of small third-world business enterprises—the same ones who had not even been able to agree on seating arrangements at Albany thirty years earlier. The problem of course could only worsen, as the new states did more and more business in the manner of the old colonies. The "revolution" in effect overthrew the royal franchise and announced that the several "states" were going into business for themselves, which naturally only increased their competitive behavior. Everyone henceforward had better look out for their own interest.

What saved the American revolutionists and their uneasy union, finally, was not George Washington crossing a river, but something more like the mythic credibility we lend him every time we spend a dollar. That is, the image of the patriarchal head of state and the ingenuity to endow it with public faith.

The task of selling the United States to its creditors went not to a general but to a financier, Robert Morris, whom Hamilton had originally recommended to Congress as its Superintendent of Finance. In 1781, with independence still a doubtful issue, and despite laws demanding its acceptance, no one would be caught dead with a U.S. bill of credit. It was simply not taken as a serious offer in any exchange. The nation needed a credit reference, and it was only natural that the businessmen of Congress would select one of their best-rated friends. Willing, Morris & Co. were eminently eligible for the job, having performed this sort of service when the

Pennsylvania Council of Safety was looking for a banker and supplier of arms in the summer of '75. If this dual role of finance and armaments sounds eerily like the unholy alliance that has brought us within a fool's whim of destruction, it was not troubling enough to keep the congressional commissioners from contracting for these same services some months later.

6. THE REMARKS ON MORRIS
are gathered from his entry
in *Dictionary of American
Biography*.

"Bold and enterprising."[6] "Of great mercantile knowledge." "Fertile in expedients and an able financier." "Very popular in and out of Congress." "Grown extremely rich." This was the appraisal of Morris by his peers. His efforts on behalf of the revolution were widely recognized, and as its first great public tycoon he naturally was offered the job of Washington's Secretary of the Treasury, an honor he refused. The realm of private finance was his true calling, and the extenuations of credit his real genius. "The least breach of faith must ruin us all," he said prophetically, as he guided the finances of the revolution. He inspired such belief that he could get tobacco—that *primum mobile* of surplus produce—out of the fields, past a blockade, and into European markets, receiving critically needed war supplies in return. On his personal credit he bought supplies with borrowed money when Congress was forced to flee Philadelphia. He managed to collect federal taxes in specie to pay interest on the spiraling debt and made requisitions from the tight-fisted states of enough hard cash to carry on the war. In the new year of 1782, with a timely loan of $200,000 specie brought in by the French fleet, he opened the doors of the Bank of North America and financed the battle of Yorktown. "I am determined," wrote Morris to John Jay, "that the bank shall be well supported, until it can support itself, and then it will support us."

The founding of the union of former colonies was thus conceived of as a stock offering, which would require some investors and reward them—particularly those who were part of the initial offering—with a rather handsome return on their money. After the war, Morris resigned his congressional post, but continued to defend the bank as one of its stockholders, even hiring the writing talents of a former adversary of his methods, Tom Paine, to establish its credibility. Morris was also at this time a member of the Pennsylvania assembly and would soon be a United States senator and the holder of a lucrative monopoly on the tobacco trade with France.

In the end, the American victory came down to a highly bid and highly leveraged buyout. When a group of Seneca warriors came to Georgetown in the fall of 1783, after another summer of forest warfare that still held the frontier at bay, the news they heard must have come with all the force of having been sold. The king had looked into his royal treasury, talked to his bankers, and decided to cut his losses. The offer of reservation lands in Canada hardly compensated for the surrender of their ancient homelands, as if the Iroquois had been his mercenaries and their country a fiefdom of the Crown. Although the ensuing treaty agreements were never accepted or ratified by the now-divided Iroquois nations, the more or less confederate states were only too happy to receive their lands as spoils of conquest. They had a lot of bills to pay. Partly because of the brilliant financing that won the war, the new nation was undergoing a serious (as we now say) downturn of the business cycle. Along with it, even Morris's financial affairs had grown increasingly desperate. Both he and his country had issued enormous promises which they could not possibly redeem. Naturally, they turned to the only wealth they could come up with—the lands they had just claimed. They started selling the farm.

The worthless currency with which the troops had been paid was depreciated to somewhere near its exchange value and in a wave of postwar patriotic gratitude was made redeemable in confiscated land. Some of this land was also set aside as outright gift, a return on services rendered. Besides these tracts of "depreciation land" and "donation land," there were millions of acres for which large land-company developers received pieces of paper, belonging to stockholders expecting to see profits. Morris himself held preemption rights to thousands of acres of western New York, which he sold to a coalition of Dutch bankers.

Inconveniently, these promises could not be redeemed while the land was still occupied by its ancient inhabitants. The Six Nations, however divided, were still determined to continue both their tenure of the earth and the forms of agreement by which they were bound to it. A paper signed in Paris or Amsterdam was not in itself going to change these conservative arrangements. What could not be declared by fiat and won by war—at least not without further great expense of money and blood—would have to be acquired by more delicate means. The confederacy of western tribes would struggle for another decade after Britain's surrender—partly still instigated by British trading interests, who stirred discontent much as the French had done against them, and partly by the continued outrages of the frontier Big Knives—but for the most part the new government in Philadelphia was looking for a cheaper solution. "I have every reason," wrote Washington to James Duane, the Continental Congress's commissioner of Indian affairs,

7. WASHINGTON TO DUANE, 7 September, 1783; reprinted in Herbert M. Lloyd's annotated edition of Morgan's *League of the Iroquois*, 2:197.

> to believe from my inquiries, and the information I have received, that they will not suffer their country (if it were our policy to take it before we could settle it) to be wrested from them without another struggle. That they would compromise for a part of it, I have very little doubt; and that it would be the cheapest way of coming at it, I have no doubt at all. . . . That it is the cheapest, as well as the least distressing way of dealing with them, none, who is acquainted with the nature of Indian warfare, and has ever been at the trouble of estimating the expense of one, and comparing it with the cost of purchasing their lands, will hesitate to acknowledge.[7]

The *Washington Covenant* belt, one of the largest and most elaborate of extant wampum agreements, documents the implementation of these policies. In a beaded picture more than six feet long and fifteen beads wide, fifteen figures stand clasping each other by the hand. They are separated at the center by a single house with an open door. Its roof extends on either side to cover the two figures next to it. They are by most accounts said to be Washington and Adodarhoh— as if he were the "president" of the Iroquois Confederacy— the thirteen remaining figures being the states. This is the new picture, the new Longhouse of North America. The belt is much admired by curators for its workmanship, as well as its elaborate representational style and obvious European influence. Apart from the year, museum notes make no mention of the treaty to which it refers.

The 1789 treaty of Fort Harmar was later repudiated as being little more than a land grab, in return for which the Six Nations were given moth-eaten blankets and certain "chiefs" rewarded with money and private tracts of land. The policy of compromise and purchase was made easier by the fact that the Confederacy lay in ruins, its fire out and its agreements scattered, unanimity gone. Brant, forced from the western end of the Longhouse, had gone into Canada with the remaining Mohawk and had little to say in this postwar division of spoils. Cornplanter, so far down the road of accommodation that his life was more than once threatened by his own people, accepted and turned into cash whatever settlements he was offered.

The proliferation of these backroom treaties, accompanied by payments of money, are testimony not only of George Washington's buyout strategy, but also of the desperate measures needed to save the new constitutional government. Most of these treaties of course were offered with the influence of rum or coercion of arms, not unlike the bribes and strong-arm tactics still employed by the BIA and FBI. The U.S. Commissioners of Indian Affairs no longer bothered to disguise the racist insolence that had lain beneath their former show of respect toward the ceremonies of the Longhouse. The exchange of wampum was quickly dispensed with.

According to the policies of Duane, their status as a sovereign people was to be denied at every opportunity:

> I would never suffer the word 'Nation' or 'Six nations,' or 'Confederates,' or 'Council Fire at Onondago' or any other form which would revive or seem to confirm their former ideas of independence, to escape.... they are used to be called Brethren, Sachems & Warriors of the Six Nations. I hope it will never be repeated. It is sufficient to make them sensible that they are spoken to without complimenting twenty or thirty Mohawks as a nation, and a few more Tuscaroras & Onondagas as distinct nations.[8]

By the time the last shot was fired in the Ohio—say twenty years after that famous initial volley, and dwarfing the relative losses of the two officially combatant nations—the Iroquois are estimated to have lost half their population, as well as the bulk of their nation's territory. It cannot have been too difficult to convince many that they had ceased to exist.

But again, it was not likely that the Six Nations would go away because of an Indian commissioner saying so. As a weaker nation being put upon by a weak nation, they knew that their adversary was also in no shape to absorb further damage. The new constitutional government could ill afford an Indian war and risk a repetition of the economic collapse that had so quickly overtaken the short-lived confederacy of states. Even defenders of that experiment had had to recognize the financial debacle that came with the overdue bills for the war, and the wars before that one—requisitions for payment, according to George Mason of Virginia, "for more gold and silver than were in the United States." So that even though made with less of the former respect, the would-be proprietors of North America fell back on their founding principles—presents to Indians.

By the 1790s Robert Morris, the financier of the revolution, was so pressed by his creditors that he could not leave

8. FROM *PROCEEDINGS OF the Commissioners of Indian Affairs* (Albany, 1861), quoted in Wallace's *Death and Rebirth*, 197.

9. THE SENECA ACCOUNT of Morris's dealings, in Wallace's *Death and Rebirth,* 179–83, makes it clear that in terms of spiritual desperation, manifest as heartless greed, the nation's founders were not far advanced from their Puritan and Cavalier grandfathers. There seems little doubt that, in any sense of the word, Morris was possessed.

his home. His already constrained business ventures had felt the paralyzing effects of the Napoleonic Wars, which would bring due the bills of an age of speculative expansion and the deficit financing of empire. His Dutch backers would not part with cash until they saw a signed paper for the thousands of acres of western New York he claimed were his, New World properties being a well-known hustle by now.

The financial wizard was cornered and desperate, and so possessed by monetary need that the Seneca regarded him as an evil conjuror, his great girth a sign of unnatural appetites. "We are much disturbed in our dreams," said the Seneca Red Jacket, "about the great Eater with a big Belly endeavoring to devour our lands."[9]

Unable to travel, Morris sent his son Thomas among the Seneca with the usual wagon loads of dry goods and gunpowder, a generous 750 gallons of rum, and $100,000 in bills. This last, after many days of negotiation, was offered to the Seneca women with the argument that it would feed and clothe them and their children more adequately than their men were able to. It effectively set the clan mothers against the warrior societies (many war chiefs were bribed privately, and the nation's sachems were not even a party to the final deal). The outcome was predictable, with the men finally saving only some hunting tracts that are the basis of present-day reservations.

But even this outrageous land grab, dignified with the title Treaty of Big Tree, was not enough to save Morris from ruin. In February of 1798, a victim of the first national cycle of mania and insolvency, he was arrested for debt. Unable to sell what he still possessed and unable to meet interest payments and taxes, he served three and a half years in prison. Released under liberalized federal bankruptcy laws, he died five years later in poverty and obscurity. His ideas of centralized finance lived on in Hamilton's National Bank, and his misfortune and the failure of public credit encouraged a period of fiscal restraint that lasted until the bank's twenty-year charter expired—when another age of expansion would begin, with another cycle of cheap money backed by cheap land said to lie beyond the Ohio country. The $100,000 paid by Morris to the Seneca turned out to be in the form of stock in Hamilton's bank, and when it ceased to function Congress had to replace the worthless paper with what they assured them again was good money.

"You ask me," wrote John Adams to Horatio Gates, "what you are to think of Robert Morris? I think he has a masterly Understanding, an open Temper and an honest Heart. He also has vast designs in the mercantile way. And no doubt pursues mercantile ends, which are always gain; but he is an excellent member of our body."

The valley of the Hudson slides by outside the day coach window, lush and green again, looking as though it had never been otherwise. It is as if the land had no memory and were indifferent to the words and actions of nations. The book beside me on my trip back downriver is Anthony F. C. Wallace's *Death and Rebirth of the Seneca*, which scrupulously documents the survival of a nation within the emerging American state. I keep my place in the book even though I'm staring at the passing landscape more than I'm actually reading. Like Wilson's *Apologies* and the knapsack of books I travel with, I've been through its pages before and apparently carry the dog-eared paperback as a kind of reassurance—a palpable sign and witness to a history that might otherwise be lost. This is of course utterly mistaken—the land remembers everything. The loss is ours, because we have lost the ways to redeem loss itself and to renew and reestablish the gift that once was ours —the land, as Robert Frost said, that was ours before we belonged to the land.

At dinner the night before, Amy's mother, eighty years old, sitting before her half-eaten food, drifting away from her family's talk of everyday living and growing, suddenly recalled by a question, a little embarrassed, said, "I was just thinking. How if you could go back and do things right that you'd done wrong." Yes, we all seemed to murmur in assent, without saying anything, finishing our dinner now, Amy clearing the table and asking who was ready for dessert. It was all sad and sweet, the evening, the people at dinner, the people in the graveyard that day, lovers in the dark of the moon, all of us wishing for nothing more, really, than to recover a little of what was lost. It is for this we are lacking a currency.

It was hardly more than a year before our mutual friends were gone. Their passing, as they say, untimely. But as their friends and family would be the first to tell you, either might easily have succumbed years ago. Bonnie one day, coughing her cough, having her glass of white wine and ultra-filter cigarettes at the bar, going home and going to shop on the way. Saying as we always do: see you later.

That had to be after Ray died, because I remember how terribly hard she took it, far more than the grieving writers and readers who only knew that a redeeming public voice had been lost. And more than as a friend, simply. Like the way she devoted herself to kids as a teacher, being somehow part of her devotion to those not always grown-up adults who give us the thing we call writing. And so first Ray, within the year, his last piece a college commencement taking its text from Saint Theresa: "Words lead to deeds. . . . They prepare the soul, make it ready, and move it to tenderness." He was ready, maybe because he'd outlived by more than a decade a life many friends thought would be the end of him. Give the guy a year, maybe two. Probably finished as a writer. He had sustained through the ensuing years and books the sweet humor of the survivor, that deep-touching note I'd heard in Doug's books as well, and in his family's beautiful sad voices. Lord knows what the graduates of Hartford thought they were being told. Four years of college hardly prepare you for such directness.

And that other word: soul—call it spirit if you want, if it
makes it easier to claim the territory. Don't forget that
either. Pay attention to the spirit of your words, your
deeds. That's preparation enough. No more words.[10]

The territory. The heart of the territory. And the path to
get there. This is what was meant by the thing we now call
money, the pledge of spirit in our words and deeds. What our
truest and deepest accountants—our poets and storytellers—
have been saying to us: the path to and from the heart. A way
to get from the act to the spirit of the act, and from words to
the deed. In the end, our only deeds the land will honor.

I put away the book and lay my pack and bedroll on the
seat beside me as the first ruins of Hamilton's city come into
view. The only way out is through it.

10. "GRADUATION ADDRESS,
Hartford College," in the
posthumous collection:
Raymond Carver, *No
Heroics Please: Uncollected
Writings,* ed. William L. Stull
(New York, 1992).

THE FINE ART OF
MAKING MONEY

A Saturday afternoon in May, in the churchyard of St. Marks in the Bowery, the poets are talking and walking. New leaves throw a dappled shade on the paving stones, heaved and gently tilted by the roots of old trees. I'm sitting on a bench having a smoke, and more people begin to come outside for an intermission in the reading. They gather around the poets to express their praise or cleverness. The reading so far has been uproarious enough that no one is taking themselves too solemnly. There is a welcome sense of ease and comfort here, alien again among aliens.

After a day back in the city, I had decided that I needed to move down here to the poets' part of town. This despite a convenient apartment available in the upper avenues, where for the rest of my sojourn in the east, except for an invisible roommate, I could have a place to myself. My host, in the week I'd been upstate, had sprung himself from detox and was already back in again. But my own reentry into Manhattan had been less than triumphant, and I associated the ensuing depression with the middle and upper parts of town. I would squeeze instead into a lower Broadway loft with a family of three, friends of a friend, who would generously lend me a bed for a few nights.

According to my original travel plans I should have been on my way to the Smithsonian, to examine their bead collection, but the depredations of research had left me without the price of a ticket to D.C.—or anywhere beyond Newark, where I had a flight out in a week. Not far south of that city, which its citizens were burning down when I was last in this region, the small brick Italian town with the formerly Dutch college where I'd developed my obsession for old texts, and to which a long-outstanding student loan was the least of my indebtedness. I had to call and say I wasn't going to make it. The debt would have to be redeemed, if at all, by practice on the texts at hand.

I had walked out of Grand Central Station with more than the usual tourist's disorientation. My researches into the heart of the Empire State had been hasty and only marginally productive. I was looking toward an evening's dinner with an editor who held an envelope in which I was increasingly certain only my doom was sealed. As if I needed to further this pilgrimage to loss, I hiked up and across town, pack and books and bedroll humped along, taking in art museums on the way. Maybe, my desperation reasoned, the missing link between money and reality is somewhere in modern art. After all, only last week a painting by Vincent van Gogh had sold for a record-breaking 53 million plus, and it's a well known romantic fact that he received nothing at all for the work of his brief, tormented, ecstatic life. If something were missing, it might easily have fallen into the resounding emptiness between Vincent's art and Vincent's pocket.

But as I walked and stared, stood and stared, and sat in sculpture gardens with people who looked as if they belonged there, it seemed that the artists had vowed this failure in marketing would never again befall them. Prices in the art mart were at all-time record levels, the museums had become galleries to the galleries, and the only serious issues seemed to be how large to make the ugly new addition to the Whitney or the Guggenheim. The Met, with taxpayers' money and a bequest from a mass tabloid, had already come down on the side of Very Large Indeed, with a whopping 50K square feet of contemporary art space. MOMA was of course standing pat with its present holdings, having shortsightedly sold the space above itself for condos. It would continue to store most of its 65,000 pieces, secure in the knowledge that modern art was firmly in hand.

Museums and corporations and galleries and banks— curators and dealers, directors and collectors, financiers and trustees—all of these functions have merged to such a degree that you hardly know the nature of the product being seen. Having learned, being modern, not to ask *what* a picture represents, now we just ask *how much*. "Our ideal transaction starts at $100K," is the aesthetic appraisal of a Rosenthal Art Equities spokesman. "But we'll do $50K as a starter to develop the relationship."

And not only does art now refer to money, but according to a New York judge it is now legally a negotiable form of wealth. Reasoning that the buyers of Dali prints (which turned out to have been photoreproduced) had been referred to by their broker as "investors" and their purchase as "an investment," the judge ruled that they therefore qualified as securities and were subject to SEC rules. As if to intentionally compound this confusion of money and merchandise, the most recent *Art News* reports a show that opened this spring in New Orleans called "The Fine Art of Making Money."[1] Besides attracting artists who regularly work with paper money as a medium, the competition featured many redesigners of currency and included one postmodern dollar that carried a corporate ad space, the revenue to be applied to the national debt. Judges included the director of the Fine Arts Program of the Federal Reserve Board.

Much of this confusion resulted from the whirlwind of money set loose by the deregulation of finance in 1980, and the perception that art was a socially approved way to invest the otherwise obscenely high profits. The inflation brought on by massive borrowing and highly leveraged (junk) bonds made much of this increase illusory—but of course imagination is here the solidest of commodities. The same issue of the *News*, in its regular "Art Market" column, reports this blur of valuations as if it made perfect sense:

1. MAY 1987. THE ISSUES OF March and April also epitomize the art market at the peak of this period of acquisition. Two sides of the art coin in 1987: the death of Andy Warhol, whose reputation was made in the art of commodities (his portrayal of the idols of commerce subsequently brought record prices at Christie's); and the Secret Service's confiscation of what it called "counterfeit cash" by J. S. G. Boggs of Pittsburgh, who draws and reproduces U.S. bills and "spends" them as an art performance (his bills carry his signature and read, "The Unit of State of Bohemia").

Cantor noted that Christie's did well with some artists who were "basically untried in the market and had only recently had gallery showings," such as transcendentalist artist Ed Gorman (his #213 Abstract, 1941, sold for $12,000 after an estimate of $7,000 to $9,000); Emil J. Bisstram (whose Duality #2, 1938, *brought $18,700 after an estimate of $10,000 to $15,000); and lesser-known names such as Harry Roseland, whose striking view of a jammed beach,* Beach Scene, Coney Island, *1891, brought $66,000 (estimate: $15,0000 to $25,000) on its pictorial merit alone.*

2. *THE CANTOS OF EZRA Pound,* Canto XLV. "With usura," Pound insists, "all arts decay." His note to this canto defines usury: "a charge for the use of purchasing power, levied without regard to production; often without regard to the possibilities of production. (Hence the failure of the Medici bank.)"

The subversion of aesthetic by monetary value is hardly recent—Ezra Pound sounded the alarm loudly for this century in his tracts and in the *Cantos:*

> *no picture is made to endure nor to live with*
> *but it is made to sell and sell quickly*[2]

—but what is poignantly postmodern and late American is the merging of such extreme abstraction with such titanic power and wealth. The similarity to downtown money markets—mergers, insider trading, inflated value, fast and big, thank you—need hardly be pointed out. What is of note is that they not only *seem* to be the same but *are.* Art is the money of money. Museums are the banks of banks. Corporations are image upon image. So much unsecured paper is chasing so little earned reality that *contemporary* has had to move over for *contemporary* contemporary, and then to *ultra* contemporary in the rush to fill the vacuum of market lag.

Despite the great number of homeless—Pound again: "and no man can find site for his dwelling"—there appears to be abundant housing of art. Exhibition rooms of 10,000 square feet have become an industry standard, requiring shows of thirty to forty "substantial" pieces. Speed and bigness are crucial. "Established" in their twenties, artists are having "major retrospectives" in their early thirties. The

3. MAUREEN MULLARKEY
("Tuesday at the Met,"
Hudson Review 40
[Summer 1987]: 193–205).
Saatchi, the London-
based ad firm for clients
such as Prime Minister
Thatcher, included in its
review of operations
the quoted corporate
dictum of R. C. Clarke,
managing director,
United Biscuits.

product becomes inevitably neo and geo and decorative, a form of wealth display for the grand emptiness of corporate lobbies. One of the world's largest ad agencies is thus of course also one of the world's largest holders of hot contemporary art. So that the *Hudson Review*'s art critic finds it necessary to quote their annual business report to explain what we see on walls:

> *Buildings age and become dilapidated. Machines wear out. Cars rust. People die. But what lives on are the brands.*[3]

As with the other kind of wealth, however, unfortunately not everyone can belong to the timeless economy of corporate logos. Its business practice, like its art, is a guarantee of scarcity. While the art product has appreciated substantially, there has been a flood of new devotees to the enhanced opportunities of the market—and in accord with its law of surplus labor, the masses of brush-wiping drudges in garrets are no better off than before.

Imagine, then, the alienation of the garrets' former tenants, the poets, who have seen the market for language fall below its historic lows and find they can't even afford the urban rat holes they've been perishing in for three centuries. Although publishing tycoons have been around almost as long as the hacks they employed, the newest mania of acquisition and merger has drastically reduced the venues for writing, meaning of course even less of a sop to the verse-mongers. Even the Vandals here—the graffiti artists—achieve comparative wealth and fame while the poets are told, Hey, go with the market—hip-hop or ad copy? A friend who'd just signed a contract with Simon and Schuster to publish his first novel mentioned that he also wrote poetry. He was treated with sympathy, if not pity, though they kindly stopped short of recommending professional help.

This complaint is now so familiar and accepted as to hardly be talked about. No one would buy a book about it. With fewer and larger publishers chasing a smaller and less literate audience, the surefire blockbuster is naturally what's expected: mass shipments to mass distributors, a preselection by the Book of the Month Club, and stand-up displays at the B. Dalton or Waldenbooks of every major shopping mall. And poetry? Virtually a handful of working poets in this country are able to make a living by their art—and that's counting at least one well-known charlatan. The remainder are employed by institutions that absorb them into their name-enhancing Creative Writing programs, with a consequent outpouring of even more young makers of serviceable but eerily similar poems chasing the same few publishers and prizes. I had heard on the car radio last week, driving back from Onondaga, that the present administration had created for itself yet another trapping of empire, a Poet Laureate, and I was embarrassed to learn they had selected someone I thought had long since died.

After intermission, the featured reader was Edward Dorn. Years ago I'd had the opportunity to review the first book of his *Gunslinger* epic and had been a serious reader of his work ever since. I knew little about him—he'd been at Black Mountain College, was a student of Olson's, and last I knew was publishing a poetry magazine out of Colorado. Where Olson looked out east from Gloucester, Dorn took the projective method inward toward the rocky spine of the continent. His cast of voice was western, shaped by the weird spaces of this late century and the morning slope of the Great Divide. These inner continental distances had always sounded a congenial note to my ear.

But today Dorn was reading something more recent and topical and light. His poems about the Independent Women of Boulder were arch and insightful, and perhaps wisely delivered to an audience in another town. I found myself disappointed with the selection—here was a poet whose voice had ranged up and down the cordillera, from Lemhi Pass to

4. *The Collected Poems
1956–1974* (Bolinas, 1975).
The brief preface affirms a
commitment to persons
rather than publishing
houses, and a similar
commitment to readers
who have followed his
work. My alien sense at
this reading is one that
recurs: both of having
fallen outside that
magic circle, and of
falling into its
diminishing radius of
discourse. It is
exile either way.

Mesilla, echoing through time from the pre-Socratics to Geronimo to the blazed-out sixties, and now it was the late '80s and he was talking about the habits of women who drive BMWs. Obviously my expectations were out of line with the day and the times. I had usually considered myself included in Dorn's brief preface to his collected poems—"My true readers have known exactly what I assumed"[4]—but today I felt myself one of those oppressed inhabitants of a ghetto, who can at last speak only to one another.

I didn't stay for the other featured readers, though I had paid my four dollars and wanted to hear them. I had to admit that I didn't have the heart or attention for it and was looking for more consolation than poetry readings are meant to provide. Instead I wandered among the shoppers and hustlers crowding the ample sidewalks of 14th Street, letting myself be absorbed by the throng of commerce. Compared to where I'd been lately, the prices of souls seemed about right. Money was walking and talking. The spirit of things alive on the street, maybe still represented by the things themselves. A woman stops to put a dollar on the folding table. The man turns the card. She walks away.

Turning down into the east village, the streets narrow, the dress becomes more late '80s, the commerce more artful. Walking ahead of me, a young woman in leather jacket and multicolored topknot is carrying a large cat which is meowing loudly. She stops, turns to the mohawked young man, also in black leather, who leans against a lamp post, and asks him if he wants a cat. What do I want with a cat, he asks her. I have a pimple. She says nothing. The cat meows. What would I feed it? She looks at him. Feed it the pimple, she says, walking away, the cat meowing loudly over her shoulder.

❀ ❀ ❀

*Theirs—and ours—was the age of monopoly capitalism,
an economic form whose code expected and rewarded the
conversion of gift wealth to market wealth (the natural*

*gifts of the New World, in particular—the forests,
wildlife and fossil fuels—were "sold in perpetuity" and
converted into private fortunes). In a land that feels no
reciprocity toward nature, in an age when the rich imagine themselves to be self-made, we should not be surprised to find the interior poverty of the gifted state
replicated in the actual poverty of the gifted.*[5]

Lewis Hyde, here summarizing the lives and times of
American poets Walt Whitman and Ezra Pound, has taken the
socioeconomic tradition of Mauss's *Essay on the Gift* as his
point of inquiry into money and the life of the imagination.
The Gift defines "gift wealth" much as Mauss did, with the
added ethnographic insight of works like Sahlins's *Stone Age
Economics.* Far more deeply personal and interior, though,
Lewis Hyde brings to this data a poet's literary sensibility, the
Jungian reading of archetypal story, and some years of work in
an alcohol detox center. He has experienced the gift in action,
and describes the way it moves. He describes market wealth as
he has also seen it, and learned to redeem and live with it.

Ezra Pound's legendary generosity, like Whitman's, had
another, darker side. Where Whitman's "expansiveness" took
him into the hospitals of the Civil War, Pound went to Europe
and began overturning things. On this heroic quest for the
heart of value, clearing away the worthless debris of history
and dead language, he endowed our century's poetry with its
characteristic image and music. But that was not enough. He
wanted a market wealth that would acknowledge the other
kind of riches, this finely wrought labor of the spirit. And he
would do this, not with the gifts of Eros and imagination, but
in the market's own terms of Logos and rationality. He would
institute a poet's economy, that is, using the political machine
of a fascist dictator. Anyone who has struggled with the shrill
didacticism of *Jefferson and/or Mussolini* can attest to the disastrous results. Neither he nor his *Cantos* came back from the
journey to Hades's kingdom, where money is said to dwell.

The admonition ought to be clear. In searching for what

5. LEWIS HYDE, *THE GIFT:
Imagination and the Erotic Life
of Property* (New York, 1983),
280. When Hyde's book
appeared—as the chapter
"The Gift Must Always
Move," *Coevolution
Quarterly* (Fall 1982)—I
was at first chagrined that
my own investigations were
taking such a slow, tortuous
route—and then relieved
and grateful, considering
someone else had done
the work. Anyone who cares
for the wealth of the spirit
will wish they'd written *The
Gift.* Regrettably, I found I
had to tell this story in a
more literal way, and to
chronicle the exchange of
promises, and the beads
and notes intended to mark
them, transaction by painful
transaction. Hyde's is a
cogent study of the roots of
such obsession, while still
lamenting with us that there
is no love in our money.

Hyde includes a note (*The
Gift,* 271) in which Pound
corrects his own earlier
note: "Re USURY. I was out
of focus, taking a symptom
for a cause. The cause
is AVARICE." That is, the
problem is not one that
rational money laws alone
will cure; the problem is
in the heart.

Mauss described as "the total social phenomenon"—the gift relation that satisfies both the soul's and the household's economy—latter-day artist errants should be extremely wary. First, by recognizing that they are "merely" artists—that is, however well they master the terms of academy and market, their only power is finally the gift itself. And that it is the heart's gift, and they only its messengers. Such an artist might know before starting out that all the data and texts he can carry back will prove only to confirm what he knew when he left.

So that finally, as in the old fairy tales, the gift lies in knowing one's self, which typically comes late in the story. In my own confused helplessness and arrogance concerning money, this journey was conceived as the acknowledgment of a gift, which had turned out to be long overdue, and both communal and far more personal than I had expected. I had willfully added to that a tougher, practical, New York motive —of selling the gift, and writing a book about love of money. In the process of travel and research, however, I had obviously become more indebted every day for shared information, access to treasures and rare materials, as well as the basic needs of food and a roof over my head. And so was left more than ever where I began, with a sense of indebtedness only the book in my heart could repay. "Between the time a gift comes to us and the time we pass it along," says Lewis Hyde, "we suffer gratitude." Perhaps, then, I'd been a long-term sufferer of chronic gratitude, and had simply come looking for what would bring relief.

It was not money. Not even poetry. And it surely wasn't art.

The only paintings I recall "seeing" that first afternoon in Manhattan were two: a deKooning portrait of a woman that brought my appraiser's tour of the Modern to an abrupt stop, literally stunned by it—and a western landscape, bold and blunt as a logger's suspenders, a swamp in whose many black-branched trees sat a wild constellation of red-winged blackbirds. Somehow it had gotten into the Whitney's much-hyped Biennial. Everything else that day, the Kandinsky color geometry, the Mirós bed-springing down the Guggenheim walls, the fascist decorative motifs so eternally in vogue, all these guys putting their modern money so heavily on the side of Logos, willfully throwing out the erotic baby with the sentimental bath.

"You saw that?" my hosts had then said that evening. The daughter—her daughter, I supposed—went with the guy who painted the blackbirds. Amazing, I said. It reminded me of the paintings of a close friend, I told them. I was back in the small province of Manhattan. I was here for dinner. We were going out for Chinese. Fine, I said.

It was the get-together we said we'd have when I got back from my research in Albany and Onondaga. Afterward I supposed we guys would talk and he would give me his editorial opinion of the writing I'd left here. In the time since I'd handed it to him, a week ago, the pages of the manuscript had appeared to me as a succession of white ghosts, all now possessed of a startling clarity that had been altogether lacking in their brief former lives. I was now convinced that it was just awful. In the nearly two years I'd been trying to imagine somebody else's idea of a book, I had produced a fast-forward twenty-year diorama of a personal and cultural life still struggling to create itself, deeply distrustful of everything this city stood for, in a form I thought one of its major publishing houses would buy. The problem might have been foreseen. Expectations of the market had more than once had this effect on my writing, so it was all the more inexcusable that I hadn't been able to see its posture of how-I-was-lost-and-now-am-found nor hear the insufferably correct voice of the communal "we." Until I'd let go of it, that is.

The actual dinner took less time than the driving and parking, although it seemed but a short distance. And the

talking afterward took even less time than the Chinese food.
He poured us both a serviceable glass of bourbon. We sipped it
in the study and hit on the pinner I'd rolled up earlier. It was
an obligatory part of the stereotype I seemed to be presenting, though I hadn't brought any to sell. I knew from our correspondence that he held seriously conflicting views on the
substance, as well as the culture that produced it. I should
have brought more, or none.

He finally picked up the envelope from the desk and
handed it to me. I had thought I'd known all along what he
would say. After all, if I'd lost track of my voice in these two
years of transcontinental draft and revision, it was partly because I had missed the sense of an audience. I frankly had no
idea who these guys were—not this editor who'd published
my late '60s ravings, and even less the people he now called
his editors, to whom he said he couldn't show my work. I
clearly didn't know what they wanted, except to market my
prose, which either no longer conveyed my views or did so
too well.

None of this, I had to admit again, should have surprised
me. Nevertheless, I felt an old rage bubbling up beneath the
bourbon. It may have been at myself, and my foolish waste
of time. Or it may have been that remark about finding a
more West Coast publisher. Or maybe it was just the
Chinese food. If I said anything, it was going to come out as a
scream about whose lunatic idea this was in the first place,
and what did he mean waving the prospect of money before
impoverished writers—but I knew better than to start. It had
gone too far already. I got my coat, gave my regards to all,
thanked him for dinner, and left. I wandered the streets for
some hours before I came back to some sense of where I was
and what I was doing here. I kept repeating in my head the
chorus of Robert Johnson's "All My Love in Vain." But self-
pity was no more satisfying than anger. Johnson died young,
after all, that slow poison in his dinner mercifully swift compared to this.

The fate of its artists is the fate of a culture. A country that does not pay its debts will eventually have no art, and then no topsoil, and no money. All the forms of wealth, spiritual and material, natural or manufactured, are essentially one. Its source is the gift of the earth itself, again both of spirit and coin. Where the money does not honor that gift, the blues musicians are only the first to go.

It was Pound's insistence on natural facts that first drew me to his work. His demands of economy, concreteness, and fidelity to spoken idiom are like a window opened in stale schoolrooms. His idea of material economy—"CREDIT rests *in ultima* on THE ABUNDANCE OF NATURE"—is an extension of his poetic theory, insisting that a culture, its money as well as its language, is only as sound as its basis in nature's gifts. His own roots, particularly nineteenth-century America for its sloppy writing and poor bookkeeping, received most of his outrage. It appears to have literally driven him crazy. Again and again in the *Cantos* and essays, with growing desperation and failing coherence, he returns to the first half-century of the United States to preach the lesson of their error. His prose like a staccato hammering, the poetry gone utterly flat, his mind like the nation's first principles appeared to divide against itself.

To say, as Pound did, "It began here"[6] is always an arbitrary proposition—but if we ignore the wartime financial chicanery of Robert Morris and his associates and overlook the earlier scandal of the Redemption—it was enacted to redeem at full value notes issued by the Continental Congress, now heavily discounted and considered all but worthless; before news of this scheme could reach the public, insiders bought up the discounted notes and turned a handsome profit—if we can get past this we can say, as Pound did, that our troubles began with the Assumption Act. This "fiscal maneuver" by Hamilton, as Jefferson later recalled it, was the transaction

6. THE HISTORY OF THE National Bank and its successors can be found throughout the *Cantos* and in any account of money in America. The essential issues were laid out in the papers prepared by Jefferson and Hamilton in response to Washington's request for their opinions on the matter. Jefferson, in "Recollections of the Hamiltonian System" (1818), gave his inside view of the Assumption scandal. His remarks— "even in this, the birth of our government, some members were found sordid enough to bend their duty to their interest" —seem innocent to this age of institutionalized self-interest.

that set the Secretary of the Treasury firmly in control of the new nation's direction. Like the suppression of the Shays and Whiskey Rebellions, it established the federal government as the central disburser and collector of money.

Somewhat similar in spirit to the previous scandal, the Assumption Act proposed that the federal government adopt the war debts incurred by the several states during the struggle for independence. A fair enough sounding principle—except that estimates of what amount was due, and to whom, varied in the extreme, and there was apparently no way to ascertain the validity of the claims. But never mind: the amount was set arbitrarily at twenty million dollars, and the money went to those who supported the treasurer and his coalition of monarchists and stockjobbers. To quell another threatened secession—and this only 1790—the southern states who were dragged into the deal were appeased by moving the nation's capitol to the Potomac. The twenty mil was naturally in stocks and stayed here in Hamilton's home town. In the same year he would use this alliance of federalists and opportunists to establish the National Bank, its charter to extend to 1811.

Hamilton's bank outlived him by seven years, but the bullet that ended his ambitions did little to change the insider trading system he had set in motion. The renewal of the bank's charter failed by one vote in the House after a tie in the Senate, but this lapse was due less to the decline of Federalist influence, or the rise of Jeffersonian democracy, than to the utter disregard of the Hamiltonian party for even its own principles and institutions. Embodying the Hobbesian notion that people were to be governed only by force or self-interest, the party of easy money had followed the western migration and was in effect carrying out the second plundering of North America, stirring a constant ferment of rebellion not against Europe but against the "old" money of the eastern seaboard.

The new America First party did not want or need a central East Coast bank—it had plenty of its own banks, thank you. Hundreds of impromptu financial institutions sprang up throughout the western states, in churches, taverns, and shops, and in the five years before the central bank was reinstated their private notes of issue doubled. Banks proliferated like Protestant sects, every man a secretary to his own treasury. This process would continue, with intermittent panics and depressions, till at the outbreak of the Civil War there would be about seven thousand varieties of banknotes in circulation, and another estimated five thousand that were outright counterfeit.

The Federal Treasury was no laggard in this inflation process and during that same five years of cheap money increased the national debt from 45 to 127 millions of dollars. The justification was again war, again with England, and though only one battle in that conflict was won by the now belligerent states—and that after a treaty of peace had been signed—the jingoists declared themselves victorious and were convinced they had restored both honor and credit. This brought a brief and illusory bloom to the depressed western frontier, which was struggling to make its land payments but had very poor market connections. When it was eventually seen that both public and private debt were seriously out of control, the central bank was reinstated—but it was too late. The sudden introduction of responsible credit policies brought on the new nation's first large-scale financial panic.

Then as now, the public memory was wonderfully brief, and before long another inflationary spiral would lead to an even more stupendous crash. But what was most forgotten, or put out of mind, was what made the whole process work at all—the massive appropriation and sale of land. As during the struggle for "independence," the real loser of the war of 1812 was not England, just as the real issue was not the Atlantic balance of trade, and certainly not the nation's honor. The defeat of Tecumseh's confederate forces by Harrison at the Thames; the destruction of the Creek nation by Jackson's army at Horseshoe Bend; the failure again of the British to support their allies at this extremity—the "war" was a violent and deliberate seizure of land that opened the west for the next wave of colonization. Blood for land, land for money, money to redeem the promises and fill the empty coffers of the banks and the national treasury. The Creeks were forced to surrender some twenty-five million acres, land that the Georgia legislature had already tried to sell to land jobbers for a little over two hundred thou. The treaty of Fort Wango opened another three million acres of Illinois bottomland for a paltry seven thou, including a small annuity to the Miami, Delaware, and Wea. And then the administration that came into office on a promise of limiting federal power constructed the first national highway to move the new occupants in. It's today's back-page news.

"Old America seems to be breaking up,"[7] recorded Morris Birbeck, a European who traveled the Cumberland road when it was the continent's first interstate—"breaking up and moving westward. We are seldom out of sight, as we travel on this grand track, toward the Ohio, of family groups, behind and before us."

> *A small waggon (so light that you might almost carry it, yet strong enough to carry a good load of bedding, utensils and provisions, and a swarm of young citizens,—and to sustain marvelous shocks in its passage over these rocky heights) with two small horses; sometimes a cow or two, comprises their all; excepting a little store of hard-earned cash for the land office of the district; where they may obtain a title for as many acres as they possess half dollars, being one fourth of the purchase money.*

So at two and a half dollars per acre, the Land Act of 1800 provided for the sale of these now "public" lands on the following terms: 320 acres minimum, one-quarter down, with the balance due in four years. At these rock-bottom prices, during inflationary times, even at the jobber's price of $1.25 down, the land was guaranteed to pay itself off the first year. Here are the figures, provided by the developer of your new farm on the Wabash, "fenced in the ordinary method, and containing a house upon it like the plan":

DR

To 640 acres of land, at $1 25, is	$ 800 00
Four miles, or 1,280 rods, at 20 rails to the	
rod, gives 25,600 rails, to which add for enclosures,	
cribs, &c., 1,400 rails. Total of rails is 27,000,	
which, at $3 50 per hundred, gives	945 00
Breaking up 640 acres, at $2 25 per acre	1,440 00
House like plan, laying up fence, and well	300 00
Harrowing and sowing seed, at 60 cents	
per acre	384 00
Mowing, raking and pressing 960 tons, (one	
and a half ton per acre,) at $2 50	2,400 00
Transportation of 960 tons of hay to New	
Orleans, at $8 per ton, is	7,680 00
Amount	$13,949 00

CR

By sale of 960 tons of hay, at $25 per ton, is	$19,200 00
Income, as above	19,200 00
Expenditures	13,949 00
Profit	$ 5,251 00[8]

8. FROM HENRY W. Ellsworth, *The Valley of the Upper Wabash* (New York, 1838), reproduced in Billington, *America's Frontier Story* (NY, 1969), 301.

Hardly any wonder that these offers created one of the greatest migrations in the history of human wandering. Cheap land. Cheap money. Pay later. It became difficult to know the real value of anything, and almost impossible to distinguish the private from the public interest. Large tracts of land, set aside by a signature and one-quarter down, turned out to have only one owner where there appeared to be many. Private developers found their own land options being bought up by smaller jobbers, who also had many false names. Both Massachusetts and Connecticut sold their largely illusory claims to western New York and the Ohio, and these vast tracts of land ended up in the hands of insiders to the deal. Six million acres of western New York went to

9. "'Tis very droll to hear
the comic stories of the
rising values here, which,
ludicrous though they
seem, are justified by facts
presently" (Journals of
Ralph Waldo Emerson
[Boston, 1913], 9:76).

Dutch and English consortiums, the Ohio lands to the ill-disguised Connecticut Land Company. With no limit to credit, no troublesome Indians and no king's commissioners, the West was open for business. Those who saw the opportunity and ventured out of the forests onto the open prairie, were like prospectors striking it rich.

It was the closest thing to something for nothing that an immigrant could imagine—particular an immigrant with a little Old-World money to invest. "The profits on capital employed any way in this country are marvelous," Birbeck reported back from the farm he had purchased. Land and the money to buy it seemed to increase exponentially, as the new country adopted new habits and expectations of wealth. In the mid-1830s bank loans increased from 13.7 to 525 million dollars, banknote circulation went from 48 to 149 million, and the number of banks more than doubled. Annual receipts for government land increased from 2 to 25 million dollars, swelling the treasury and actually paying off the national debt for the first and only time in the nation's history. Even Emerson, on a visit to Chicago at this time,[9] shared in the general hilarity and disbelief at such great and sudden fortune. Imagine the surprise, then, when on May 10, 1837, the New York banks closed their doors. Amid all the paper abundance, it turned out there was little actual wealth. The money had not been representative of the facts. It was the monetary equivalent of a Fenimore Cooper romance, or the vast canvas landscapes of the Hudson Valley school. Our present equivalents you can easily name.

As to actual wealth, a great portion of the new western immigrants were refugees not from Europe but from the agricultural practices that had left the soils of New England and the South almost incapable of production. This was simply the farmer's way of doing what the banks were doing—where *usury* meant, as Pound had said, making wealth from nothing, with no attachment to the land and the growing grass. It was only a bubble. All it had taken to puncture it was for the Indian fighter then in the office of President to miscalculate slightly in his power struggle with the banks. All payments for government land would henceforth be in specie, he declared, and not in bank-issued notes of credit. Insisting that minted coin be the only money, not promises based on the speculative value of real estate. But then it turned out there was not enough in the banks to cover even a third of their notes, so that when this requirement was enacted as law and federal inspectors sent to look into vaults, it was not unheard of for the money to pass the inspector on the highway, on the way to his next bank.

For twenty-five years following the Great Panic of '37, the government paid and collected its bills in hard cash and had no part in the banking business—until the great conflict over how best to commoditize labor, with credit and wage slavery winning out over the Roman *familia* of live-in household bondage. By the end of the Civil War, the nation's debt had gone from $65 million to $3 billion[10]—as if the Treasury had printed so many invitations to the gilded age that followed. As the cycles of inflation and panic began to be shorter and more severe, further centralized control of banking and markets became a necessity—until only the Secretary of the Treasury, backed by greed and enforced by fear, could issue the greenback we occasionally see in our beggars' cups today.

It's not too terribly complicated, this story of buying in cheap and selling out dear, making your money make nothing but money. If that is where your talent lies. Speculators in land, art, or money differ only superficially from ordinary thieves—except that the thieves, like the poets, often believe the wealth is "in" the deeds or canvas or coin. A successful seller of bonds, for example, works the distance *between* the signs and the thing they represent—so that a commercial piece of investment art, to take the other side of the coin, will never have the vitality of everyday subway graffiti. Where the interest lies in keeping true costs from being acknowledged, living will have little affect and the erotic life will wither and die. Culture, which includes our government and

10. THIS OTHERWISE forgotten history was noted shortly after the inauguration of the present Chief Executive, in a *San Francisco Chronicle* piece (2/7/93) speculating on what he would do about the current deficit. Under the two previous administrations, whose policies were in effect during this research trip, the debt had increased by three trillion dollars.

While the Civil War ostensibly limited the degree to which persons can be considered a commodity, it firmly established modern forms of production, marketing, and centralized finance, which in effect return workers to commodity status, with government welfare replacing the plantation household. See *Harvey Wasserman's History of the United States* (New York, 1972) for the political economy that followed.

money as well as our arts, will be left to business. And we know what happens when business is left to those for whom life—particularly the lives of others—is only business.

Secretary of War Calhoun reported to President James Monroe in 1825 that in his estimation the removal to the Indian territory (present-day Oklahoma) of the Five Civilized Tribes (Cherokee, Choctaw, Chickasaw, Creek, Seminole), could be accomplished for the sum of $95,000, with an additional 3oK if a conference were required "to explain to them the views of the Government, and to pledge the faith of the nation to the arrangements that might be adopted."[11]

11. *AMERICA'S FRONTIER STORY* also reproduces an account of how faithfully this pledge was fulfilled in the forced emigration westward: "Frequent appeals were made to me to clothe their nakedness and to protect their lacerated feet. To these I could do no more than what came within the provisions of the Contract" (283–86). It might be said that this was the nation's most nicely observed contract with the nations it displaced.

I cannot find that this was the amount approved, but it is certain that a contract was let to the Alabama Emigrating Company, which was then skimmed and subcontracted at barely profitable terms. The supply wagons could not afford to wait for those who couldn't keep up. No allowance made for blankets against the November storms nor for footwear against the frozen ground. Since some thousands consequently died, the per diem eventually made the operation cost effective.

So now the continent lay empty, and ready for colonization as far as the Mississippi. To fill its emptiness would come churches and banks, parks and art museums, farms and industry. It would all be made of money, the money based on promises. And the promises, and the land, would prove once again to be empty.

🦑 🦑 🦑

I don't know how many miles I walked that night, hat turned down and collar up, walking I suppose like I'd seen the street crazies walk, driven and mad and straight ahead, mumbling something from the blues. I passed others the same and was sure for one instant that a small man in a raincoat was García Lorca, still wandering the streets searching for Walt Whitman. I didn't look again and didn't stop at any of the bars I passed—for once at least avoiding this final crash of the inner and outer economies I was trying to keep balanced. Besides, I'd spent the day's budget on art museums.

When I let myself into the apartment, the roommate was just finishing packing a nylon overnight case. He was going for the weekend, to his girlfriend's place I gathered. He said he'd talked to John this afternoon, and that maybe the back-to-back sessions in detox had had a good effect. He seemed more in touch. Great. I said I'd had a long day. Walked too many miles. He said I'd have the place to myself, but I told him I was moving tomorrow. I couldn't afford life on these upper avenues. At least downtown they'd only steal my things, and let me keep the names.

WHEN IN ROME

On a downtown street corner a man stands among the hurrying crowd yelling *Help—Help!* over and over at the passing midday traffic. He appears to be in no more danger than the rest of us. An everyday cry of loss, alienation. A block farther on, a woman is screaming at a poster on a brick wall. No response. No contact. No firsthand sense. In the middle of Broadway a guy in a greasy suit cries again and again to the people on the sidewalks: *You're gonna burn. You're all gonna burn.* No one even looks. A beggar on the subway stairs: *Be human. Have pity.* No one listens. Another lies unconscious in a puddle of urine on the sidewalk. Nobody stops. Nobody can afford to.

Everything, sooner or later, gets paid for. As everyone knows, later is always more expensive. For most of our time on earth, human transactions have been accompanied by exacting and graceful methods of paying this price, as it came due. What the colonists of the New World called "Indian giving," and then the anthropologists something more polite—like "reciprocal prestation"—was a gradually dawning redisclosure of their own ancient ways of doing business. In culture after culture, for uncounted ages, ways have been found to honor the principle of the gift, which is the source of all life and wealth. Almost universally, the medium of this exchange was beads made of shells.

Shell currency was magic, a contract with the mysteries

which redeem life from death. Shells paid the blood price, for death at the hands of another, the first down payment on the social contract, assuring peace. Shells compensated for the "giving away" of offspring in adoption or marriage, returning the gift and opening exchange between families or tribes. And so shells came to mark agreement between neighbors, and between neighboring nations to be trading partners. Not money, but the mark of a transaction, by which debts got worked out, and agreement was renewed.

But the gift exchange was not invented by ethnographers and conchologists. Its terms were always negotiable, and highly circumstantial. Shell currency was not minted money and differed not only in size and shape but also in its history of previous transactions, and even in its gender. It might have so many relations to its "owner"—with whose family or clan it resided—that it remained a magical object. As a talisman, it continued to be a sign of the procreative abundance of the gods, as we see in those portrayals of Aphrodite arising from a seashell, or the Latin name of the quahog clam, *Venus mercenaria*. One did not lightly "spend" such spiritual "capital." On the other hand, the shell might be ornament, its "use" value—where beauty is accorded its own economic function— precluding its value as currency. So there was always something to work out. It required a great willingness to bargain, and agreement to come to some agreement. It was the token of that good will. Carried or worn on the person, it was a desirable object and expressed the desire for "exchange"—a token recalling the erotic root of all economy and the spirit of natural increase that is the ultimate source of wealth.

I had toured the shell exhibits at the Museum of Natural History, with a friend from home who was also in Manhattan this week. Lunch in the museum restaurant had of course been gorgeous. All glassed-in sunshine and new spring hats and flowers. Even the food was light. Unfortunately, the twelve-dollar tab ate most of that day's living allowance and so included an even lighter dinner. I hoped my dismay was not obvious, but she knew of my general impoverishment and with her usual generosity paid our admission to the museum. Or her museum membership had covered it, because she just gave the man at the door a plastic card and we went on in. We got to spend a long time among the artifacts of the Northwestern tribes, in a room that was said to replicate a Haida council house and the culture of the potlatch. Reminded of the wealth of our rainy coastal home, we would walk and talk the breezy afternoon away, finding ourselves at last footweary and surprised that we had come to the southern tip of the island, watching the ferry boats come and go.

But before we could get out of the museum, like another, heartier lunch, I'd had to feed my obsession, and while she browsed among the moribund flora and fauna, I hovered greedily around the *Man and Mollusk* exhibit, like an otter in an abalone bed. This hunger was something I was still calling "research," though increasingly uncertain where it came from, and what it was for. I had begun to understand that it was something tucked away deep in my own museums. On the first morning back in town, after my somewhat failed pilgrimage into the Iroquois gift economy, I'd awakened with the dream sensation of having held a woven belt of beads. Wampum beads, made of clamshell, heavy, palpable. This dream imparted a sense of solidity that I think carried me through the week that followed, and through the combined onslaught of inner and outer bills come due. For anyone who's chosen live-in exile—or had no choice—the confrontation with Gotham both confirms one's alien status and brings home its personal costs.

It was a comfort to share both dream and alienation with another outsider. At the end of our afternoon's walk, she sweetly dragged me along to the apartment of friends, where I gathered a few hors d'oeuvres with my cocktail and looked out over the wilderness we'd been wandering in. The buildings began to be lighted as evening came on, and the city assumed its jeweled opulence. I knew that she belonged to this lofty world, having inherited a Midwestern hybrid seed patent—but she'd also been endowed with wonderfully generous politics and consistently changed market wealth into gift, much to the benefit of her community. Because of this, and perhaps her blonde hair, I'd always thought she was a reincarnated Corn Goddess, though she considered herself very human and would have been embarrassed by such pretension. I thanked her and our hosts and said good-bye, feeling a renewed sense of perspective, and very well nourished. She even gave me the number of an editor friend to call, and although he would tell me what I already knew—Go home and write your book—I felt better with the paper in my pocket. See you back home, I said, and hummed to myself in the hallway, leaning on the Down button, the chorus of *Baby You're a Rich Man*.

Fortuitously abandoned here by circumstance and bad budgeting, I continued to feed at the lunch counter of public memory, still served in the libraries and museums dedicated to its ongoing credibility. The official version. Every institution, and its popular superstitions, rests upon the mythic bedrock of its founding. That what is actually in the museums and libraries contradicts these public advertisements seems to occur to only a few disturbed scholars and Indians who read treaties. Exhausted by walking, I began to travel the subways, dropping in my tokens at the turnstiles as I came and went beneath the city.

A circulating coinage, even when our pockets are empty of it, is taken for granted as a staple of human life—one of those unseen inventions like a written character or the notation of number that we can't imagine being without. Because money is a comparatively recent invention, and because it merged with or overlaid an older system of exchange, its nature and history are almost invisible to us, found if at all in the darkness of archetypal memory and the obfuscations of money managers. But in general, no one asks—until the day someone refuses to accept or pay our money. We are then supremely surprised, as if all the words in our books had had their meanings altered. Only then do we ask where it came from, and where it went. And if this is called inflation, why do we feel depressed?

The first coins to circulate generally among the western city-states were minted in Tyre, carried and exchanged principally by Phoenician traders.[1] The coin bore an image of a shell that had been highly valued and widely exchanged for the "royal" purple dye that it contained. On the reverse of the coin was the dolphin, the trickster-trader, Hermes of the sea. About the same time, roughly half a millennium before the present era, an emperor in China issued a currency of bronze cowrie shells, as well as miniature bronze agricultural tools, as tokens of the actual shells and tools that had been exchanged traditionally. Many centuries later Marco Polo noted the shells still circulating alongside gold and silver, so it seems that the symbolic marker was never allowed to wholly replace the object of exchange. The Chinese would be the first to experiment with a paper currency, from the ninth century till the fifteenth, when it was abandoned because of the emperors' consistent and disastrous inability to resist its overissue.

What we call coinage is usually considered to have begun when the Mediterranean city-states affixed their official seal to ingots as an assurance of purity and weight. These public assurances began to circulate in the form of coins, referring not only to their commodity value but to the credibility of the issuing body. The images they bore were at first of sacred animals. The stater of Asia minor carried a stag, later a ram. Lydian coins bore the image of the lion, the bull, and the bee. The Athenian owl circulated as widely as the city's cultural influence. It was Alexander the Great who first made a coinage uniform throughout his realm, a brass denomination stamped with the assurance of his own Macedonian likeness. Julius Caesar of course could do no less, and a subsequently imperial Augustus would do it in gold—and from that very beginning, the credit and credibility of the empire began their

1. THE HISTORY THAT follows is based on "Man and Mollusk" and "The World of Coins," displays and accompanying texts at the Museum of Natural History and the American Numismatic Society's Museum, and again on Angell's popular history, *The Story of Money* (Garden City, 1929). Far more clearly than the history of "economics"— what people *thought* they were doing—the history of money reveals a human notation system that at first tries to imitate certain obvious laws of nature— e.g., everything gets paid for—and sooner or later succumbs to the temptation to circumvent those laws and consequently fails, often with disastrous effects. It appears to be a cyclic process, such as that of prey and predator populations, whose increase and decrease has a certain lag time, with consequent die-offs and the belated wisdom of new economic theories.

long and famous decline, at last collapsing under the massive overissue of a copper coinage. The difference—as well as the likeness—between the thing, the spirit of the thing, and the sign of the thing appears to be one too many for people to keep track of.

You would suppose a lesson had been learned, but apparently there is no adaptive mechanism that inoculates human populations against money. So skip a mere two centuries, and Justinian is refinancing imperial credit with a coin that carries the likeness of Christ. Only another century brings us to Charlemagne, whose silver penny would for four hundred years be one of western civilization's most stable tokens of value. Then the Crusades and the plunder of the New World put tons of coinage into royal coffers—often minted on site, as the Spanish preferred, and shipped back as ready money—and of course every coin carried a portrait of the head of state, so its citizens would suppose that to be where wealth originated. They did not see they had come upon their own New World likeness: early economies of the sun and moon, linked to the earth by the constant remittance of its brightest gifts. Centralized city-states—Cuzco, Tenochtitlán—waiting like a ransom to the gods of time.

And then there is the other, material side of the coin, on which the image of a commodity was represented. For a long time before there was money—and between times, when there was none again—a surplus commodity would often serve money's purposes. Apparently the cow was the first such living certificate of wealth, replacing the shell as pastoralists replaced hunters and gatherers. Although the process was far more complex than a narrative of museum displays can suggest, there is a clear general outline of an increasing capacity for, and interest in, the accumulation of wealth—and a need to indicate quantities too large to easily store or exchange. As with the later agrarian utensil-money, a symbolic object was at first substituted for the actual thing. A cowhide represented in bronze was already in circulation during the Homeric age, long before the bull's and ram's head coinage that would be current during the millennium or so of range wars that were to follow. Among agriculturalists the image would be of the olive, the sheaf of barley, the wine cup. A coastal city would stamp a tuna on its coinage, a manufacturing town the image of the bronze double axe. All of these—at first in fact, and later in theory—redeemable in the thing itself.

The invention of money appears to be coterminous, first with grazing and farming, and subsequently with the rise of the state. The highly centralized empires of Egypt and China, however, did without its use or tried and abandoned it as too dangerous an expedient. Merchants for some millennium and a half did without it, substituting such devices as clay promissory notes for the actual commodity. The Greek *symbolon* was such a note, broken into two pieces that could be redeemed only against the other half. While the dynastic city-states did issue coins of gold or electrum, they appear to have been diplomatic symbols of power as much as denominators of trade. The Athenians, with access to silver mines, issued a coinage that was remarkably stable over a long period of time, with all the appearance of sound democratic monetary principles. Of course, as with democracy itself, they also experienced some remarkable failures—so that before Solon's laws, it was not unusual for fields to appear to be growing stone mortgage columns rather than crops. The Spartans, fearing similar disaster, specifically prohibited its use. The fable of Midas and an abundance of ancient lore provided eloquent testimony as to the dangers of metallic wealth.

But say that money is roughly coincident with certain conditions that gave rise to the state. It came about as part of that great and relatively recent break in the continuity of human culture that we distinguish—perhaps prematurely—as the end of the Stone Age. Where in broad terms we can see that property-owning, patrilineal, bronze-wielding cultures supplanted the communal, matrilineal, gift-exchanging cultures—arrangements that had gotten us through the difficulties of the ages, including those that money won't buy us out of. If we take dictatorial materialism as its ultimate expression, and plutonium as its ultimate commodity, it may be that money is one of those evolutionary dead ends that the pale-ontologists puzzle over. At best it is an experiment, with so far few encouraging results.

The experience of Rome, as it rose and fell, appears to be typical. It began with a coinage that was part of the social contract, as much a part of the *res publica* as its laws and gra-naries, a device for allocating the common wealth. But the old household gods began to be alienated from the *familia,* and real property to be distinguished from personal. As it let go its agreements with the spirit of the gift, residing in all things, the state abandoned its plain brass coinage and be-came enamored of gold. Under the irresistible promises of gold, money became an end rather than a means—as if the spirit resided only in that bright coin—and a still-remem-bered orgy of materialism gave rise to the wild speculative device they called *moneta.* These confusions of money with wealth created many conditions familiar to our present state, with the same consequent erosion of value and enduring de-pression. Gold and silver eventually went into the private hoards that are still being dug up today, and the brass coinage became so debased that it had to be exchanged by weight rather than number. Thus the empire returned to regional barter—that is to say, there was no longer an empire.

But the inability to deal with the money abstraction is usually a failure to control either term of the symbolic equa-tion. So not only were Rome's valuations skewed by avarice, but the imperial mines in Spain and Greece eventually played out, with a consequent dearth of silver and gold that lasted till the crusades and the conquest of Mexico and Peru. This dou-ble bind, where things inflate and disappear along with the spirit of things, was of course compounded by the urgent and great expense of the wars required to keep the whole system —both credit and credibility—moving along on an imperial scale. Read about it in the *Times.*

Although money has disastrously failed us on countless occasions, we suppose there's no choice but to give it our faith and, as willing victims of mass delusion, endow it with a greater reality than the wealth it was supposed to represent. Whoever then controls it, controls our lives. When Germany was stricken with devastating inflation in the 1920s, after paying its huge war indemnities, those who carried marks in wheelbarrows to the bakery were reported to be unaware their currency had collapsed. To them, it seemed the value of bread had unaccountably risen by a factor of some thousands. Probably our understanding in these matters has not progressed much beyond that of the ancient Carthaginians, who issued a metal coin enclosed in a sealed wrapping of parchment or leather, on which was declared its value. And perhaps the words Don't Ask—because if the seal had been broken, because you doubted or shaved off some of that value—then your money was no good. But even Carthage did not heed this wisdom for long and was rich in gold and silver coin when plundered and destroyed.

2. WITH ITS REMAINING museum collection (now in the custody of the Smithsonian) moved to newer quarters, scholars will no doubt miss the library's gothic atmosphere, the picturesque ride there on the Pelham Bay, and the sociological charm of its old Bronx neighborhood. The Stock Exchange, the Museum of Natural History, and the Museum of the City of New York, where the rest of this story was gathered, so far as I know still occupy their former locations.

❀ ❀ ❀

For a week I wandered the New York boroughs visiting the open shrines of language and money. I rode the subways till the tiled walls began to look like rows of shell beads between destinations. From the library of the Heye Foundation[2]—an old brick edifice in the Bronx where an ancient doorkeeper at last was convinced that I had an appointment and let me into the dim rows of oak tables and drawers of index cards—to the public frenzy of the stock exchange floor, where traders behind bulletproof glass jumped and shouted inaudibly to electronic impulses, hundreds of excited messengers crowded together in a great room, pushing or talking on phones or staring at lit-up boards, standing amid the litter of short-lived information strewn everywhere.

It appears that once it had "bought in" with shell beads, the economic practice of the old world readily transplanted to the new—where there was abundant natural wealth to cover its habitual deficits. We witness the same struggle to keep a credible face on its currency, the public espousal of republican virtues while slavery and plunder fill the treasury, a widening gap between imperial symbols and colonial realities—a gap enlarged now by the new "freedom" from old moral restraints—it all appears to describe a seamless, continuous artifact of human illusion, from the days of Croesus to the appearance of the first Diner's Card. The City is a monument to that illusion, to the space between the show-biz glitz and the actual do-re-mi—that space always inhabited by those souls preferring to trade inside.

It began as an agreement between certain white commercial gentlemen. In Federal Hall, down at Wall and Broad Streets, the first Congress of the United States had issued $80 million in stock (we would say government bonds) to pay the debts of its war with the king. In the following year, a similar issue created the capital of Secretary Hamilton's National Bank. To fill the need for a marketplace in which to exchange these notes of security, on the 17th of May, 1792, under a sycamore on Wall Street, another group of some two dozen patriots instituted the New York Stock Exchange. Their principal place of business for a time would be the Tontine Coffee House, named after the twelfth-century Italian banker who invented the classic monetary pact of brotherhood—keep it in the family. In the name of the new nation, although its legislative functions were moved south, the island of Manhattan retained the financial status of a city-state. During the early years of the nineteenth century, the city would issue its own paper notes for the trading convenience of its citizens. Some of the first securities traded on its exchange were those of the city's waterworks, the Manhattan Company, which later became Chase Manhattan, collecting and dispensing an even more liquid medium. Most of the securities were purchased, then as now, by foreign interests, who must have considered they had not lost a colony but gained an investment. The first woman was admitted to the exchange in 1967, the history adds as an afterthought. Nothing is said of Indians.

A tourist asked our guide through the exchange if the

ticker tape ever stopped, and she said in an absolute tone: *NO.*
It was as if we were in the presence of an immortal. A great,
inflated hungry device of the human mind, its importance
magnified in the words it uses to talk about itself. It refers to
"a total Facilities Upgrade program, currently in progress."
Eleven computers were being installed, creating systemic
acronyms that are spoken like the names of deities. DOT is
the Designated Order Turnaround system. ITS is not the
neuter possessive, but Intermarket Trading System. Within
five months, on a Black Monday in October, this foolproof
market would crash 508 points, a fall exacerbated by this
computerized trading system, along with yet another ingenious device known as portfolio insurance, guaranteeing
against exactly such losses. These occasional financial epipha-
nies—a sudden awareness that the whole structure is a lunatic human creation that thrives on abstraction, distortion,
and the creation and selling of privileged information—seem
to linger only briefly in the public consciousness. Memory
loss is apparently one of the symptoms of this public demen-
tia, and it seems to affect the mind of everyone who carries
the delusion in their pockets and purses.

My hosts' lower Broadway loft doubles as a photo studio, and
while I'm away all day a cottage industry pays the bills.
When I return, business is winding down, their daughter has
been picked up from her school, and dinner is being discussed. One night they generously invited me to join them,
and afterward Mike and I sat at the table talking about the
need for money, why and how much, and where the need
comes from. In the morning he asked me if I'd pose for some
shots, and as a grateful guest I naturally obliged. Another
night I had dinner with his sister who I remembered meeting
once out West. We went to a restaurant in Soho that advertised California cuisine. It resembled nothing I recalled eating
in California, at prices neither coast could afford. But we were

both feeling impoverished and, with the curious logic of the noncommercial classes, felt the need to squander what little we had.

She and her husband were in tight circumstances—literally, the apartment too small, their bills too much, their lives too intense, she had explained when I'd called looking for places to stay. Despite the fact that their cost of living was already too high, however, they were going to move to a place down here where it was even more expensive. Developers were putting unbearable pressure on their block, not to mention the pressures within of having to make so much money just to pay back the money they already owed for the taxes and drugs you had to pay for if you wanted to make enough money to keep living. He couldn't join us for dinner because he was working late in the sound studio for the Japanese recording company that was not going to pay unless they got their digitally remastered tapes done *now*. We split the forty-dollar tab, and to help digest it she walked me by the windows of local shops, full of beautiful and very expensive artifacts and commodities. Where the insiders shop, I supposed, and the rest of us wander the sidewalk museums looking in.

She turned out to be a knowledgeable and streetwise guide to the ways of the city-state. She pointed out the women with curiously large purses, capacious enough to hold the high heels they carried while on the street, where they wore running shoes. She stopped me from giving change to a beggar on a corner—"With that location? He's making more than both of us." When I got back to my cot in the sewing room, I felt somewhat happy and deranged. The food had been unimaginative, the beautiful things not particularly desirable, but something about walking amid the wealth display with a charming and vibrant woman created a wonderful illusion of richness. On the bedside table was a release form for the photos, granting permission to reproduce my likeness. I felt my moment of wealth and fame.

There are psychologists whose practice is exclusively the counseling of those who suffer from the neuroses of money.

3. FROM HARRISON'S *Messages and Letters* (1922) quoted in Billington, *America's Frontier Story*, 258–60. Following the usual pattern, once the invaders purchase a foothold, they dispense with the ritual of presents, drop the supply of trade goods, and take up the more lucrative market of supplying the new settlers' dependencies. In the final stage of relations, the appeal for gunsmiths is a constant note of two centuries of frontier transactions. The fatal irony of this dependence appears to have gone largely unremarked.

It is so addictive that it draws even casual users into delusional and obsessive modes of behavior. This is traditional lore, as old as the idea of easily convertible wealth. What I would ask the money doctors, if I could afford the treatment, is how this public and private madness overwhelmed the New World, colonized and bought and sold this land and its inhabitants and left us here in our present poverty. And how —and with what—are we possibly going to redeem this indebtedness of the spirit?

And doesn't the doctor always then ask: When did you begin to experience this condition?

🌼 🌼 🌼

Brother. Do not believe that I came here to get presents from you; if you offer us anything we will not take it. By taking goods from you you will hereafter say that with them you purchased another piece of land from us.[3]

Tecumseh's speech to General Harrison reads like a farewell address from the bead-exchanging nations east of the Mississippi. It was delivered at Vincennes, territorial capitol of Indiana, in the late summer of 1810, in response to the "treaty" that appropriated their lands. The Shawnee had learned too late the distinction between "giving" and "buying." But the speech also makes it clear that they are no longer able to disentangle themselves from the economy of alienable wealth.

If we want anything we are able to buy it, from your traders. Since the land was sold to you no traders come among us. I now wish you would clear all the roads and let the traders come among us. Then perhaps some of our young men will occasionally call upon you to get their guns repaired. This is all the assistance we ask of you.

This mixture of defiance and appeal came with the too-late

recognition of who they were dealing with—Tecumseh has to
ask General Harrison, How can we believe you people who
have murdered your own prophet and laugh at "the shaken
among you"—a perception accompanied by the helpless acknowledgment of the dependencies the Europeans had
brought them.

With his back to the Mississippi, his British allies of
doubtful allegiance, I imagine in Tecumseh's speech a gestur-
ing hand, now threatening and now offering and now implor-
ing by turns. With typical openness, he describes his plans for
alliance, saying they will gather at the Huron Village, "where
the great Belts of all the tribes are kept." This is the only
mention of the shell beads that fifty years earlier would have
outlined and given unity of tone to a less impossible set of
choices. A little over a year later, while Tecumseh was still out
exchanging war belts and gathering allies, his brother the
Prophet led a premature raid against the Americans. Harrison
seized upon this motive for the war he had been trying to
provoke and systematically attacked and destroyed the
Shawnee towns of the upper Wabash. This action would later
earn him the presidency of a grateful United States. Two
years later, Tecumseh would be dead, the confederate nations
scattered and in exile.

The devolution of the bead exchange in North America
has much in common with the economic decline of modern
nations, where material value deteriorates along with the
failure of the social contract. Here is the ethnonumismatic account:

*Although the United States government continued to
use wampum in its dealings with the tribes of the Mississippi valley until about 1830, the value of shell beads
dropped rapidly. During the years 1802–1811, grey and
white wampum sold in the U.S. Government fur trading
posts at varying prices. In 1806 the grey (purple)
wampum sold at $3.75 per thousand beads while white
wampum was $2.25 per thousand. The government*

ordered beads in large quantities, some orders going as high as 28,000 beads, and on special occasions running into the hundreds of thousands. In 1810, grey wampum was $3.00 per thousand and white, $1.75 per thousand. By the 1830s and 1840s, wampum beads supplied to Indians west of the Mississippi and around the Great Lakes were used primarily as ornaments.[4]

4. ARTHUR WOODWARD, *The Denominators of the Fur Trade* (Pasadena, 1970)—summarizes the varied symbolic uses of wampum but confuses its abandonment as a coinage of trade with spiritual demise: "Wampum, as such, has virtually passed out of existence but the term is perpetuated in our language and future generations will know it in name only." As if it were the Vanishing American's disappearing coin trick.

When the Campbell Brothers' bead factory in New Jersey closed its doors with the waning of the nineteenth century, it had done its work thoroughly. At the end, wampum was produced on a machine that made six beads at a time. The last of the local indigenous people were no longer employed there, having been removed to a reservation in the Dakotas. The factory briefly reopened in 1905 to produce enough wampum beads to satisfy the demands of museums and collectors.

So the beads became valued as works of art, objects of adornment, the prize of collectors and "cultural presenters"— like old coins we would put under glass or wear as jewelry. A dead currency. But it should be clear by now that there are many who consider the beads still current and alive, and representative of contracts that remain in effect. That the words and things and spirit may still be strung together. It is not surprising that this claim should be resisted by our public institutions. The despiritualizing of wampum was only the first stage of a larger, still ongoing misappropriation. The "killing" of the gift contract is in fact the prototype of modern economic warfare, whereby one nation purposely destabilizes the economy of another. It is a literal devaluation of its social bonds, weakening its resistance to more overt invasions— such as Hitler's Germany, with all it had learned about hyperinflation, inflicted upon neighboring Austria. Or our CIA, upon people too numerous to mention. What is less visible is its internal application, where populations within a state are so attacked, and their souls go one way and the money goes the other. And this does not apply only to Indian reservations —the streets of the city are now the edge of this internal frontier. The trading post is run by the real emperor of the Empire State, who does for his customers on a daily basis. He's the man with the hand in every transaction. The ticket from the image to the real thing, in his hand. Today the soul's currency is crack cocaine, but it could just as well be bread and spectacle, gin for the London poor, opium for the Chinese —or if you prefer, government wampum. The deterioration of material value almost as fast as the failure of social bonds. The shell game has not changed nor have its effects.

🐚 🐚 🐚

I left my downtown hosts, with heartfelt thanks and the gift of a thin chapbook of poems. I said nothing about the photo release, which had proved impossible to sign after all and lay still on the night table. I hated to appear ungrateful but was feeling weird and paranoid about soul loss, perhaps because I placed too much value on my likeness. Lord knows I had laid some serious debits to that person's account lately. My last night in town I moved back up to the west nineties, bone weary and glad to be going. My ventures out into the City had become more cautious and circumscribed as I gradually understood where I was. I'd had a close encounter in the Bowery, wandering at half tilt on a full-moon night where I shouldn't have been. I was keeping an eye out for the guys to my left, leaning against a beat-up yellow Pontiac—only the day before I'd slid into a departing train just ahead of another such likely bunch of young entrepreneurs on a Bronx subway platform.

So I didn't see the werewolf until he was just over my right shoulder. Before the reflex even reached the fight-or-flight area of my somewhat distracted brain, two blue sleeves with hands gripping a nightstick came over his head and yanked him backward by the throat. The sudden rush of con-flicting messages must have canceled each other, because I didn't break my pace or look to either side, and only later did I become sensible enough to realize I should have been scared. All this time carrying a traveling stash among people who could probably smell it.

And now this morning as I gathered up my belongings— I'd mailed home most of the books I'd been collecting and carrying and had just come up from the basement with clean laundry—I was already moving around with the slow, stunned gait of the habitually battered and depressed, when the screaming started coming up from the street below. It came up nine floors as if from across the street, a woman's terrified and repeated *No . . . No . . . No,* and after what seemed a long time a man's voice from somewhere, apparently shouting at her assailant, *Stop it . . . Stop it . . . ,* on and on, her voice and then his, until the screams grew quiet and the man stopped yelling. By the time I'd finished packing and left a note for my host, who this time had apparently stayed in detox, a police car had arrived, its siren a low and weary moan echoing up between the hundreds of empty windows. From the bedroom I could see little knots of neighbors standing on the opposite sidewalk and corner. I couldn't see what had happened, and I was grateful. I tried to summon up the dream of only a week ago, that sense of a thing solid and paid for, so that someone or something wasn't always at our backs coming to collect. And I prayed to be taken out of this pile of mortgage stones, this IOU to the gods.

THE ORIGIN OF THE FAMILY

We'd gotten ours, the woman next to me recalled, as we leaned against the fender of the station wagon and looked out over the valley and the swollen spring river below us. She was known for a rather mordant sense of irony.

We were standing on a high bluff overlooking the upper Mississippi valley, in southern Minnesota where in summer you can throw a rock across the river. Way down below at the river's edge was the small town of Winona, last wood-loading stop for the paddle steamers bound upstream. Now one of those out-of-the way towns that became resettlement areas following the deflowering of the sixties, and then a haven for shopkeepers and cultural impresarios in the acquisitive times that followed.

Up there on the bluff, a brass plate attached to a large piece of granite describes the merits of Wapasha or Wabasha, a northern Sioux warrior who helped the U.S. army overcome their traditional Sauk adversaries. Together they annihilated Black Hawk's people, who made the mistake of coming back across the river to reclaim their former agricultural lands. It was the early 1830s, still plenty of time before the Great Panic. People were intent on getting rich. It was a new generation of Americans, and they were going to get what was theirs—even if it wasn't theirs.

Looking out at the now peaceful seeming land, I had to

agree that she and I probably got what we had coming. We had spent a year or so of intense craziness together—or not together—and beneath our abiding affection for each other was a determination not to reenact the damage of those days and nights of smoke and mirrors. She had her infant daughter now, as well as the older boy, and as handholder and godfather I'd seen from the beginning how the child helped her get her life back on center—including her move here, back to where she'd once built a house and had a life, to this peaceful source of inland waters, a healthy distance from that broken Pacific edge. I had envied many of my hosts the security and comfort of their lives but hadn't expected to feel that here. I had detoured out of Chicago on the way home in order to check out her new life, see how they were doing. Now I wondered if my own couldn't use some of this stability. She was even engaged to be married, to a wealthy Chicago lawyer who had been proposing for years. Sometimes it seems like the only economy is the enormous carrying charges of our wandering affections.

Her ex, the one she'd built the house with, asked if I knew about the so-called Black Hawk War. No, I hadn't read much about it but remembered a note of the Reverend Beauchamp to the effect that Black Hawk had been the last to use wampum belts to make alliances. That was 1832. A period of great national spending and speculation was at full flood. Relations with the inhabitants had passed to the new westerners, a generation of self-serving jingoists who regarded them as intruders in their own country. East of the Mississippi, there was simply no place for Indians. Progress had come to rule, and progress was measured by the money it cost to secure possession of the land. Bruce gave me some documents of the transaction:

> *I have paid sixty-seven of your Sioux; the remainder, thirty-one will be here, it is said, in a few days. I found it impossible to get all at one time. The first who came with whom was Wabashaw; the French Crow, and most of the*

principal men wanted me to give them the money with-
out division and they would divide it. When convinced
that I would not do that they received their portions with
much complaining as to the quantity and they say
inequality of the division.

They . . . desired I would say to you and to their
Great Father that they wanted to be placed under my
agency; or in other words, "we want you for our father;
and we want you to pay us our money, to take the man-
agement of our shop, and of our agricultural establish-
ment." They also complained of the want of oxen etc. I
briefly answered that I would let you know their wishes,
and—if their G.F. directed—I would be their agent, etc.[1]

1. RETURN I. HOLCOMBE, *Minnesota in Three Centuries* (Publishing Society of Minnesota, 1908), 193–94. This official version, the letter of U.S. Indian Agent Joseph Street, continues, "they are a discontented people and hard to please," which would apparently justify the economic paternalism of the "G.F." who replaces the exchange relations of warrior society.

This picture of Indian/white relations, in which the cash economy has completely replaced the bead exchange, is a process by now familiar. But where it once was content to leave internal relations to the confederate or independent nations, the character of the newborn American had apparently acquired a spiritual hunger that would prove to be nearly unanswerable, except by a devouring—an incorporation—of land and wealth that would eventually leave us the reservation system and the warfare-welfare state. Even the Iroquois, who had made their peace with the pre-United States generations, found they were not immune from this process of de-personalizing and despiritualizing the land, and the removal of all but monetary values. What is presently referred to as "ethnic cleansing," or simply genocide, followed by the usual appropriations of vacant property.

Some control system apparently failed to function, not just in the horrible slaughter of presumably soulless indi-genes that characterized the initial invasions of the Americas but as a national policy that called for the extermination or expulsion of everything not like itself—of everything, that is, unprofitable. Outrageous land claims were revived—the six million acres, for example, supposed to have been ceded to Plymouth colony by James I and then ceded to New York by

Massachusetts in 1786, was again discounted by its Dutch holders and wholesaled to the Ogden Land Company—which with the usual bags of money and barrels of whiskey went about purchasing what remained of the reservations granted the Iroquois after the revolution. A group of some two hundred Seneca even agreed to be bought out entirely and moved to Kansas, where many of them died, and whence the remainder returned complaining bitterly of the climate and hostile inhabitants.

The devastation of native material life, in the pursuit of material gain for the Euro-American, was not without its spiritual side. An enormous outpouring of sympathy for Indians seems to have sprung up almost as fast as they were being removed—sometimes at the same moment. A Lieutenant Anderson, among the troops attacking Black Hawk's people on the Wisconsin shore, where the steamboat *Warrior* prevented them from crossing back over the Mississippi, sent the following account of the "battle" to a popular periodical:

> *When our troops charged the enemy in their defiles near the bank of the Mississippi, men, women, and children were soon mixed together in such a manner as to render it difficult to kill one and save the other. A young squaw of about nineteen stood in the grass at a short distance from our line, holding her little girl in her arms, about four years old. While thus, standing, apparently unconcerned, a ball struck the right arm of the child above the elbow and shattered the bone, passing into the breast of its young mother, who instantly fell to the ground. She fell upon the child and confined it to the ground also. During the rest of the battle the child was heard to groan and call for relief, but none had come to offer it, when, however, the Indians had retreated from the spot, and the battle had nearly finished, Lieutenant Anderson (the writer) of the United States army, went to the spot and took from under the dead mother her wounded daughter and brought it to the place we had selected for surgical*

aid. It was soon ascertained that its arm must come off,
and the operation was performed without drawing a tear
or a shriek. The child was eating a piece of hard biscuit
during the operation. It was brought to Prairie du Chien
and we learn that it has nearly recovered. This was
among the many scenes calculated to draw forth a sym-
pathetic tear for human misery.[2]

This gruesome piety, though it may spare an injured child or
two, can only be seen now as the dissociation of a violent psy-
chotic. The reality—that an army of iron-age speculator/
farmers is brutally annihilating and forcefully appropriating
the territory of a band of stone-age agriculturist/hunters—is
lost in the blur of patriotic sympathies. A certain amount of
schizophrenia was probably required to get the job done. Not
too surprisingly, at about the same time as this great outpouring of emotion based on public images of Indians—appropriating the cult of the Savage, as well as his property—the
populace of the new nation was undergoing a prolonged spell
of religious awakenings and revival.

Upstate New York appears to have been a principal fountain of this spiritual rebirth, and Joseph Smith was certainly
the quintessential type of its receivers. His vision, inspired in
part by ancient burial mounds, traced the word of God from
its origins to Elmira, New York, by way of the lost tribes of
Israel popularly supposed to be the ancestor of these remnants of the Iroquois scattered on reservations. Again with
that psychic dissociation which was apparently necessary to
"the establishment of American civilization," federal soldiers
and Indian agents were removing all material sign of the
land's inhabitants, while prophets and popular writers appropriated what were taken to be their spiritual roots. Lewis
Henry Morgan and the anthropology industry began as a
natural outgrowth of this economic and spiritual vampirism.

The final irony of this unconscious process occurs when
the born-again Euro-American then takes up a collection to
send missionaries to save the souls of Indians. During the

2. THE OFFICIAL VERSION
again (*Minnesota in Three
Centuries*, 196). "In all
its gory," as Bruce Hittner
inscribed the copy he
generously mailed me
later—"another view
of the Black Hawk war."
Holcombe, the Minnesota
historian, proudly offers
Lt. Anderson's account
as a piece of western
Americana—already
reprinted in the *Niles
Register*, as if that were a
new gospel. Note that this
policy of disinformation
and propaganda
(dissociation and denial,
to put it clinically) was
developed two centuries
earlier in the extermination
of New England's
indigenous population.

The life and work of
Bruce Hittner (1950–94)
acknowledged this "lost"
regional history and
incorporated it into
our present lives.

3. RED JACKET'S SPEECH IS
quoted in Wallace, *Death
and Rebirth of the Seneca*,
206, from Samuel
Drake's *Biography and
History* (1837).

1830s, at the peak of this period of material and spiritual inflation, three or four missionary groups were competing for
Indian souls in western New York State. This in addition to
the Quakers, who had been working among the Iroquois since
the 1790s. The traditional response to these spiritual overtures
was stated with clarity by the Seneca chief Red Jacket:

> *Brother, you say you have not come to get our land or
> our money, but to enlighten our minds. I will now tell
> you that I have been at your meetings and saw you col-
> lecting money from the meeting. I cannot tell what this
> money was intended for, but suppose it was for your
> minister, and if we should conform to your way of think-
> ing, perhaps you may want some from us.*
>
> *Brother, we are told that you have been preaching to
> white people in this place: these people are our neighbors,
> we are acquainted with them: we will wait a little while
> and see what effect your teaching has upon them. If we
> find it does them good, makes them honest, and less dis-
> posed to cheat Indians, we will then consider again what
> you have said.*[3]

But many native people, under the influence of exceptional
individuals, did adopt Christian ways. Well before the revolution, all the Oneida and many among the other nations had
become Christianized. Long before that, a number of Mohawk
had moved north under the influence of the Jesuits, and the
martyred Kateri Tekanawitha is still the namesake of many
reservation churches. These changes of theology did not nec-
essarily conflict with the ceremonies of the Longhouse, although in practice traditional customs were looked down on
by the missionaries and their converts. Perhaps the deepest effect of the missionaries was this new cultural self-conscious-
ness—no doubt instilled partly by the spiritual lectures of
their self-appointed saviors—but also by the sheer psychic
shock of the collective encounter with the aliens.

Euro-American culture, such as there was, and although it

got a lot wrong, was also strongly influenced by native culture, and even by the way Indians regarded its odd and nasty
habits. The shock was mutual and is still being felt. But it arrived suddenly and almost irresistibly for the indigenous culture. Seeing themselves as they were seen, the inhabitants
eventually abandoned the practice of ritual torture and cannibalism—clearly, it enacted satisfactions in a manner much too
direct for most Europeans, without the sanction of religious
or political inquisition. Just as later, because it was hardly
consonant with the picture of the noble savage in a sentimental pastoral, the Christianized Iroquois altogether abandoned
the white dog feast.

But while the Christian and Indian pantheons accepted
each other with some slight alterations to the spiritual longhouse—somewhat as the political League went about "adding
rafters" to accommodate newly adopted agreements—in the
realm of everyday material practice there were some serious
details to be worked out. Since no distinction was made between religious theory and the way one lived, conversion for
the inhabitants became synonymous with the abandonment
of the stone-age economy at its source—in its transactions
with the spirit world. Of course there were advocates of doing
exactly that, and the dispute was bitter and sometimes divi-
sive and continues to this day. But the missionaries were the
agents of changes that were probably inevitable for a culture
that had just gotten a crash course in fifty centuries of
Western Civilization and then been left on reservations and
told to change or die. The government sent small annuities
and under George Washington took some steps toward technical assistance. It was felt that this would not only set indigenous people farming, but as Secretary of War Philander Chase
Knox put it, teach them "a love for exclusive property."

It was the Society of Friends, of Philadelphia, who seemed
best to grasp what was needed and stepped in when the half-
hearted government assistance programs failed. To the
Seneca they proposed a four-year incentive plan:

Brothers, We will give to every Indian Man, living on this river, who shall raise 25 Bushels of Wheat or Rye in one year, on his own land, not worked by white people, the sum of two Dollars.

2. For every 50 Bushel of Indian Corn raised by any one Indian Man, in like manner aforesaid the sum of two dollars.

3. For every 50 Bushel of Potatoes raised by any one Indian Man, in like manner aforesaid, the sum of two Dollars.

4. For every 2 Tons of Hay raised as aforesaid, and put into a stack or Barn, not being mown or drawn in by white people, the sum of two Dollars.

5. For every 12 yards of linen Cloth, made by any Indian woman, out of flax raised on her own, or her husbands land, & spun in her own house, the sum of two Dollars to be paid to the Woman.

6. For every 12 yards of woolen Cloth, or linsey made by any Indian woman, out of the wool of her own, or her husband's sheep, & Spun in her own house the sum of two Dollars, to be paid to the Woman.[4]

The proposal to plow and spin for dollars was no doubt as ridiculous then as now, but it did at least address the issue of how to live among people who kept accounts in this manner. It obviously appealed to the women's interest in keeping a distinct power in the household economy—they were surrendering, after all, the essential role of agricultural providers. On the other hand, it held little appeal for young warriors who not long before would have been ridiculed by the women for doing their work and told to wear a dress. They gave little weight to old Cornplanter's urging of white people's ways—even he acknowledged he had let himself be cheated by the whites out of much of their former hunting grounds.

But the Quakers were as resourceful in argument as in practical affairs. They countered that similar difficulties had been overcome in even more desperate cases. The Quakers told them of "a people who lived beyond the great waters in another island, who many years ago lived much like they do now," yet who had woven some of the linen they were wearing. Meaning, we are to suppose, that if the Irish tribes could be civilized and made useful, there was hope for the Iroquois. After some negotiation, model farm and technical assistance programs were undertaken, which had a lasting and beneficial effect on material life. The inner life, the Quakers considered, would speak for itself.

The picture of a European paying an Indian to grow corn is dark with historical irony. But its deepest shades are to be found in the issue of who was doing the planting. If the gift transaction with the spirit world is the soul of economy, its heart is the production and sharing of food. The tribal people who undertook to live among whites were faced with a revolutionary realignment of men's and women's roles in domestic life. From earliest contact, European male observers had been struck by the authority of women in the New World. In the domestic, religious, and political life of the Longhouse, it appeared that women wielded all the decision-making powers, that men owned practically nothing and when not on the hunt or war path seemed to be rather indolent and irresponsible dependents.

Marriages were arranged by the matrons of each family, the ceremony a simple gift exchange of venison and corn; if a marriage was dissolved by one or both parties, the woman retained both her property and her children. Women owned not only the household and its furnishings but the earth itself, and although men might clear new fields for their shifting mode of agriculture and participate in the harvest and corn-shucking ceremony, it was the matrons of each longhouse who directed the storage and disposition of food among its several fires and families. Seed and agricultural implements and the modes of production were theirs, and no feast or ceremony or expedition could go forward without their provisioning. This is the deeper power beneath their political and religious "rights," which were considerable: to nominate and depose the councillors of the League, to choose from among themselves and the men the "faith-keepers" who directed ceremonial life, and to select the officers of medicine societies that assured personal and collective well-being.

When Red Jacket announced in council with the Americans, "We are the owners of the land, and it is ours," he was not speaking for the male Council of Chiefs, but for the women whose representatives they were. But neither was he referring to the "right" of ownership, as we commonly understand it in terms of private property. Women had "economic" power not so much because they "owned" the means of production but because they embodied the principles of hospitality for which the Longhouse was noted, and the deeper principle of nature's own generosity. Ceremonial life consisted in great part of festivals of thanksgiving, celebrating the Three Sisters—corn, beans, and squash—as well as the maple, the strawberry, and the life-giving abundance of a feminine nature. Thus along with the store of food, the matrons also kept furs and quill- and feather-work and belts of wampum. Women were keepers of the gift. And when, for example, at the end of the Ritual of Condolence, the condoling moiety lets "escape" its women to the mourners, it is a gift relation that does not presuppose ownership, no more than if it were the earth herself.

But by the 1830s American culture had no memory of these relations and had created in their stead the familiar sexual and cultural scripts of the modern Wild West show, with all the basic features of our present foreign policy and domestic life. If it were not already evident in the destruction of the Shawnee alliance, or along the Trail of Tears, the Black Hawk War gave clear testimony of a new devaluation of everything not like this new America, and of the tactics of simple genocide that would enforce it.

Despite the rifles of the sentimental but utterly merciless "Indian fighters"—and the cannon mounted on the steamboat they had named *Warrior*—a few of Black Hawk's people made it back across the Mississippi. It was too much for Wabasha and his mercenaries, who had no heart for such massacre and withdrew from the battle. Only when goaded and shamed by the American officers did they join in the butcher and scalping of the survivors.

5. THE OFFICIAL HISTORY
and tone of the frontier
again, where *give* might
be translated *take from.*

"Go home to your squaws and hoe corn," said General Street to Wabasha and the already shamed warriors.

> *Your Great Father gives you some flour and pork to eat;*
> *you have no stomachs for war. Go home to your squaws*
> *and hoe corn.*[5]

Clearly a great change has taken place, where it appears that in the space of generations a great transition of power has swept away all recognition of the feminine principle that governed North America. The self-consciously Indianesque rhetoric, the posturing Great Father who usurps the female role of food provider, the demeaning implications of "your squaws"—all this reveals that the issue of Whose Land is deeply tied to questions of male authority. And that the patriarchal domination of land and life has come about through its overturning of economy at its root, in the roles and relations of domestic life. If for no other reason, tribal people had to be removed because they provided an example that ran contrary to this new patriarchal doctrine, an attribution of gifts that Western Civilization had gone to considerable trouble to suppress.

We'd had a couple of years to get over it, a Saturday afternoon to drive around and look across the river to the Wisconsin shore and talk about it, and now in the middle of May a june-bug Sunday afternoon to sit on the porch and laugh at what remained. A foolish bar-life affair, not conducted with great

brilliance or discretion, it was made worse by betrayals and ill-
ness and the drugs of choice that balled up all the pain and put
it off till later. After a year or so of this emotional pinball, we
had careened off at our different tangents, looking for people
and places to hold us safely, and finding of course only more of
the instability we carried within us. I'd had to see that this trip
was partly an attempt to briefly escape that cycle. I told myself
I was here for the distance.

By the time our time together was done, we'd gone from
intense combatants to a couple of retired generals who could
sit on the porch and rock the baby and discuss the strategy
and tactics of love and domesticity. It was the issue of living
together that had most driven us apart, whenever we needed
an issue. I was caretaking—it wasn't in the deal, I pleaded. I
was getting to live in the house as partial payment for having
worked as a carpenter to build it. I was receiving unemployment and looked forward to getting some writing done. She
on the other hand worked nights as a bartender and days as a
reader, making nickels and dimes that were duly deducted
from her AFDC—all to support her and her young son in the
cute little bungalow that rented for a fortune, and cost another to keep her back injury as warm as she thought
California should be. It drove me nuts to think about, and
even more nuts to think of doing anything about it, and that's
where it ended.

So then two or three years later—over the waffle and coffee and cigarettes we regularly shared, at a restaurant that offered neutral space and all the blandness of Christian cuisine
—this same woman is telling me she's going to have another
child and didn't I think that was a good idea. Right, I said,
knowing I had nothing to say about it anyway. Only she didn't
want the father to know. Right again, I said, realizing I'd just
become a godparent. And then it turned out that motherhood
transformed her into a model of organization and sobriety.
She'd even stopped smoking, and now would only let me
smoke on the porch. Fine, I said. I'm quitting anyway.

And so there we sat, in this valley of an upper Mississippi afternoon, under the shade of an already leafing elm, her infant daughter beside her on her son's lap, and she the smiling ironic madonna at the center of our portrait of domesticity. That's me in the distance.

❀ ❀ ❀

When Lewis Henry Morgan began his researches in upstate New York, it was certain universals of community life he was looking for—initially as a model for his men's "lodge," then later as a model of society itself. Because the Iroquois helped invent anthropology, their ways were often assumed to be universals of early human development. Since then, the subject has of course grown steadily more complex, particularly as the Euro-Americans began to learn how much of their own history was lost or missing. That their culture had as little solidity as the economic bubbles that supported it. It was that gnawing sense of something not there—a series of questions becoming louder and more insistent among both the anthropologists and their informants. Hasn't this "civilization" taken a terribly wrong turn somewhere? Doesn't it seem in fact to be costing a great deal and making life somewhat worse? Where did it go wrong? And along with this, a vast yearning for antiquities, bogus fossils, and a quest for the lost origins of nearly everything.

Well, the answer came back: things went wrong very early on, and it started right at home. This would be Engels now, reading the notes Marx had made in Morgan's *Ancient Society*, which drew on his Iroquois studies and the scraps of available ethnographic data to put together a picture of ancestors not recognizably related to the people seated in Victorian parlors. Nor was it like the children at hard labor, the urban destitute, the exhausted land and starving husbandman. Engels's assembled notes and readings of Marx's gloss became *The Origin of the Family, Private Property, and the*

State, a monograph that has achieved a persistent notoriety—as communist text and doctrine, as an example of poor anthropological method, and as a feminist sermon preached by a nineteenth-century German male. Although not entirely wrong about the place of women and the primacy of home economics, in the light of history Engels has come to seem a little like the Quaker telling the Indian how to grow corn. What was indisputably true, however, and is hardly more understood today than when it was pointed out a century ago, is the revelation that these institutions—family, property, state —the very underpinnings of society, have not been around very long. And might not, Engels added, be around very much longer. "The state," he was pleased to announce, "has not existed from all eternity."

What Morgan had discovered in the Iroquois Longhouse was an ancestral form of political economy—a history the Euro-Americans now realized they had also experienced but had suppressed and forgotten. But more important—and probably what he and Marx had supposed to begin with—was that the transition from the earlier mode of organization had involved a major cultural shift involving all our social patterns, from money to monogamy:

> The stage of commodity production with which civilization begins is distinguished economically by the introduction of (1) metal money and with it money capital, interest and usury, (2) merchants as the class of intermediaries between the producers, (3) private ownership of land and the mortgage system, (4) slave labour as the dominant form of production. The form of family corresponding to civilization and coming to definite supremacy with it is monogamy, the domination of the man over the woman and the single family as the economic unit of society.[6]

Morgan, Marx, and Engels were working with a suddenly expanded sense of human history, and they tended sometimes

6. FRIEDRICH ENGELS, *The Origin of the Family, Private Property, and the State* (1884), edited by Lawrence and Wishart and introduced by Michelle Barret (Harmondsworth, 1985), who summarizes the history of Engels's reworking of Marx's notes on Morgan's evolutionary anthropology —somewhat moderating Lenin's "This is one of the fundamental works of modern socialism, every sentence of which can be accepted with confidence." From the perspective of modern feminist anthropology the work is flawed in obvious ways, but it retains the value of its original insights.

to project into the future as far as they now saw into their own past. In their vision of domestic life, there was a note of the familiar lusting after "primitive" sexual arrangements, not too different from the vastly popular literature of white women abducted and adopted by savages. In their vision of "liberty, equality, and fraternity"—it is Morgan who invokes this phrase at the end of his study of the Iroquois—they were carried away by Victorian notions of progress and missed a great deal in supposing that increased control over nature and the bringing of slaves and women into public industry would somehow mean the end of the capitalist mode of production. It was also the error of Hamilton, of course, who predicted the same conditions would be the capitalist's salvation.

Morgan's observations of matrilineal clans, as both Marx and Engels realized, were as much a "discovery" as Darwin's of our long-term history. But even more directly to their source, the insights of these three Victorian males are of present value because of the particular women they were talking about:

> *The unusual role of Iroquois women in politics, religion and domestic life cannot be dismissed simply as a histor-ical curiosity. It cannot be explained by Iroquois kinship structure, nor can it be attributed to the size of women's contribution to Iroquois subsistence. The powerful posi-tion of Iroquois women was the result of their control over the economic organization of their tribe.*[7]

But rather than seeing these as prophetic texts, to be judged according to the extent they have "come true," they ought to be regarded as early works of discovery in the tradi-tion of Mauss's *Essay on the Gift*. What this tradition of inquiry is seeking in the customs of "savages"—in the democracy of the tribe, collective ownership of land and its biotic wealth, the recognition of the mother right—is a rela-tionship to the world that has been missed, a spirit that is lacking in both public and domestic exchange. And it suggests that we look again at our modes of government and see they

7. JUDITH K. BROWN, "Iroquois Women: an ethnohistoric note," in *Toward an Anthropology of Women,* ed. Rayne R. Reiter (New York, 1975). For an account of how the status of Iroquois women influenced the beginnings of the modern feminist movement, see Sally Roesch Wagner, "The Iroquois Influence on Women's Rights," *Akwekon Journal* (Spring 1992).

are not separate from our habits of exchange and ownership—
and that these in turn are not separate from the way we live
and keep house. Property is theft, as they say, and it applies to
persons as well as things. We need something with which to
repay this act of misappropriation, and might well begin with
an equitable and sustainable home economics.

But before the first ethnographers could get to the Stone
Age to recover some of these losses of memory, the Quakers
had already set about to bring the Iroquois into the nineteenth century. They saw that material salvation required
precisely that "fall" from primitive grace that Morgan and
Marx would later lament. But the Quakers evenhandedly
threw out both civilized and stone-age vices, condemning
drinking and cardplaying as well as communal dances and
unthrifty spending. For the most part they concerned themselves with purely technical assistance, as usual supposing
that if the outer person were taken care of, the inner person's
light would keep it on the path. With their example and help,
the old fenced settlements were abandoned for isolated frame
houses on land individually cultivated, replacing the previous
combination of communal and private plots. The man worked
the fields and made contracts for its surplus. The woman had
charge of the house and domestic economy. Both individual
income from the sale of surplus produce and the collective
annuities paid by the government were invested in capital
improvements.

In many outward respects, like the Creeks who became
prosperous slaveholding plantation owners, the Iroquois were
more successful at rural agrarian life than many of their
white neighbors, who were only that much more in favor of
government programs for removal. But from within, also,
there were signs that the Quakers had succeeded perhaps too
well and that the soul might be feeling the effects of these
material changes. The old carved likeness of Tarachiawagon,
the spirit of good and creation, came down—but unaccountably there were outbreaks of magic, accusations of witchcraft,
and troubled dreams. Despite the miracle of material adapta-

tion, amid the plowing and spinning and outward success, the economy of the spirit began to feel what we commonly refer to as depression, with all the usual symptoms of dependency and domestic confusion.

🍀 🍀 🍀

"Teach your mama to suck eggs," she was saying to her son. He was trying to tell her how to hold his baby sister. He was being very sweet and responsible. I was sipping iced tea and reading the Sunday supplement. It was full of the self-satisfied complacent poison of people who got and held on to more than they would ever understand, for less than they will ever know of its real value. "Listen to this," I groaned and read another proof that they will spare no nastiness to cash in what's left. How can anybody live among such people and stay sane. "Sane?" She got up to take the sleeping baby into the house.

It was the beginning of the end of my trip. The next afternoon found us in a cafe, behind large tinted-glass windows, escaping from the humidity and the children, sucking up the largest double gin bloody marys I'd ever seen. I recall they were only two bucks apiece, although I believe we had six of them. But I had given up keeping a daily account of my travel expenses—I had a ticket and enough to get home on, and the little that remained was gravy. We drank and talked. She had told me her plans: marry the lawyer who was calling her daily to come down and set a date to pick out the big house in the suburb. Right, I said. So what if she didn't seem to particularly love the guy—it was a practical move, and I sure didn't have a better idea.

I said I was going to go home and write the book I had started out to write. Who needs New York. Right, she agreed. She knew I knew almost as little about money as I did about love. That I had this problem with home economics. And except for the occasional accident of a poem, hardly knew even my own heart. I told her how I'd started this trip thinking I could save this relationship, despite many miles of difficult

geography between us, if I could just get some perspective—
and how instead I found I was in love with this painter whose
grandparents' grave I had just been to visit. "Sounds like it
was time to get out of Dodge," she said. "You sure it's safe to
go back?" I had to admit she was still the funniest woman I
knew. It was with considerable hilarity and difficulty that we
made our way back to the little house in the haunted valley of
the mother of rivers.

THE DREAM
EXCHANGE

Mom and the kids in the station wagon, I waved good-bye as I crossed the runway to the A.M. Chicago commuter—like a last sweet twist on the dream of the American family that so obviously was not working out, and surely was not us. The family that never was, and at this point clearly never will be.

Walk into any airport. Get on a plane. Look around. Caught between the Stone Age and the millennial American present, it will prove as impossible to go forward as back. Modest advances will be followed by great backsliding. Small material gains by deep spiritual breakdown. Naturally this will occur within both the group and the individual. Lack of money, domestic discord, addiction—then as now, the usual symptoms. Traders and missionaries promising comfort and salvation, neglecting to mention the price of souls. People drifting from one spiritual dependency to another.

Of the various missions[1] to the early victims of the American invasion, it was the genius of the Quakers to rely on the "inner light," where Christian doctrine and material reform had failed to reverse the effects of traumatic cultural shock. Much as "money" still bore a resemblance to the bead exchange, the Quakers' "light" corresponded (as the Jesuits had

1. THIS PERIOD OF transition, like the events preceding it, is well documented by Wallace, *Death and Rebirth of the Seneca* (New York, 1969). While not the last word on Seneca history, as some of its subjects have pointed out, Wallace's account is doubly insightful of their economic and spiritual adaptations of Quaker ways. Implicit in this history are a number of ways the Quakers were also influenced by the exchange.

recognized early on) to a central mechanism of Iroquois psychology and religion—the dream exchange. Speaking of the Seneca, Father Jacques Fremin reported that dreaming appeared to be their divinity and acting out dreams their principal form of worship:

> . . . whatever it be that they think they have done in their dreams, they believe themselves absolutely obliged to execute at the earliest moment. The other nations content themselves with observing those of their dreams which are the most important; but this people, which has the reputation of living more religiously than its neighbors, would think itself guilty of a great crime if it failed in its observance of a single dream.[2]

The dream was a spiritual resource, which both the individual and the collective might draw upon. And by the practice of guessing and acting out dreams, that resource appears to have been constantly nourished and replenished.

> The people think only of that, they talk of nothing else, and all their cabins are filled with their dreams. They spare no pains, no industry, to show their attachment thereto, and their folly in this particular goes to such an excess as would be hard to imagine.

The priests were amused but also jealously aware they were witnessing an economy of the soul's deepest transactions. It was the spiritual counterpart of other indigenous metaphors of exchange: the string of beads, the forest trail, the chain of alliance—the open path to the heart. Even the Quakers had to admit it was excellent mental hygiene. Where a dream came in response to crisis, as would naturally occur, it served as a catalyst of atonement, spiritual reform, and personal change. When Cornplanter was in disgrace among his people because of bad deals he'd made with the whites, it is told that he went from house to house at the midwinter ceremonies clad only in rags, till it was guessed: he'd dreamed of having all vestiges of his chief's title taken from him. Naturally, the custom

2. FREMIN'S OBSERVATION was noted in Wilson, *Apologies to the Iroquois.* From *The Jesuit Relations* for 1642, 54:97–98. As a corrective see James Hillman's work (e.g., *The Dream and the Underworld* [New York, 1979]), which shows the traffic between dream and waking to be both an ancient commerce and a gift our clinical psychology is much in need of. Thus the Jesuit might have seen he was confronting the source of the Word he had come to preach.

sometimes took very personal and bizarre forms of unconscious acting out. The good Quakers must have noticed that the inner light sometimes cast dark and peculiar shadows.

But it was the public dream life of Cornplanter's half brother that most deeply affected the Iroquois nation at that critical juncture, as it was attempting to transform and reconcile itself to a life surrounded by nineteenth-century Americans. Probably because they were geographically isolated even among the Seneca, who were conservative even by the Iroquois' own conservative standards, the people of Cornplanter's Town had kept many of the traditional feasts of thanksgiving. Like the Ritual of Condolence—the ceremony of mourning that ends in recovery and restoration of the collective loss—these expressions of gratitude usually concluded with the guessing of dreams. Ceremonies of thanksgiving enact the "spending" half of our reciprocal transactions with the gods—as dreams represent, like food, our most commonplace "income." We send them smoke and incense, with prayer and songs of thankfulness; they return an abundance of provision and a rich inner life, which both community and individual may draw on at need.

So when Ganio-dai'yo, wasted by prolonged dissipation and drink and depression, collapsed and died in his daughter-in-law's arms, only to revive and reveal a great vision message, the first sign of this impending visitation was a profound sense of gratitude. He and his culture had hit bottom. The winter's peltry had been squandered on rum, the houses lay in ruin, the women had removed themselves from the drunken violence, and only hungry dogs roamed the village.

But now it is spring, and he has miraculously returned from the other world. Something as simple as the sun shining in at the doorway seems a great gift. Outside, life is returning to the earth. He is overfilled with thankfulness. He hears his name called. He is on his way out the door when he collapses.

Some one spoke and said, 'Come out awhile' and said
this three times. Now since I saw no one speaking I

3. ARTHUR C. PARKER, *THE Code of Handsome Lake*, Bulletin of the State Museum (Albany, 1913), 24. Included with his study of maize and the Constitution in *Parker on the Iroquois*, the text draws on written sources. Around 1860 several oral versions were compared and found to differ. Chief John Jacket was chosen to write it out in Seneca using an orthography taught by the Presbyterian minister Asher Wright, and it was then rememorized. When the script was lost page by page, and the narrative about to be lost again, Chief Edward Cornplanter had begun to write it out again in the minute book of the Seneca Lacrosse Club when he met Parker in 1903. In an ecumenical spirit, this reading of the Good Message was then translated by William Bluesky, the lay preacher of the local Baptist church, while Parker wrote it down. William Fenton's introduction reports that "its readers are both Iroquois, who need the book, and anthropologists, psychologists, and a host of other academicians, who study messianic movements, of which this has become one of the classic types"—a remark somewhat classic in its own right.

thought that in my sickness I myself was speaking but I thought again and found that it was not my voice. So I called out boldly, 'Niio!' and arose and went out and there standing in the clear swept space I saw three men clothed in fine clean raiment. Their cheeks were painted red and it seemed that they had been painted the day before. Only a few feathers were in their bonnets. All three were alike and all seemed middle aged. Never before have I seen such handsome commanding men and they had in one hand bows and arrows as canes. Now in their other hands were huckleberry bushes and the berries were of every color.[3]

The Messengers have been sent by the Creator, who is aware of the dreamer's newfound sense of the gift. They have come to instruct him, and unless he wishes to suffer great torment and death he is to follow and repeat their message. He is to eat of the berries and to tell the people to make juice of the strawberries, of which all should drink. They leave him with a warning against four "words" that make the Creator unhappy —whiskey, witchcraft, love potions, and abortion/sterility medicines. A fourth messenger will come at another time and continue his instruction. This occurs the following August.

Still not recovered by then, Ganio-dai'yo tells Cornplanter that he may appear to die but that he will actually be in a trance. While in the dream state, he is taken by his guide on a journey along the sky road. On the path they see the vices of materialism, disbelief in the old ways, and the white man's institutions of punishment and worship, which are not meant for Indians. Halfway to heaven, he sees George Washington sitting on his porch with his dog, and along the road Jesus shows the dreamer what the white people did to their prophet. He wishes him better luck. Then, almost to heaven, they come to the turnoff to hell, and in the great iron lodge of "the Punisher" they review the retribution visited upon drunkards, witches, wife-beaters, promiscuous fornicators, fiddlers, and cardplayers.

The dreamer is then conducted along the narrow road to the country of the Creator. There Ganio-dai'yo meets his dog, sacrificed at the last midwinter New Year; then his deceased son, infant grandson, and, still great with child, his niece whose recent death had contributed to his breakdown. The dream is in this regard an internalized condolence ceremony, and it seems appropriate that the niece should attempt to restore relations among the living. Her father, Cornplanter, and her brother Henry were at opposite poles of the argument between traditional and civilized ways—she tells the dreamer that the younger Philadelphia-educated man ought to obey his father. The Messenger was making it clear that those who listened to the Quakers had strayed too far.

The Gai'wiio—the Good Message—continued to be delivered in a third vision the following year and with frequent additions till the death of Ganio-dai'yo in 1815. On the subject of backsliders and unbelievers, on his role as prophet, on certain land sales and his visit to President Jefferson in 1801—there appears to have been an ongoing channel of communication with the Messengers. The note was in general conservative yet finding ways to accommodate what was useful or inevitable. It is as if the dreamer were a channel to that collective resource, the messages a curative for the schizophrenic malaise in which the community found itself. It was the note of recovery: stay sober, give thanks for every day, care for elders and children, practice kindness toward animals, honor your traditions—virtues the Quakers might have preached but here expressed in an idiom that was ancient and familiar.

The name Ganio-dai'yo translates roughly "It is a handsome lake," or Handsome Lake, as he is usually called. It was a hereditary title belonging to the Wolf clan of the Seneca. It refers to that lake from which Dekanawida obtained the wampum shells used to establish the Great Peace.

Dekanawidah was ordered by the Creator to use the shells found on the shores of the water that flow from the earth to carry messages of happiness and peace. With these shells the people could talk with the Creator and all words spoken while they were held came from the heart. Words then spoken would be true, and any promise made while holding the shells must be kept forever. Some beads were set aside for "repenting" by Dekanawidah.[4]

4. SNYDERMAN, "THE Function of Wampum," 601. Snyderman, as noted earlier, was an observer of Tonawanda ceremonies in 1951. His informant here is identified only as Sherman Redeye. Snyderman also reports a tradition that, like Dekanawida/Hayonhwatha, Handsome Lake found a lake with shores of wampum, which he had previously dreamed.

The prophet and his spokesperson Hayonhwatha would also have had historical reverberations for Handsome Lake and his half brother Cornplanter. In their complementary functions they would recall a division of prophetic roles that was common far beyond the Longhouse. A generation before, Neolin and Pontiac had enacted these same roles of seer and public voice. Even at the time, Handsome Lake was known as the "peace prophet" to distinguish him from the twin brother of Tecumseh, the "war prophet." And prophecy itself was taken to be a natural extension of the customs of dream enactment. In these same years, there was said to be a female prophet among the Tuscarora, and a similar visionary to the Mohawk. Long after Handsome Lake's death, the Four Messengers appeared to other prophets to confirm his vision.

Not all of Handsome Lake's doctrines and actions were accepted or approved, however. He was not able to abolish the medicine societies, such as the False Faces, whose ceremonies of healing and acting-out dealt with those dark forces which the Christians had excluded from the pantheon. While he encouraged some role changes that were necessary to the new agrarian life, his attempts to break down the mother-daughter relation—asserting instead the primacy of the husband-wife relation, and legislating love and abortion—were resisted with the traditional strength of the clan matrons. He attempted to suppress destructive witchcraft—a community that lives with its collective unconscious on open display is ripe for internal mischief in difficult times—but his responsibility for the killing of several alleged witches caused lasting resentment and led to his moving several times to another town, most notably Tonawanda, near Buffalo. These setbacks, combined with recent jealousies and the traditional mistrust of autocratic power, eventually led him to establish a pattern of pastoral visits, concluding finally with a last journey to the heart of the Longhouse at Onondaga—his ending thus again invoking the beginnings of the Great Peace.

So the blessings of the dream were somewhat mixed, and even the vision of recovery had to be reenvisioned. As important as the dream was the way it got incorporated into everyday life. There were many details, affecting both the family and national life, that had to be worked out by a political economy already under serious stress. Handsome Lake's vision, however subject to argument, provided the initial practical terms by which the white man's economy could be incorporated into traditional communal life:

> The educational and technological customs of the whites were to be integrated into a Seneca society that retained as a social value the village communalism, reserved land title to the nation itself, and depended upon traditional reciprocal gift-giving rather than commercial sale as the mechanism of internal distribution. The moral restraints of modesty and of kindness to animals were levied in such a way as to preclude, in theory at least, the development of the profit motive and rural capitalism.[5]

It seems odd now that Morgan, then Engels and Marx, could not see that the Iroquois—as deeply flint-rock conservative as any upstate Republican—had undertaken by necessity and inspiration to make, within a capitalist economy, a radical experiment in communal living arrangements. Apparently all these early ethnologists could see was the accepted picture of a noble vanished race, perhaps because it was their own past they were looking for. And since they considered they were dealing with an extinct ("disappearing") culture—much like a naturalist preserving perishable specimens—they failed to see that the Iroquois could accomplish such remarkable outward change because they still had access to living root traditions, which were brought present again by dream and prophecy. Thus the principles of this reformation would be kept by a

5. WALLACE HERE DESCRIBES (*Death and Rebirth*, 282) a transition that should be required study for anyone undertaking "rural development," of other nations' people or their own.

kind of Indian "church," based on the Good Message, as it was reestablished by the matrons of the clans in the years after Handsome Lake's death—but its foundation was a spiritual economy older than the Longhouse. And it is still open for business and will be paying out steady dividends long after the banks are closed.

🐚 🐚 🐚

I took the airport bus in from SFO, stashed my baggage in a downtown Greyhound locker, and caught the 14 Mission up to where friends lived. Up to that sunny bohemian barrio with a congenial coffee and wine bar, and a couch to hang out on till it opened. By eleven, I'd be ready for the all-night dog.

The proprietor of the place allowed poetry and poets to occupy the back room most evenings and had the jazz up front. He drew me a glass of beer to start with, and we talked a little about my trip and how it was back east. The springtime had been beautiful, I said, and Manhattan as treacherous as ever. But I hardly knew how to tell him what I'd found out. It had been like a dream. I had been through a city where people go to steal from one another. I was in a vault where a great treasure was kept from its rightful owners. It would be restored, and much would be redeemed by it.

But I still only dimly understood what this dream meant —that the source of all treasure is in the heart, which opens and is restored both in giving and receiving. And that this was the blessing I sought in the origin of "economics"—a kind of currency that would pay all the dues. If I could have just said this, I'm sure Alvin would have understood.

The principal ceremonial feature of the meetings of the Longhouse or Handsome Lake religion is the four-day recitation of the Code, recounting the vision and all the sayings delivered by the Messengers. The ceremony thus revives and reenacts the ceremonial "readings" that had anciently sustained both the civil and religious life of the Iroquois Confederacy. The recitation was recovered from the last of

Handsome Lake's followers who still recalled the "Way," and
taught to another generation of Speakers and Prompters. Its
forms and laws were entrusted to Faith-keepers, again reviving an old function of the Longhouse and adapting it, like the
frame building with a chimney, to available materials and
tools. Although the Messengers had told Handsome Lake that
their words should be written down—and approved of liter-
acy to the extent that two people of each of the Six Nations
should learn to read, in order to know what the white people
were really saying—the Code was instead committed to memory and keyed to strings of white shell beads. At the founding
council the rules for the reading were woven into a belt of
wampum, "so these truths would remain forever."[6]

The internal truths of the Longhouse religion also continue to be enacted ceremonially, in the confession of sins and
the promise to mend. The sinner holds strings of white
wampum while speaking. The confessor has as part of his du-
ties to send out a string of wampum to recall an errant soul—
much as clans traditionally sent a string of beads to ask a
wandering person's return. Again, the newly adopted forms
were not an innovation but a revival, with new emphasis on
old practices—such as the ceremonial strawberry juice and
the guessing of dreams—that had been part of the principal
feasts of thanksgiving. Wallace's account of a Six Nations ceremony in the 1950s describes their continuing vitality:

> When at last she takes hold of the strings of white
> wampum handed to her by the confessor, her whole body
> quivers. She speaks slowly, almost inaudibly, while her
> fingers stroke and caress the wampum as if it were her
> sole support. She confesses that she left the longhouse to
> become a Catholic; now she repents and wants to return
> to the longhouse. Tears roll down her cheeks; from time
> to time she dabs at her eyes with a handkerchief.[7]

We come back to the heart, then. The reopening of the
path to the heart. Through the changes of five centuries, this
essential transaction continues. Still sometimes marked by

6. SNYDERMAN ("THE
Function of Wampum")
identifies this as the *Ga
Jus'towaneh* or *Big Fire*
or *Big Light* belt. He also
draws a sharp distinction
between such "private"
religious belts and
"public" message
or confession strings.

7. (*DEATH AND REBIRTH*, 12).

the beads of wampum, it is a transaction between the past and the future, redeeming the individual, the human collective, and the body and spirit of the heart's informing gift. It recounts the losses, keeps the account of what's due, and makes returns to the source of life and economy. It may prove, in the history of the reinhabitation of North America, to be our best model of personal and cultural redemption.

The wampum beads are used both by the adherents of the Longhouse "church," and the chiefs of the Six Nations in the "election" ceremony that renews the body politic. The forces of history have altered the seamless beadwork of the ancient Confederacy, and civil functions are divided between Onondaga and Grand River, Ontario. The use of beads in religious life, so far as outsiders need inquire, is carried on wherever the Longhouse members gather. Just as their wampum was appropriated to the state, the Council of Chiefs was outlawed and discredited by the governments of both the United States and Canada, and "democratically" elected chiefs sometimes installed in their place. Consequently the council meetings became clandestine and the investiture wampum kept hidden. Handsome Lake's wampum, along with the *Big Light* or *Big Fire* belt that marks the rekindling of his vision, is said to be kept where no anthropologists have seen it. The best account I've found of the current use of wampum is that of the poet Joseph Bruchac, in a beautiful little chapbook, *The Good Message of Handsome Lake:*

> *At Tonowanda*
> *they may be brought out*
> *once each two years*
> *at the beginning*
> *of the long circuit of preaching*
> *the prophet's words*
> *from Longhouse to Longhouse*
> *which begins each fall.*
> *He who bears the title Ganio-dai'yo*
> *is their custodian.*

Yet if even one cloud
is in the sky,
the strings may not
be brought into the open.
Whenever an anthropologist
is present at
that meeting,
there is always
one small cloud
which can be found.[8]

8. JOSEPH BRUCHAC, "Tonawanda," *The Good Message of Handsome Lake* (Unicorn Press, Greensboro, 1979).

9. THE END OF THE LAST poem of Bruchac's collection, "Not a Thing of Paint or Feathers."

Like the string of white beads, the Iroquois belts belong to an enactment of belief and require no further documenting or validation. Their "meaning," as a currency of the spirit, suggests that the anthropologist and scholar look instead someplace closer to home.

The heart makes its promise and with this marker says, I pledge my faith. Here is my word: I will begin again.

. . . their belief
is not a thing of paint or feathers
but of the heart.[9]

I waken with the poet's small book on my lap, the reading light still on. It is first dawn, and the northbound all-night bus out of San Francisco is now swaying to the familiar curves of rivers. Out the white-line window I can just make out the silhouette of madrone and fir on the ridges above the Eel. Down below, silvery willow on the banks, behind them dark and ancient columns of redwood. Strands of fog hang suspended in the trees and above the swift current. A faint, rippled reflection of sky, the river sweeps along with us, full of having been somewhere, almost home. An hour more will bring us out at the Pacific.

I return to home as I left it, trying to hold together the

pieces.[10] To the casual traveler's eye, we are following a thread of serpentine water through the groves of an emerald forest. But behind this green curtain, the land is in a state of exhaustion, the forest at the bottom of a third cycle of depletion and recovery, the human community wondering what it's going to do for money. Each time, less comes back—because too much has been taken, and too little *given* back. The long-term balance of accounts is visible beneath the river's reflection, in the silted water and the erosion-choked riverbed. It is not as easily seen, however, where it touches our human business most closely—in the web of living things that has been broken and scattered and spent. It was this inquiry that set me on the present quest: How can we redeem such enormous loss? For all that land and life, with what shall we make return?

When I began to examine our accounts[11] with the spirit of this place, I found that they had been kept by a shell economy predating the arrival of the American dollar by some centuries. The shells called "Indian money" are still regarded as family wealth and are displayed in ceremonies of healing and renewal. Its present custodians are only recently recognized to exist, let alone given a reservation or rancheria to exist on. The dentalia shell remains, nevertheless, a working description of a natural economy that the prevailing idea of wealth has nearly bankrupt. For more than twenty years, a regional power company has diverted the greater part of this river into a neighboring watershed, by way of turbines that shred every salmon and steelhead fortunate enough to make it that far—it would not be cost-effective to install a screen, say company spokesmen. And the last privately owned stand of these old-growth redwood—they're the object of a hostile takeover by a Texas junk bond magnate; because he raided his own savings and loan to finance, cutting has doubled to increase liquidity. Because of such insanity, and because the shell exchange is predicated on long-term returns to both body and spirit, it will probably outlive the dollar by as many centuries more.

I gradually came to understand that this more ancient way of doing business had once been almost universal and

10. THE FULL MEANING OF what I'm arriving at is only beginning to appear in books. It is tentatively expressed in *Home: A Bioregional Reader* (Philadelphia, 1990). This anthology brings us one step past the crisis response that has characterized the "environmental movement," a necessary, ongoing, but largely defensive action. A "bioregionalist," so far as I get it, is an environmentalist who has moved in, put a lifetime down, and started making payments. Studying, monitoring, and attempting to restore natural systems while learning to work and live and sustain family and community on those same terms—and then render some account of it—these writers give an eloquent current record of that experiment. The result, judging from that, is a good deal of practical wisdom, insight, and humility. It begins to describe, that is, the only terms on which the earth will continue to support us.

11. THIS HAS BY NO MEANS been a solitary or recent endeavor. I would add to the above reference Peter Berg, ed., *Reinhabiting a Separate Country: A Bioregional Anthology of Northern California* (San Francisco, 1978), and acknowledge a particular indebtedness to Dr. Loon's "Tusk Shell, Gold Dollar, Pulp Note and Weed: Four Economies in the Six Rivers Region."

that we survive at all because it is the root stock of our hy-
bridized, chemically dependent money tree. It is the "bible"
to which even our most dismal social sciences seek to return.
Its basic tenet is again the law of reciprocity, by which we
constantly recognize and repay our obligation to the source
of our gifts. The irony of "New World" history is that it remembered things Europe had long forgotten—but the invaders' money still bore an ancestral resemblance to the
economy it encountered here, and that resemblance opened
the door of North America—only to find that the stranger's
coin had lost its spirit and was a soulless device to buy and incorporate by deed the land and all it contained.

Here then an ancient way of accounting had been overwhelmed by a more recent, short-term method of keeping
books. But I found that this process had its own long story—
of how the money economy came about, how it subverted the
earth's oldest contracts, and how it was then employed as a
form of warfare that has brought us to our present impoverishment. I wished to recount, one transaction at a time, how it
had come to this. And to then look again at this other way of
keeping accounts, which has been too long put off as primitive, outmoded, or dead. The aboriginal nations of North
America, bound together by the ceremonies of beaded agreement, are the founders of our essential contract with this continent, which a small group of Euro-American gentlemen
only partly succeeded in imitating. It now appears their
"freedoms" were purchased on credit, at a price we have only
begun to repay.

I have undertaken, then, as Jefferson said we should, a recourse to fundamental principles—but with a deeper and more
inclusive sense of where those principles originate. Deeper
than money, and inclusive of more than beads. When I began
to string together the story of wampum and the Iroquois
Confederacy, I saw in each transaction with the Europeans a
misunderstanding seized upon by greed and opportunity. To a
large degree, that is the history we must acknowledge and redeem. It provides a prototypical example of how the money

12. NEW YORK TIMES,
13 August 1989. The twelve
belts returned were not
identified; presumably,
they included all those of
the nature of civil contracts
of the Longhouse. The
state allowed it had been
the custodian, not the
owner, of the wampum.
Subsequent accounts of
repatriation and return
of lands are from the pages
of the Times, 1987–94.

economy destroys indigenous gift economies. But a deeper sense of this transaction evolved over the years, as the path of my research began to partake of the long term, and I reexperienced in the present some of the truths I had found in old documents. That economy and ecology are not different, that what your money's worth and how you live are an inextricable knot, and that body and spirit fall apart and require, one by the other, constant acts of redemption. These, I would say to Tom Jefferson, are the principles to which we urgently need recourse.

It is traditional wisdom that we waken from a dream to the same world we went to sleep in. It is only in its personal and communal enactment, again one transaction at a time, that the dream world can enter this one. It is neither the Salvation nor the New Deal that is so often promised but is woven from the history of all our transactions that preceded. It is a vision that every day's acts must affirm. As remarkable as the Good Message—which continues to be a bright fire in the bloody darkness of recent history—as remarkable and of equal importance to our desperate present, is the Iroquois example of survival and recovery by the enactment of a dream. Only by accepting his own soul's indebtedness could the keeper of books begin to understand this. And only in the making of his own book begin to put back some of what was lost.

🦉 🦉 🦉

"These belts are our archives," the Times quoted Raymond Gonyea saying, on the occasion of their return to the Onondaga two years after my visit there.[12] At the time I met him, and he generously conducted me to see the New York State Museum's wampum collection, he was negotiating the repatriation of a dozen belts that represented the essential contracts of his nation. When I last inquired, his address was the Repatriation Office, in the Bronx, of the Museum of the American Indian—which the year after my visit there returned eleven belts to the custody of the chiefs at Grand River. I would like to think that inquiries by peculiar scholars, bill collectors, and potential thieves helped to hasten this process, but in fact credit goes to the persistence of Six Nations representatives and their more steadfast allies.

Over the objection of scholars, who say it is like the removal of rare books from libraries, other museums have begun to follow this example. Partly under threat of federal legislation, or more direct action, the repositories of indigenous artifacts have begun to open their hoards for an accounting. The Smithsonian appears to have established a model for the return of these ransomed beads and bones: "To repatriate, by request, funerary objects, communally owned property, ceremonial and religious objects, and objects transferred to or acquired by the museum illegally." Behind this legal boilerplate lies a misappropriation of such enormity that perhaps shame is as much a motive here as a desire for justice. The museums themselves must have been shocked at the cumulative inventory of the vast charnel house they had created. Tens and tens of thousands of indigenous people's remains, as if to incorporate land and life itself had not been enough; as if a nation of ghoulish orphans had to steal and lock away the ancestral bones it lacked.

These grisly treasures will of course not be surrendered lightly and will continue to be guarded by the professional dragons of public institutions. While the city and state museums of New York have agreed they were the custodians rather than the owners of their wampum collections, they continue to quarrel with one another and private and federal jurisdictions for the possession of the vast remainder. The George Gustav Heye Center of the National Museum of the American Indian has moved into new quarters, which I'm told are as impressive as its name. Neither the Museum of Natural History nor a short Texas billionaire were successful in their bids to acquire the holdings. Representatives of its old neighborhood, however, objected to its flight downtown, so it still maintains an annex up on 155th. It still oversees the world's largest collection of indigenous artifacts but shares its abundance with the Smithsonian in Washington, whose own Indian Museum was scaled down from the original $80 million plan. Wealth and grandeur are still the essence of what these museums display, and in this they differ little from the other institutions by which the nations's reigning valuations are maintained. The museum's present location, on Bowling Green, was available only because the federal government, at a briefly scandalous price in the billions, moved its bankruptcy courts to Foley Square.

Clearly, money is as much the cause as the cure of our indebtedness, and it is commonplace wisdom that "throwing" it at a problem usually makes it worse. It is a useful but always dangerous human invention, meant originally to acknowledge something received, and to make return. A language, and like language itself, it lives or dies with the breath and heart of its transactions. In common with all human agreements, to remain current and living it cannot remain in vaults and museums, nor can it be indiscriminately dropped from the towers of Babel. Its "meaning"—and the meaning of the wealth it represents—is thereby cheapened and lost. It is of course heartening to see that the Wampanoag who survived King Philip's War are now pulling down a billion dollars just from the spinoffs of their Massachusetts gambling operations—but one wishes that once wealthy tribe all their traditional wisdom, for they will surely need it. But who can gainsay the Pequot the million a day they are clearing from their own Las Vegas in Connecticut? Under the guise of concern for Indians' souls, missionaries and soldiers have surely saved them sufficiently from the temptations of materialism. It may be that high-stakes bingo will yield more tangible comfort than all our belatedly recalled treaties and reparations will ever amount to.

Money puts human contracts to the severest test, and our own is witness to the fact that they don't always withstand its temptations. There is still truth in the truism that money is only as good as the people who use it—the *way* they use it.

Adding some "profit" to the Indian side of the books is not by itself going to settle their account. No more than the misguided imitation and appropriation of their culture by the new-age Wanabee tribe. Using money unconsciously—so as to cheapen the meaning of beads, for example, while making them too expensive for Indians to buy—is as deadly an act of spiritual greed as stealing people's ancestors. And giving back some land or bones or artifacts—if it is no more than a reconveyance of stolen property—misses the point entirely. However essential such repayments to long overdue accounts, they are not going to buy absolution. According to most indigenous teaching, there is no such thing—no erasing of history follows from a confession of sins. The point is the resolution to do better, to live differently. We can redeem the past—both our word and our credit—only by deeds in the present. We might begin by honoring at least our own treaties and laws, and by staying on the path of which these reparations are the first shaky steps.

This will require nothing less than a change of heart.

The web of our essential acts keeps changing and moving— my journey only touched on a moment of it, in the two-hundredth year of a contract gone desperately wrong. It is but one of many transactions reread on the run, by a scholar without credential, not altogether clear of heart, in a time of enormous lies and public borrowing. But if conclusions are consequently hard to come by, I would simply point to what indigenous people have been saying all along: that the contract needs to be renegotiated. It is time this advice was heard.

The man I traveled to Onondaga to see, and missed, is now an envoy to the United Nations as well as a custodian of the Longhouse. Chief Oren Lyons is presently active in the international alliance of Non-Government Organizations (the NGOs) that has begun to give a collective voice to the resurgent indigenous nations of the earth. As noted at its first

13. "INDIGENOUS PHILOSOPHY
and the Land," Report of
Commission II of the
International NGO
Conference on Indigenous
People and the Land,
15–18 September
1981 (*Treaty Council
News* 3, no. 5 [1981]).

Geneva conference some fifteen years ago, it was formed in response to worldwide dispossession and genocide inflicted by states and multinational corporations. It proposes that first people offer an alternative and sustainable model for humanity's future and that its basis is in the gift relationship:

> *Being is a spiritual proposition. Gaining is a material act. Traditionally, American Indian people have always attempted to be the best people they could. Part of that spiritual process was and is to give away wealth, to discard wealth in order not to gain. Material gain is an indicator of false status among traditional people, while it is "proof that the system works" to Europeans.*
>
> *In terms of the despiritualization of the universe, the mental process works so that it becomes virtuous to destroy the planet.... Ultimately, the whole universe is open—in the European view—to this sort of insanity.*
>
> *Most important here, perhaps, is the fact that Europeans feel no sense of loss in all this.*[13]

And where loss is felt, no ritual of recovery to give it enactment. These are the sad terms of the present, much as they were at the opening of the Bead Wars some centuries ago. Dream fulfillment has not been the same as wish fulfillment, and so the sense of loss is still borne largely by the Indians. Noted by the news as occasional and disconnected uprisings, the war is usually in the breaking and forgetting of contracts —and when necessary, by the forms and methods established wherever there was a "frontier." Only when there is active resistance to these ongoing misappropriations does it appear in the *Times:* the month-long Mohawk blockade of the Mercier Bridge, protesting the taking of ancestral lands for a golf course; the closing of the New York Thruway by Seneca in response to violations of their public treaties—but such skirmishes at the Longhouse doors are hardly news, and not even recent tactics. They are of a piece with the history of the Americas and can be recited as part of a litany that includes Wounded Knee and Chiapas, James Bay and Black Mountain and the Amazon. The sad shame is that we hear none of these names till the Indians begin to shoot back.

The active example of the Six Nations continues to remind us of their founding principles: that any social and spiritual economy that hopes for continuance has to be based on a contract with the earth and its gifts, and supported by a great deal of patience and courage and inspiration and hard work. It has to partake of natural law and thereby be capable of nature's powers of recovery and renewal. Not only all people, but all living things, must have full economic status in the greater web of transactions. There has to be a way to account for loss as well as gain; to let go of not just illusory wealth but our spiritual dependence on it; to return the gift, knowing it will return again, and so buy back our public indebtedness and our desolate hearts.

I returned from my pilgrimage to begin life again. And again, it was the life I had left: no one was waiting at the station when I got off the bus. I had mailed most of my books and papers and so easily walked the few blocks up to where I lived at the edge of town. I don't recall unpacking or being glad to be home. I was still a pilgrim, impatient for the journey to begin. It would come out, not just at this account, but at what a life might become if lived according to its map.

It would take some years to sort out the pieces and, between odd jobs of teaching and carpentry and caretaking, more years to string them together. To all outward appearance, the journey would have been a failure. The project of selling a book about the '60s, and so turning love into money, had met the fate it probably deserved. The book about money, on the other hand, which had taken me to see a man who was not home, would turn out to be a story of the heart, and of its powers of renewal and recovery.

The journey, then, as with any pilgrimage, was one of acknowledgment—of reconnecting with essential accounts and beginning to transact them. So I would add, finally, to the texts of the gift exchange, the ongoing business of the present day—and the otherwise poor example of my life—as signs that its economy is still at work among us. Those whose hospitality allowed me to survive my researches into money—who continue to live with it and work for its institutions, with the grace of their survival—they lead me to believe that money was created just to prove there are things it can't buy. And so they are still providing and sustaining.

My host in upper Manhattan, during the crisis of getting straight, met an old love, and after much difficulty and breaking of old dependencies they married. My partners at lunch and dinner have written books, made music, become teachers and parents—and so are still sharing their gifts. My friend in western Massachusetts is still rebuilding the big old house he lives in and, as courageously as those who would repair our house of state, is counting the losses and hoping some day to break even. The writers of Albany still manage to give honest account of that city—unearthing its past, as in William Kennedy's *Very Old Bones*—much as Hendrick urged more than two centuries ago. Doug Unger has again written a book of witness, this to the tens of thousands of Argentinian disappeared, which after great difficulty has finally found a publisher. He now teaches in Las Vegas, where they apparently can afford to support writers.

Not long after my visit to Minnesota, my friend broke off her engagement to financial security, and she and the children moved back to the coast. We can still make each other laugh at the invincible ignorance of our hearts, and the persistent emptiness of our pockets. As to my own, the poet and the painter were spiritual partners and loving protagonists for some years following my unconscious paying of respects to her living and dead. Not long after this journey, I became the owner of an old house near hers, with a loan from the generous friend who treated me to the shell exhibit that day in Manhattan. But because I then took in my aged mother—who was slowly losing all memory—and because of disagreements about money and gifts, we were never able to put our households together. Once a week we would go to town and pay a third party to listen to our dreams and condole our losses, but it didn't seem to improve our waking lives. While being care provider to my mother, subsisting largely on her social security check, this book was written.

Gift to money to gift again. Life's reciprocity, still at work. Somehow its redemptive transactions continue. Despite daily reports of decline and fall, individual example still renews one's general faith. Family and friends bravely turn their lives around and give me some hope for my own. The recovery that comes from within and saves our souls even at the farthest margin, continues to ripple outward. It extends to a larger circle of familial and collective well-being and continues out into the place we live, returning as a life that surrounds and supports our own. Fragile and damaged as it may be, it is what is literally meant by culture. For almost a quarter century I have watched and participated in this conscious and difficult cycle of exchange, struggling to return life's talents and energies to their source. It is a literal act of charity and, like the journey, begins and ends at home.

Located on the verge of a narrow strip of unstable coastal dunes, both the land and the little working-class village to the east of me have taken their share of damage and displacement. Much of my time is devoted to caring for both the little house and the larger one. I am sustained in this work not so much by money—which is a subject that still often eludes me —as by the wealth of that larger household and its daily economy. Upriver, I know there are people moving rocks around in streambeds, stabilizing old log roads and landslides, chainsawing massive jams of debris, reconstructing a river, as if such a thing were possible. Downriver at flood, acting from sheer desperation and faith, capturing salmon whose eggs will perhaps keep the native stock alive until their spawning habitat is restored. Up on the river bars, every summer more of the ancient dances and regalia come back. Down in the towns, in offices and storefronts and warehouses, a commerce that makes some return to the spirit. And anywhere they can, some still using the herb for money, in spite of Hamilton's revenue agents and mercenaries.

With every gain, there has been more than abundant loss, and more than a few misjudgments. It would be a miracle to break even. Increasingly, for those who have dedicated themselves to this life of stewardship, reparation, and recovery, the lesson is one of perseverance, with frequent teachings of humility. And the investment is in longer-term bonds—in communities where kinship means both family and place; in watersheds where salmon are the primary indicator of riches. And always, as if a constant remittance of dues, in community centers and kitchens and school rooms and public buildings, the meetings—the incessant and endless meetings. Coming to understand that this labor of restoration, if it can succeed at all, is the task of generations. That we come to it as aging children, learning as I've begun to do here, to read some ancient notes that tell the way again to North America—how do they live there, and what is their law; how do they marry, how mourn; what is their art, what do they play—and what do they use for money.

We have undertaken, with our lives, the negotiation of a new contract with each other and the earth—and though it will go by the names of conservation biology and environmental ethics, family counseling, and community building, it is at heart the reopening of the gift relationship. At heart, and from there outward.

Here are the pieces. Text and dream: this is how it began.

Cover design by Judy Hicks, using a photograph by Joan A. Martien. Text design and production by Thomas Christensen, in Adobe Aldus and Zapf Humanist; David Peattie and Sarah Weld assisted with the production. Alan Bernheimer, Thomas Christensen, Edith Gladstone, Kirsten Janene-Nelson, and Sarah Rosenthal contributed to the editing and proofreading. Bill Nelson prepared the maps. Data Reproductions did the printing, on Glatefelter Opaque recycled paper, and the binding.